The Symmetry of the Tiger

Works by Eugene Benson

Plays

The Gunner's Rope
Joan of Arc's Violin

Novels

The Bulls of Ronda
Power Game

Libretti

Heloise and Abelard
The Summoning of Everyman
Psycho Red
Earnest, the Importance of Being
The Auction
A Tale of Two Cities

Non-Fiction

J.M. Synge
English-Canadian Theatre (with L.W. Conolly)
The Oxford Companion to Canadian Theatre (with L.W. Conolly)
Routledge Encyclopedia of Post-Colonial Literatures in English (with L.W. Conolly)
The Oxford Companion to Canadian Literature (with W. Toye)

The Symmetry of the Tiger

A Memoir

Eugene Benson

Rock's Mills Press
Oakville, Ontario

Published by
ROCK'S MILLS PRESS
www.rocksmillspress.com

Copyright © 2019 by Eugene Benson.
Published by arrangement with the author. All rights reserved.

For information, please contact the publisher:
customer.service@rocksmillspress.com

ISBN-13: 978-1-77244-177-2

For Ormonde and Shaun

Contents

Lambeg Drums and Sir Edward Carson / 1

College Days and Irish Nationalism / 13

Saint Thomas Aquinas and Ravel's Boléro / 25

The Coils of Venus / 41

Saskatchewan / 55

The People of the Sun / 70

The Rain in Spain and NATO Pilots / 90

Cold Bacon and Doctoral Studies / 106

The Wandering Scholar / 124

Marriage, Politics, and Marshall McLuhan / 139

Of Canadian Opera and Irish Poets / 160

The Bulls of Ronda / 176

Landscapes of the Mind / 191

Can Lit and the Colonial Cringe / 209

PEN and the Sword / 227

The Importance of Being a Writer / 240

L'Envoi / 256

Lambeg Drums and Sir Edward Carson

On the 14th April 1921 my uncle Francis Benson, head constable in the Royal Irish Constabulary, was assassinated by the Irish Republican Army. He was a victim of Ireland's war for independence from British rule. The tragic consequence of that war was the partitioning of Ireland a year later when the northeastern part of the country became Northern Ireland where I was born. As I write this in my ninetieth year I realize how profoundly the events of that time influenced my life and career and why I feel the need now to write down my story. But how to capture in a few hundred pages the multitudinous impressions that have impinged upon those ninety years, how to convey the experiences of life in many cities and countries, how to communicate the joys and sorrows that are part of the human condition and that are yet uniquely mine? And how can I distinguish what is significant and what is not? Take the year 1933. It is a Sunday morning, sunny, the church bells ringing, I am five years old and my mother and I are on our way to morning Mass. I am running in front of her, almost dancing, calling out my pleasure at the new pair of shoes I have just gotten. I feel I can run as fast as the wind, that my mother is the most beautiful person in the whole world, that this is the best day of my life. Why should that sunlit morning return to me so often?

While I intend to tell the truth about my life, the unvarnished truth as the cliché has it, autobiography is the most chameleon of genres. The very choice of the autobiographical form involves a paradoxical form of censorship since what I privilege can displace or supplant other forms of revelation—the biography, for example—over which I do not have control. President Eisenhower wrote a voluminous book about his "crusade" in Europe when he was the Commander-in-Chief of all Allied Forces in the second world war. But there was no mention of the most important personal influence in his life at that time, his love affair with his military driver, a young Irish woman named Kay Summersby. I am not suggesting that I have suppressed material as dramatic as this—I merely point out that the exercise of writing an autobiography is sometimes an exercise in evasion. The best thing to do—without evasion—is to begin at the beginning, that is, on 6 July 1928 when I was born at 7 Bonavista Terrace, Larne, Northern Ireland. My first memories are of being in my pram with my twin sister Bernadette and hearing the ceaseless surge of the Irish Sea and the crying of seabirds in the sky above me. We were a large family consisting of my father, John Joseph, my mother born Isabella Green, my sister Mai, brothers Charlie, Hugh, Jackie (his twin sister Daisy died of pneumonia at age one), Françoise, Bernadette, Gerard, and finally Philomena. My mother, before she married, was a nurse and a midwife who spent a great many of her nursing years staying with rich families in England and Scotland while she cared for her pregnant patients, assisting with the birth, and remaining with mother and child for a few weeks. Before the year 1921 my father had been an officer in the Royal Irish Constabulary (his family came from the west of Ireland), but when Northern Ireland was established he transferred north to join the Royal Ulster Constabulary (R.U.C.). I suspect he did this because my mother was born in the north of Ireland, and because she saw no future for them in southern Ireland, where R.U.C. police officers had been regularly murdered. My father's first posting as an R.U.C. officer was to Irvingstown, County Fermanagh, which was a dangerous place since its population, predominantly Catholic, was violently opposed to the R.U.C. and the dominant British presence. My mother had a loaded gun to protect herself and the family when my father was on patrol and they had an agreed upon signal so that she knew when it was safe to open the door to him. It was against this background of political betrayal and violence that I grew up in a rump state where the rights of the minority Catholics were brutally suppressed and the Protestant majority retreated into a garrison-like mentality fed by ignorance and bigotry ("Home Rule is Rome Rule," "Ulster will fight and Ulster will be right"). Sir Edward Carson, a lawyer who had acted for the Marquis of Queensberry against Oscar Wilde, masterminded the partition of the ancient country of Ireland. Sometime in the mid 1930s my father was transferred from Larne to Ballymena, an inland town not many miles from Larne whose most famous citizen, Timothy Eaton, founded the flagship Eaton's department store in Toronto followed by a string of department stores across Canada. When I emigrated to Canada in 1954 my mother told me to look him up because, she claimed, anyone from Ballymena who asked for a job was never turned down. I dismissed this as motherly concern combined with hearsay but was surprised to learn many years later that this policy was in fact partially true—the policy did not, however, extend to Catholics seeking work. Another famous or infamous son was the Rev Ian Paisley. It was fitting that he should have been educated in Ballymena, which is often compared to the right wing, South Bible belt of the USA with its fundamentalist religious sects. Throughout his life Paisley publicly denounced the Pope as the Whore of Babylon and the Anti-Christ, he was violently opposed to gay rights ("Save Ulster from Sodomy"), and he fomented sectarian violence by his attacks upon Catholics. The British Government rewarded this clergyman's career in 2010 by conferring a peerage on him as Baron Bannside. I remember Ballymena vividly because I lived there from about the age of two until I was eleven. Most of the people in the area were originally from Scotland (transplanted there by the English who had driven out the native Irish Catholics at the beginning of the seventeenth century) and everyone spoke in a fairly thick Scottish accent. I myself used the words "yin" and "twa" as in "yin and yin makes twa" plus many other such phrases as "gie him a clobber on the gub" ("hit him on the mouth"). Every St Patrick's Day families climbed Slemish Mountain just outside Ballymena because tradition had it that St. Patrick tended sheep there as a young boy. The religious tensions also had their darkly comic side in Ballymena—when Protestant children forced Catholic children to curse the Pope, Catholic children forced Protestant children to curse King Billy. That "Billy" was the Protestant King William the Third who defeated the Catholic King James the Second in a fairly obscure Irish battle in 1690 was, I suspect, not known to many of these children. The date of the battle was the twelfth of July which was and is commemorated every year in the famous Orange processions.

    Preparations for the Twelfth of July begin months earlier when drummers start practicing on their huge Lambeg drums, lashing them with canes until often their hands bleed, while onlookers cheer them on by the light of great bonfires. The drumming reverberates menacingly for weeks throughout the cities and countryside reminding the Catholic minority of the power of the Orange Lodge. The marches on the Twelfth are an extraordinary spectacle involving hundreds of thousands of Orangemen in dark suits, orange sashes, bowler hats, and white gloves, parading under festooned arches and past homes flaunting British flags and gaily coloured streamers. Bands by the hundreds ("Kick the Pope" bands as they were known), mainly flute and drum, play patriotic songs.

> *It was old but it was beautiful*
> *And the colours they were fine...*
> *And it's on the Twelfth I love to wear*
> *The sash my father wore.*

Violence was rare during the marches, but after the music and the speeches there was a great deal of drinking that led easily to rioting. I can remember when I was about seven years old seeing drunken crowds of Orangemen surging past the windows of our house followed a little later by the police with truncheons in their hands hoping to control them. Leading the police was my father!

Against this background of political strife and the deep Depression of the 1930s our family life ran its fairly uneventful tenor. We were never poor—a police sergeant made a good salary and with care and economy we never went hungry. My mother was quite extraordinary in running a family that eventually numbered nine children. She followed the kind of household schedule that most families did at that time. If I remember rightly Monday was washing day—my mother had a washing lady who came in to help—Tuesday was ironing day, Wednesday was mending day, Thursday cleaning and dusting. Saturday night was always set aside for bathing when we used the bathroom and also a large tub placed in the kitchen. On Sunday our family (and all the other families) dressed up in our best clothes and we went to church. Sunday morning breakfast was always a little special since we got fried eggs and sausages. Our parents worked tirelessly to support their family. My father reported for duty at the police barracks every morning, five days a week, at eight a.m. for full inspection and returned home after his day ended at 6 p.m. In the evenings and especially at the weekends he cut the boys' hair, mended shoes, and cultivated a small garden to provide fresh vegetables and potatoes. In addition to all her household duties my mother was a nurse in times of illness—if, for example, one of us developed diphtheria, she set up an isolated bedroom in our house, hung sheets dipped in disinfectant on the doors, and nursed the child through the illness. Because my father came from Sligo in the west of Ireland he was raised on Irish music—jigs, reels, hornpipes—and especially Sligo fiddle music as played by neighbours Michael Coleman, James Morrison, and Paddy Killoran. This tradition was continued in our house. My brothers Charlie and Hugh were taught the violin (fiddle) by nuns and very soon they could play by ear dozens of these tunes. When my father heard a beggar playing for money in the streets of Ballymena, he would bring him home for dinner (to my mother's dismay) provided the beggar paid for his meal with Irish music. Mai, and Françoise, and Bernadette were taught Irish dancing—the very same steps basically as those jazzed up in the famous Riverdance sequence sixty years later. There were not many occasions when my parents entertained guests, but on these evenings my father would get a bottle of sherry for the ladies and a case of beer (stout) for the men—there was seldom whisky because it was expensive. There would also be tea and sandwiches and cake. Dancing and music would follow later in the evening (fiddle, piano, and harp provided by our family or by the guests)—if one did not have musical skills one could offer a recitation which was an acceptable alternative. I still remember repeated recitations of such poems as "He's gone to school, wee Hughie, and him not four…" and Percy French's long song "Abdul Abulbul Amir" sung from memory without a flaw:

> *They fought all that night neath the pale yellow moon,*
> *The din, it was heard from afar,*
> *And huge multitudes came, so great was the fame,*
> *Of Abdul and Ivan Skavar.*

I also remember one evening the excitement of my parents because they were going out to hear the world famous Irish tenor John McCormick—my mother looked very beautiful to me in her best clothes with a pearl necklace, and my father wore fashionable civilian clothes instead of his heavy black police uniform. I emphasize home entertainment because it was only in the late 1930s that we got a radio. Telephones were only for the rich. We did have movies in Ballymena and, in fact, children could pay their way in by bringing along a specified number of jam jars as payment! There were even men who travelled the towns and villages showing films—they sometimes came to our house, set up a sheet for screen, and showed (for a fee) one of the very limited number of films they had. From Spring to Fall military bands played in the parks of Ballymena—there was a very large Army barracks just outside the town. In command was a famous soldier General Adrian Carton de Wiart—we children often followed him in awe because he had a black patch over an eye he had lost in the First World War. I was also aware of the large number of men who hobbled about on crutches or who had lost an arm, victims of that war. Curiously, there were also many hanging around the main town squares who were clearly mentally deranged (they were called "idiots" by the people). They would now be hospitalized, but in those days they were accepted with extraordinary tolerance by the townsfolk and allowed to live their deranged lives in full public view. In summers we holidayed as a family in Portstewart, a northern seaside town on the Atlantic Ocean near the Giant's Causeway, where we rented a house for one month. As children we loved those holidays, swimming—there is a wonderful beach—looking for tiny fish, walking on the promenade with our parents in the evenings while a band played, and enjoying especially ice cream from the various Italian restaurants in the town. It was indicative of the times that Catholics in Northern Ireland holidayed in Portstewart while Protestants holidayed a few miles away in Portrush—a self protective ghettoization of sorts. The only time I left Northern Ireland as a child was to go to a funeral in Carrickbanagher, Sligo, in the west of Ireland. I cannot remember who in my father's family had died, but I do remember the wake when all the people from the surrounding farms came to bid farewell to the dead person who was lying in the house in an open coffin. There was much drinking (but no drunkenness), the old women smoked clay pipes, and there was much telling of stories. There were even keeners, women who were paid to weep over the diseased. In our family it was believed that when a member was about to die a ghostly woman, a *bean sidhe*, would give warning. On this occasion the family told the mourners that the *bean sidhe* had indeed appeared and no one thought to question this. I have never been surprised that the poetry of W.B. Yeats is full of ghosts and spirits—his family came from Collooney where my father's family attended the local Catholic Church.

In the late 1930s we got a radio which was installed in what we called the Front Room, a room reserved for special occasions. One such special occasion was an evening in 1938 when our family gathered to hear a speech from Prime Minister Chamberlain who had just returned from Munich, Germany, after talks with the German leader Adolf Hitler. Chamberlain gave his audience an assurance of peace in our time. Less than a year later I was fitted with a gas mask and first heard the ominous wailing of air raid sirens signaling the outbreak of war with Germany. In that same year, 1939, my father was transferred from Ballymena to the outskirts of Belfast. And so began a new phase of my life.

Belfast in 1939 was the largest city in Ireland with a population just under half a million. It was a leading industrial city on a par with English cities like Manchester and Liverpool and was known chiefly for its huge shipyard—one of the largest in the world—its building of aircraft, and its linen industry. It was here that the famous "Titanic" was built just before the 1914–18 war, when it was sent to Southampton, England, prior to making its maiden (and final) voyage to New York. But I heard little mention of "Titanic"—it was as if its sinking represented a kind of stain or an indefinable punishment for some vague crime. Belfast's shipyard also built battleships and aircraft carriers for the Royal Navy. When some years later I got to know Dublin, the capital of southern Ireland, I was struck by the great difference between both cities; Belfast was industrial, highly technical, dominated by a Protestant (Presbyterian) work ethic while Dublin seemed still a late nineteen-century city where the arts were regarded as more important than the sciences, where an oral tradition still existed as opposed to the modern communications systems of the North, and where the work ethic was much closer to that of Catholic continental countries like Italy and Spain. Despite its wealth, there was a great deal of poverty in Belfast. Unemployment ran as high as 25 percent and tuberculosis was rampant. I was saddened at the sight of hundreds of young women in shawls returning at dusk from the tobacco and linen factories that dotted the cities. They were prisoners of a dreadful work routine that cut short their youth and condemned them to lives of poverty and large families and a future without hope. The new school that I now entered in Belfast in August 1940—Newington Catholic School—close by Duncairn Gardens where our new house was situated—was very different from what I had expected. Our work in the school in Ballymena followed the curriculum set down by the Ministry of Education, but in my new school the work was far more exacting, written work far more precise, and home work (which we rarely had in Ballymena) now taking up at least an hour and a half every evening. The teachers were very well prepared and there was no undue punishment of the pupils—but there was a conviction that this school had a reputation as being the best Catholic school in Belfast and that pupils must work hard to maintain that reputation. I would like to say that I flourished in this new academic environment but I didn't. I was overwhelmed by Belfast, by the size of the city, by the strangeness of the boys I met, by their baiting me because of my accent (they did not have an accent, I did!), by my new teachers, by the high standard of the work being done by the other pupils. Gradually my marks began to drop, I worked harder and harder, but nothing seemed to help. I was saved from my misery by the intervention of Hitler's *Luftwaffe*. In 1940 Germany, having defeated the French and the British in Europe, soon occupied much of France from where their planes could attack all parts of the British Isles, including Northern Ireland. So it was that the *Luftwaffe* sent a small number of bombers in April 1941 over Belfast in preliminary bombing raids and, finding the defences negligible, mounted a huge raid on 15 April that lasted for hours. I remember that night vividly. When the sirens sounded, my mother woke us, got us dressed, and shepherded us down to the kitchen. My father was on duty on the outskirts of the city and so it was left to my mother to try to protect her family. Within a very short time of the sirens sounding the alarm, the bombs began to fall in the distance, some with a strange whistling sound one heard just before the explosions. Very soon the bombing grew nearer, enemy planes could be plainly heard, and plaster fell off the ceilings and walls of our house. At that my mother made us sit with her in a space below the kitchen stairs. Not long after our very large kitchen window was blown in with hundred of glass shards ripping into the sofa and chairs on which we had been sitting about ten minutes earlier. By this time the lights had gone out, the blackout curtains had been torn apart, and our house was full of light from burning houses all around ours. We must have sat there under the stairs for about an hour when we heard a whistle blowing and a couple of Air Raid Wardens came into the house looking to see if anyone was alive. They told us to clear out of the house and go to a school about a quarter of a mile away. It was difficult to get out because there was so much debris in the hallway, blown off the ceilings and walls. In the street outside all was smoke and flames with many of the houses collapsed. As my mother huddled us along, we heard a huge whistling which we now knew meant that a bomb was falling close by and we fell on the street. I remember thinking that if I looked back at where the bomb was falling I would be killed (like Lot's wife in the Bible who was turned into a pillar of salt). But I did look back and I saw the house opposite ours explode as it was hit. I also saw the naked foot of a woman lying on the street in front of me and I was fascinated by the slow trickle of blood that ran down her foot. When I close my eyes now, so many years later, I can still see that blood. We soon got up and walked in the direction of Antrim Road—about one hundred metres away—where we found that a concrete air shelter had collapsed. Outside it British soldiers were trying to dig out the bodies inside and again I remember being struck by their nonchalance as they smoked, dug, and passed around cups of tea. Had we followed instructions we had been given some months before in a government pamphlet we would have been in that shelter. I mention the nonchalance of the soldiers because I myself felt absolutely no fear in the face of the carnage around me. I do not put this down to courage but rather to my age—I was too young to fully understand the danger I was in. Eventually that night we arrived at a school where there was simple food and drinks and medical personnel to care for the wounded. We children (Jackie, Bernadette, Gerard, Françoise, Philomena, and I) played or dozed off early morning when we were allowed to go home. There we found my father. Again Air Raid Wardens came along and advised him that the house was too dangerous to live in, that it would have to be demolished. Somehow he found transportation and we all set off that day with a few possessions to live in the country with my Uncle Eugene. Cherry Hill farm, Ballymagin, Maralin (sometimes called Magheralin), was to be my next home.

Long after these events I learned that over two hundred German bombers had spent some six hours bombing Belfast, that the anti-aircraft batteries did not fire from fear of hitting their own British planes which did not, in fact, fly that night, that some 1000 people were killed and that 100,000 homes (more than half the city's stock of housing) was destroyed, that the Waterworks, so close to our home, was a primary target so as to immobilize firefighting activity. And much later when I married it was to a woman who as a child living in Berlin endured the thousand-bomber raids launched by "our" air forces to destroy that city and its inhabitants.

Maralin was a tiny village (perhaps two hundred people) about thirty miles from Belfast, and our Cherry Hill farm was about two miles distant from it, deep in the heart of the country. We children were familiar with the village because we often visited my mother's family there and we had heard her sing verses from an old ballad "The Ducks of Magheralin":

> *Oh it is the finest city in the real old fashioned style,*
> *A credit to the County Down, the pride of the Emerald Isle.*
> *It is the finest harbour for the bread carts to sail in,*
> *And if ever you sail to Ireland you'll sail by Magheralin.*

My Uncle Eugene was a bachelor and family myth had it that in his youth he had been deeply in love with Violet, our cousin, but she had refused his offer of marriage. Whatever the truth of the matter, it gave him a certain stature with us children—the lonely rejected bachelor who compensated for lost love by an extraordinary fondness for American cowboy stories which he devoured every night when he went to bed.

Unlike our neighbours Uncle Eugene was not a progressive farmer. He still used horses for his ploughing and threshing—great eighteen-hand high Clydesdales that he entered in competitions. We children would brush the horses until their skins shone and my sisters and mother would weave ribbons in the horses' manes. There was no running water in the farmhouse—we drew water from a deep well just outside the farmhouse door, a well so deep that it took many seconds before a dropped stone made a sound. The water was always ice cold and fresh. The floor of the kitchen and the bedrooms were of clay but when we moved in my parents arranged to have proper cement floors installed. Cooking was done over an open fire which was a terrible burden on my mother; later she got a stove. These conditions must have seemed primitive to my mother who owned a beautiful house in Larne (now leased), and our very fine Duncairn Gardens home, and who had spent so many years as a midwife in the homes of rich families in England and Scotland. Because we were on a farm we were spared the worst effects of the rationing system that the British Government had introduced as a war time measure. The standard two eggs per person and four ounces of butter per person per week represented a real hardship. After 1940 one rarely saw an orange and never bananas or grapes or any fruit that had to be imported. Margarine was used to supplement our butter rations but it was universally hated. Even clothes were rationed and silk stockings became a rarity—Mai, like other girls her age, tanned her legs with some kind of oil and used a lipstick marker (I think) to draw a line up the back of her legs.

We children walked to Maralin for church services and to school—my uncle and parents went to church in a trap or small carriage. What I found interesting about going to Mass was how the priest collected money. As each parishioner gave his donation, the amount was written down in a notebook by the collectors and about every three months the priest read out the Collection List mentioning each parishioner by name with the amount given. This list was one of the chief topics of conversation but, interestingly, the practice itself was never criticized or condemned. Our new school was quite small and consisted of two classrooms with some thirty-five students. We had the same curriculum as that in my Belfast school but I now revelled in my new surroundings. I loved the little village and life on the farm; there were only two others in the final grade, both girls, so I was not subject to bullying or ridicule. Best of all, my teacher took me under his wing within a month of my arrival marking me out as a student eager to learn. He was an older man, close to retirement he told me. He gave me extra tuition and he lent me books to read. My marks shot up. Soon, he told me, he would help me prepare to write scholarship examinations that summer. The result was increased coaching and reading, which I enjoyed and which seemed to please him. Soon the summer holidays came along and off I went to St Malachy's College in Belfast and also to St Colman's College in the town of Newry to write their scholarship tests.

Naturally we helped out on the farm and that summer of 1941 I cleaned out barns, learned how to milk a cow, weeded the turnips and pulled thistles (a job I hated), tied the corn sheaves that Uncle Eugene cut as he sat on the reaping machine with his two great horses pulling, sprayed the potatoes with bluestone. It was that summer too that I first began to feel a love of nature—to be out early in the fields when the dew was fresh, to swim in the pond that was on the farm, to hear the variety of birds that I had not known in the city—magpies, swallows, linnets, larks—and to watch out for the feral cats that haunted the barns but were rarely seen. At night the stars were clearly visible since there was no industry near us and the blackout rules meant that every house had its curtains drawn against the threat of German bombers. I had lots of time for play with my brothers and sisters—the one with whom I played most was my seven-year old sister Philomena who followed me everywhere. It was more than fifty years later when I saw a photograph of her that I realized that my beloved Philomena suffered from Down's Syndrome.

In July came news that I had won scholarships to both St Malachy's College, and St Colman's College, Newry, and my parents decided that I should go to Newry as a boarder. Soon came a letter telling me what clothes I should require and that I should also bring three serviette rings and six linen serviettes and two pairs of football boots. All these things were purchased in the nearby town of Lurgan, the summer flew by, and then it was time to leave. My Uncle saddled up the trap, my trunk with all my worldly goods (including those serviette rings) was loaded up, and with my mother we set off for the town of Lurgan where my mother and I would take the train to Newry where I would begin my new life. Everyone waved goodbye. Philomena ran after us crying for me unrestrainedly. I never saw her again and the remembrance of her tears has stayed with me all my life.

College Days
and Irish Nationalism

In August 1941, at the age of thirteen, I entered St Colman's College, Newry, about thirty miles south of Belfast. It was a warm day when my mother and I walked out of the city and up a long winding road to the College. We came to a gatehouse and an avenue that led to the College buildings on a hill in the midst of a very large estate. As we walked we passed a grotto presided over by a statue of the Virgin Mary. In the distance the College, a large red building, came in view. It housed classrooms for the pupils, separate dormitories for junior and senior boys, a library, a large study hall with a desk for each student, a dining hall, rooms for the priests who taught at the College, rooms for the nuns who looked after the cooking and operated a basic medical service. To the left as one faced the College was a chapel. To the left of the chapel there was a large house in its own grounds on a higher elevation which was known as The Bishop's House. To the right of the College were two football grounds where Gaelic football and field sports were played. This college was to be my home for the next five years.

My mother walked me to the main building where we met the President of the College, a priest by the name of Boyle, to whom my mother entrusted me. We returned along the avenue, past the grotto and its statue of the Virgin Mary, and at the gatehouse my mother kissed me goodbye with tears in her eyes. I was alone for the first time in my life. But I was not afraid. I could not imagine life here would be any different from the life I had led up to this point, a life surrounded by my brothers and sisters and loving parents. I was a part of them, I was Eugene, I was family. At St Colman's College, I thought, I was merely joining a larger family.

But life was not like that here. For a start I was no longer Eugene—I was Benson, a first-year student who knew no one, who had no friends, and who had to learn quickly the rules governing the College. And there was a host of rules that had to be followed. Up at seven in the morning, Mass in the Chapel (unheated even in winter), breakfast at eight, classes at nine, lunch at twelve, classes till three, sports from then until after four, study from five till seven, dinner at seven, followed by study, then evening prayers at nine, and so to bed with lights out at ten. The teaching staff was largely made up of priests because the College began as a seminary-boarding school for Catholic boys who could be influenced to join the priesthood. These priests, including Father Boyle, offered a curriculum in 1941 that reflected that seminary background; it included Latin and Greek, languages necessary for all entrants to Maynooth Seminary in the south of Ireland where Irish priests were trained. English and Gaelic were also offered to us and history, maths (algebra, trigonometry, arithmetic), chemistry and physics, and religious knowledge. Lay teachers offered physics and chemistry, painting (Miss Boyle, the sole woman on staff). My favourite teacher was Monsieur Delafaille, a plump little man from Belgium who was also the organist in the Cathedral in Newry. He taught singing, directed our school concerts and musicals, and he gave private lessons, for a fee, in violin and piano—I took violin lessons with him for four years. When he appeared at the operettas he directed in the College he brought his wife along, a pretty attractive woman, also plump, whom we students adored and lusted after.

The flush of the first days' excitement soon wore off and then, inevitably, homesickness set in. During the days one was so busy that one had little time to think of family. But at night, in the junior dormitory when the lights went out the sound of muffled weeping was often heard. And how could it be otherwise? We were children of a "tender" age, surrounded by strangers, overwhelmed by the loss of our parents and brothers and sisters, subjected often to bullying by older boys and to beatings by the priests. There were new subjects to be learned, new faces to meet that one hoped would not be hostile, new codes that one didn't understand and, not understanding, exposed one to mockery, to exclusion from the tribe that would protect you if only you knew what the code was. It would be weeks, months in some cases, before a carapace of endurance and self-protectiveness grew over the wounds of these students, these children. But when pain came, it would be felt even more intensely because of the rawness of these wounds. One day I was called to see Father Boyle. He had a message from home. My sister Philomena had died. Of diphtheria. I took the news calmly but when I left him I raced to the boys' toilets and locked the door. And I heard myself, not crying, but howling. Howls of pain for my dead Philomena and for my family so far away, for my loneliness, for the abuse showered on us by the priests.

But even in the worst of settings humans find modes of accommodation. The first years went by and I was taller, stronger in physique, more knowing and more known by those in the classes above me. I could defend myself. I achieved stature when I was picked for the junior football team and, special distinction, I was also (in my third year!) on the senior team. On the sports team I won respect because I had beaten all my opponents in the Northern Ireland Catholic High Schools Sports Championships in the mile event and the shot putt. I became a favourite of my teachers and so I wasn't beaten as many of the other boys were. Life offered me its blessings—books, music, sports. And soon I made friends. Laurence and Sean and Kieran and Martin and Joe and most of my classmates as well as those on my football team and the sports team and all those who discovered Keats with me and Shelley and Byron and Emily Brönte and Dickens and the movies of Hollywood. I became fifteen and, though damaged, I survived.

Life at St Colman's College in those far away 1940s was as if one lived in a monastery. We were about one hundred boys from age twelve or to eighteen who spent most of the year (except for Christmas and two months in the summer) isolated from contact with the outer world. We had no access to newspapers or to radio or to the telephone and we had little contact with those living outside the College. By rule we wrote home once a week and when our parents replied it was to give us family news. Nothing about the outside world. But rumours from the outside did seep in—Pearl Harbour (where exactly was it?) had been bombed by the Japanese, Germany's armed forces were at the gates of Moscow, U-boats were sinking great numbers of Allied ships (we learned of this when one of the students lost his brother at sea in the Mediterranean), Allied Forces had landed in North Africa, American soldiers in great numbers were flooding into Northern Ireland and the UK. One day Monsieur Delafaille brought an American soldier, Guido Avelloni, to sing for us. He had been training in San Francisco to be an opera singer before he was conscripted. His recital—a selection of arias for tenor—was a revelation to me of what the classically trained voice was capable of. I never forgot that American soldier, but although I searched for his name later among the casts of various operatic companies I never found it.

But these world events were not at the centre of our universe. It was dominated by study, examinations, sports, performing in plays and concerts, and keeping out of trouble with our teachers. They all had canes and when we were found breaking any of their rules we were beaten on the open palms of our hands. I do not remember any of the lay teachers beating the students—only some of the priests, and especially the President, Father Boyle. He beat the younger boys unmercifully and terrorized the students in his classes in Latin. We were very seldom in the company of girls but there was one occasion when we attended an event where girls from the convents in and around Newry were present. An Irish travelling theatre group called the Anew McMaster Play Company performed *Macbeth* to the hum of boys and girls whispering and giggling as they exchanged notes or flirted with each other. One of our boys, Hendry, managed to get a girl's address but when she replied to his letter, it was intercepted by Boyle who summoned the entire body of students to the central study hall and read out the girl's letter to all of us as Hendry squirmed. Labelling the correspondence salacious and disgusting, Father Boyle then expelled Hendry from St. Colman's College. I can only guess at the damage done to that boy.

I do not remember any direct evidence of homosexuality, which the priests denounced as the gravest of sins. Prefects of the two dormitories were warned that boys should never be allowed to sleep in the same bed although it was customary at that time for boys to sleep two-abed with a brother when at home. From time to time a new boy, thirteen or even younger, marked by an unreal quality of beauty, entered the College, and by some kind of telegraphic herd instinct he was instantly nicknamed "Lady." This nickname, unlike many others, was not meant to hurt or demean. Indeed, the two boys that I knew as "Lady" were given a special status in which they were observed and admired from a distance but never molested in any way. Every Saturday students had to take a shower and every Saturday, as the junior boys undressed Father Boyle, flushed of face and cane in hand, entered the dormitory ostensibly to hasten the boys to the shower rooms. Nakedness was everywhere on display as the frightened youngsters scattered trying to evade Boyle's cane and eyes.

What also isolated us from the outside world was the religious character of our environment. The liturgical year dominated our lives: Christmas—the Birth, the coming of the Wise Men, the Epiphany—Lent, Good Friday,

Easter Sunday. For these feast days the student body walked downtown to Newry Cathedral where the Bishop presided over the services. Most memorable was the Good Friday evening service when in the great Cathedral all the lights were extinguished except one candle which, symbolizing the crucified Christ, was ultimately quenched to represent his death. The liturgical singing at these liturgical events was done by priests with beautiful voices accompanied by male choirs. The vestments of the clergy complemented the various services with colours appropriate to the occasion.

A notable event of the school year was the Retreat when a visiting priest came to the College to preach to us about our salvation and to remind us of non-earthly things. This took the form of sermons on such things as Death, Hell, the Seven Deadly Sins, and so on. In James Joyce's *A Portrait of the Artist as a Young Man* there is a wonderfully accurate description of such a Retreat—little was changed in my day. I always associate those Retreats with cold dark weather and days that seemed to stretch on and on and I am still haunted by memories of these priests, dressed always in black, who came to us in the gloomy evenings to speak of damnation and sin. These sermons, full of apocalyptic warnings, were quite traumatic for some of the student body because of their relentless detail about the eternal punishments awaiting the sinner. All this was prelude to Confession in order to obtain absolution. To what sins did we confess? Since we knew by rote what the mortal sins were—Pride, Covetousness, Lust, Anger, Gluttony, Envy, and Sloth—we had a fine selection. Who has not at some time been lazy, proud, angry? And so, burdened with guilt, we confessed our sins and were forgiven. It was a religion of suppression—suppression of imagination, of creativity, of sexuality, of enquiry—but we were then too young to know that and our youth provided us a kind of protection.

Once a year the Bishop descended on us from the mysterious Bishop's House to conduct Oral Examinations in Greek and Latin. We were assembled in the Study Hall and one by one the boys in the two Senior grades were called upon to come forward and sit at a small table below the dais where the Bishop, awesome in his full episcopal robes, presided. Accompanied by the President, Father Boyle, he examined us in an exercise little changed from that of the Middle Ages when Abelard and Duns Scotus and Aquinas had been interrogated in like manner. I remember, as if it were yesterday, being asked to open my Greek text of *Seven Against Thebes* by

Aeschylus and to read from it. The Bishop then called on me to translate after which he singled out verbs and ask me to name the mood—indicative, conditional, subjunctive—whether passive or active, and he went on to select nouns that I was expected to decline. The same thing happened with Latin texts. And so Aeschylus, Xenophon, Herodotus, Caesar, Livy, Virgil and many others of the Ancients were read aloud in Ulster accents under the eye of the Holy Roman Catholic and Apostolic Church and we trembled, were praised or rebuked, and returned thankfully to our seats. For those who had a flair for languages, this was an ordeal; for those who had not these public oral examinations were a public torture, an academic *auto da fé,* to be remembered for years with revulsion.

But if the College, and the Church, had their own rules, we the students had ours—unwritten, but encompassing every area of our lives. The basic rule was that the priests of the College were our natural enemy against whom we devised elaborate strategies. At the sight of a priest coming a student would hiss "Nix" which was then passed from student to student to alert those doing what they did not wish to be seen doing—such as smoking a cigarette or playing cards. It was also understood that boys would not "squeal" on each other, or reveal to the priests who was responsible for breaking a College rule. This was important because the College used the boys to discipline themselves. Thus there was a Head Prefect responsible for the entire student body. In the Dining Room there was a Head Table at which sat the Head Prefect. The other boys sat at tables with a Prefect at the head of each table, with the most junior boys being at tables furthest removed from the Head Prefect's table. In general, these Prefects tried not to send boys to the priests to be punished.

There was also a Prefect for the junior dormitory and one for the senior dormitory. Ten o'clock was lights out but since it was difficult to get the boys to go to sleep immediately, storytelling was allowed. I do not remember why or how I was selected to be a storyteller but late in my first year I was asked by the Prefect to tell a story and thus commenced some three years of storytelling. A few minutes after the lights were turned out I began. It might be my version of various books that I had read, *The Mill on the Floss, Oliver Twist, The Hunchback of Notre Dame, The Count of Monte Cristo, Treasure Island.* I also told stories based on films I had seen—*The Adventures of Robin Hood, Captain Blood, Gone with the Wind, A Tale of Two Cities,* and many more. Like most of the boys,

I knew the names of a great many film stars—John Wayne, Tom Mix, Errol Flynn, Hopalong Cassidy, Clark Gable, Rita Hayworth, Betty Grable, Alan Ladd, and Hedy Lamar. And so, night after night, I told tales of Rita Hayworth leading Tyrone Power to destruction in *Blood and Sand*, of the horribly misshapen Quasimodo who loved the gypsy Esmeralda, of David Copperfield running away from his cruel stepfather. Within twenty minutes or so the boys would drift off to sleep and the Prefect would tell me to stop. The following night I picked up where I had left off. I do not know how long this extraordinary form of entertainment continued at the College, but I look back on my story telling with some astonishment, astonishment because it then seemed so natural a thing to do and because the telling of stories came to me so easily.

While St Colman's College was meant to influence boys to enter the priesthood on graduation, it also served another purpose in that it was a bastion of Irish Catholic nationalism. While the College followed the curriculum prescribed by the British government it was, in spirit, loyal to Dublin and not London or Belfast and this loyalty permeated every aspect of its teaching especially in such subjects as English, History, and Gaelic. Neither cricket nor soccer (the games of the Britisher) was allowed, only Gaelic football and hurling. In our History classes we learned Ireland's ancient history and of its struggles against English domination and soon I fell in love with the idealized Ireland presented so alluringly as the tragic and beautiful Dark Rosaleen by such nineteenth-century poets as James Clarence Mangan:

> O, *my Dark Rosaleen,*
> *Do not sigh, do not weep!*
> *The priests are on the ocean green,*
> *They march along the deep.*
> *There's wine from the royal Pope,*
> *Upon the ocean green;*
> *And Spanish ale shall give you hope,*
> *My Dark Rosaleen!*

Our heroes became Wolfe Tone, Robert Emmet who was hanged, drawn and quartered by the British and mourned by his sweetheart ("She is far from the land where her young hero sleeps"), and Patrick Pearse and the other men who were shot by the British in 1916 after they took over Dublin's General Post Office and proclaimed the birth of the Republic of Ireland.

When I returned home for the holidays these nationalistic ideas surfaced and my mother was shocked by my espousal of the nationalist cause (then championed most loudly by the Irish Republican Army). She argued that our family were taking the King's shilling (because my father was in the Royal Ulster Constabulary) and therefore we owed allegiance to the English King and government. Surprisingly, my father never objected to my political stance. Perhaps he shared my views. Certainly he must have felt conflicted by his position as an officer in a paramilitary force that was predominantly Protestant and anti-Catholic, and he must also have remembered with pain his brother Francis murdered by his co-religionists and countrymen. The very lively and continuing political debate between me and my mother often resembled the Christmas dinner argument so powerfully depicted in James Joyce's *A Portrait of the Artist as a Young Man* where the Dedalus family argue over the fate of Charles Parnell, famous Irish politician, and the role the Irish Catholic Church played in betraying him.

My nationalistic views were reinforced by my study of the Irish language. In my first class at St Colman's College, my teacher, Father Petit, gave me my Gaelic name—*Eoghan MacBineid*—and that was the name I went by throughout my five years in his class. In my third year I won a summer scholarship to the *Gaeltacht* in *Rann na Feirste*, Donegal, in the north west area of the Republic. I and a number of other students—boys and girls from the Catholic secondary schools of Ulster—took a train and then a bus into this very remote part of Ireland. Divided into very small groups of three or four at most we were lodged with the local farmers for whom Gaelic was their everyday language. We were warned that if we spoke *Beurla* (English) we would be immediately sent home in disgrace. For the next three weeks we attended classes every day in Irish history, Gaelic, dancing (reels, hornpipes, jigs and so on), and we learned Gaelic songs like "*An Chuilfhionn*" and "*Bheir Me Ó*".

> *I mo cláirseach ní raibh ceol*
> *I mo mheoraibh ní raibh brí*
> *Nó gur luaigh tú do rún*
> *'S fuair mé eolas ar mo dhán.*

[There was no music in my harp
No power in my fingers
Until you said you loved me
And I found my poem.]

I loved the *Gaeltacht* and especially because we now had girls in our classes—redheaded girls, blond haired girls, funny girls, clever girls, adventuresome girls—young people just like us boys. On certain evenings we were brought to various farm houses where a *seanachie* (a storyteller) recited by memory Irish tales. We set out across the hills, the sea not far distant, in the summer evening, laughing and joking and flirting until we reached the designated farm house. The *seanachie* always began with the formulaic opening, *Uair amháin agus ar feadh tamaill agus i bhfad ó shin bhi sé...* ("Once upon a time and a long time ago it was . . . ") and then proceeded at great length. We sat in the kitchen by the turf fire trying to follow what was being said while the *bean a tighe* (woman of the house) went about her chores, knitting, weaving, or baking. Such immersion quickly improved our command of the language and soon I wore a *fáinne* (gold ring) in my lapel as a sign to others that I was a Gaelic speaker and would welcome conversation in the language.

During the summer and Christmas holidays of 1942, 1943, and 1944, I returned to the farm at Ballymagin where I was very much part of the farming community. I was now a strong young teenager eager to lend a helping hand. In the summer I joined in getting in the harvest—tying the corn (wheat) as it was cut by Uncle Eugene on the horse-drawn reaper, placing it in stooks (hay stacks) to await the threshing. In this process the seed was winnowed from the corn by feeding it into a threshing machine, which was driven by two horses walking in a circle and so powering the machine. I worked with other farm laborers pitching up the sheaves to my uncle who fed the machines. This was hard and dirty work but like most teenagers I revelled in my strength and on being now accepted as an adult. There were other jobs such as the weeding of thistles from the fields, planting potatoes, "dunging out" the byres of the cows and pigs, milking the cows and sometimes a goat. I even got to plough which represented a real challenge since it meant I had to guide a huge Clydesdale horse while at the same time trying to keep the plough in a straight line.

Once my Uncle, unable to find someone older, had me hold a number of pigs while he castrated them. Farm life was tough and basic—young people soon learned the facts of life, surrounded as they were by the whole business of breeding in order to live. The cow had to be led to the bull, the mare to the stallion, the rooster was everywhere with his hens, and wild cats produced litters regularly in the lofts and byres and preyed on the plentiful farm mice.

During these months of holidays I did have access to newspapers and the radio and so learned of the progress of the war then raging around the world—the battle of Stalingrad, America's push across the islands of the Pacific in its war on Japan, the Allies landings in Italy, preparations for D-Day and invasion of Europe. Northern Ireland was now home to hundreds of thousands of American troops and popular American culture in the form of films and music was all pervasive. People learned to dance the jitterbug and the radio broadcast popular hits like "Boogie Woogie Bugle Boy" and "Coming in on a Wing and a Prayer".

My last two years in college were very pleasant for I was now very much a part of the student "establishment"—the prefect of the senior dormitory; an actor (the Major General in Gilbert and Sullivan's *Pirates of Penzance*, for example, and playing the lead role in a play written entirely in Gaelic); good at sports. All the things so terribly important in one's teens. The priest in charge of sports was a Father McGovern ("Bertie" to the students), a humane man who never beat the boys. He was later posted to the small parish of Maralin where I had attended school and there he remained as Parish Priest until he died. He is buried in front of the church thirty metres from where my parents and Philomena lie buried.

There was another priest who did not use the cane, Father Owens ("Tony") who taught English. He influenced me greatly because he was so enthusiastic about his subject and because he related literature and music to his summer travels to Rome and Salamanca in Spain. Under his guidance I began to understand more fully the nature of literature and how the words of the great writers seemed magical, offering entrance to the world of the imagination, a world that seemed somehow superior to and more challenging than the ordinariness of everyday life. One of my earliest insights into the nature of this other world came from a desire to understand more fully the imagery and symbolism of Shelley's "Ode to the West Wind." Why, I wondered, does Shelley personify the wind? And why does he seek to be identified with it: "Be thou, Spirit fierce, / My spirit." And it came gradually to me that the ode was very similar in essence to the Gregorian plain chant hymn we often sang in the College Chapel and which begins, *"Veni creator Spiritus, mentes tuorum visita"* ("Come, creative Spirit, visit our minds"); that this hymn was traditionally associated with the feast of Pentecost when to the sound of a great wind the Holy Spirit descended upon the Apostles inspiring them to go forth and transform the world. That too was Shelley's message—the poet, inspired by the creative spirit, would redeem the world through art:

> *Scatter, as from an unextinguished hearth*
> *Ashes and sparks, my words among mankind!*

Up to this time I had always thought of redemption and salvation in terms of Christian theology; now the thought that another force might offer salvation came to me very often.

In my final year I began to think seriously about what I would do with my life. Become a medical doctor? A teacher? A lawyer? A priest? The latter attracted me greatly, partly, I suspect, because the College environment was an ever-present stimulant. Our teachers were priests, our education was imbued with Catholic thought, the College Chapel was a place we attended every morning and evening, influential preachers came often to speak of non-material things. And of course at the age of seventeen I was young enough to be idealistic, to reject the rewards offered by a professional career in the world—and to ignore, or forgive, the cruelty of the priest Boyle. And so finally I decided to become a priest. But one did not become a priest in the way one became a doctor or a lawyer. The priesthood was a vocation—one had to be called by God. And it seemed to me that I was being called, not by any overt sign but by the ever growing conviction that I could help others to live a better and fuller and more spiritual life. But I would not go to Maynooth College where clerical students were trained before taking up parish life in Ireland. My idealism demanded more than that. I would seek something more challenging, something that offered a newer world and a new vision.

Came the end of my last college year with Final Examinations in June 1946 (the War in Europe and Japan now over), a period of intense study from morning to night, and then the end of the school year and my college years. In the Chapel, as always, there was a final Mass to mark the end of the school year where the organ played and we sang: *Te Deum, laudamus . . . Et laudamus nomen tuum in saeculum, et in saeculum saeculi.*" Time to say goodbye, time for me to enter another phase of my life. And I now knew what it was. I had decided to become a priest in the Society of St Patrick whose priests were destined to spend their lives and ministry in Nigeria, Africa, spreading the Gospel. Bringing the message of salvation to the heathen. I had found my challenge and my future.

Saint Thomas Aquinas and Ravel's Boléro

In September of 1946, when I had just turned eighteen, I traveled to Kiltegan, a village about twenty-five miles south of Dublin in County Wicklow where the Mother House of the Saint Patrick's Missionary Society is located. We first year students—probationary students—lived about three miles distant from the Mother House. My new home was a castle, Humewood Castle, complete with turrets, spirelets, and towers and situated in spacious grounds. Built in the nineteenth century by Member of Parliament William Hume Dick, the castle was inherited by his granddaughter Mimi, daughter-in-law of General Maxim Weygand who had been Commander-in-Chief of the Allied Armies in France in 1940. Madame Weygand had leased the Castle to St Patrick's Missionary Society for an indefinite period and so I and twenty-seven other young men took up residence here for the first year of training for the priesthood.

My new life was totally different from anything I had known up to this point. It was, in a very real sense, a spiritual boot camp. The military allusion is not accidental since our spiritual training was based on that devised by a former Spanish soldier turned priest—Ignatius of Loyola, the founder of the Jesuit Order, later canonized a Saint of the Church. We probationers were assigned three priests to shepherd us through this crucial year. One was the Vicar General of the Society who would be our Spiritual Director and mentor; the second, our Dean, a general factotum who made sure we followed the rules and who was responsible for the day-to-day running of the novitiate; the third a priest to hear our confessions. The day began with Mass at 6 a.m., breakfast at 8 a.m. followed by time for various chores. Classes commenced at 9 a.m. when we learned the history of the Society and its Constitution and our rights and obligations; lessons and practice in plain chant, the liturgical music of the Church; Church history; and studies in the lives of the saints. At two-thirty p.m. we had dinner during which a student read aloud from the Gospels or from the lives of the Saints. Such readings might include François Mauriac's life of Margaret of Cortona, the autobiography of Saint Thérèse of Lisieux, or selections from the writings of Saint Augustine, Saint Bernard of Clairvaux, and Saint Teresa of Ávila. Following dinner we worked in the grounds of the Castle mowing the lawns, raking leaves, or weeding the long avenues. Supper was at 7 p.m. with Solemn Silence beginning at 8.30 when we had evening meditation before going to bed at nine-thirty. We were allowed to receive letters, but we had no other contact with the outside world—it was even more hermetically sealed to outside influences than St. Colman's College. There were, of course, no women. Such a life might seem utterly boring but it was in fact given meaning by our fierce determination to become priests. We believed very much that we were chosen—our mentors emphasized time and time again that the word "vocation" had its etymological roots in the Latin word *vocare*, to call. Additionally, we were in the Society of our own free will—we could leave at any time if we wished.

In our second month a new phase of our spiritual boot camp began. This was a thirty-day Retreat devoted to the Spiritual Exercises set down by Loyola in a guidebook as terse and organized as a military manual. The first week would constitute an examination of the nature of sin, the second Christ's life and works, the third week His passion and death, and the fourth His resurrection. During this month a Grand Silence prevailed and talking was allowed only on the ninth and twentieth days. Classes were suspended so that the entire four weeks could be devoted to spiritual readings, examination of conscience, and prayer. Four periods were set aside daily for meditation following the four daily sermons or lectures given by the Spiritual Director. This was new and fearsome territory to us. We were asked to abandon the comfortable world we knew—family comforts, attachment to friends, the desire for worldly goods—for a world of the spirit where such things were seen as a hindrance to those seeking enlightenment. Slowly I began to understand the saying of Jesus that a man must be born again before he could enter the Kingdom of Heaven. There must be death before a new birth and this Retreat was a preparation for that death. The rarified atmosphere of the Retreat soon began to take its toll. In the first week two students left the Society, in the second week two more, four others by the end of the month.

A great deal of the stress quite obviously was caused by this new regimen in which we were called upon to learn techniques to deal with an environment that was almost totally spiritual. How does one meditate for a half hour? For an hour? Suspended in this month-long state of meditation, texts in the Gospels took on startling clarity. "What does it profit a man if he gain the whole world and suffer the loss of his soul?" I was familiar with the text, "He who is the without sin among you cast the first stone," but now what came to me with startling clarity was not only the tolerance of Christ but the fact that it was customary in His time for women to be stoned to death for adultery according to the law of Moses.

As our journey into the Exercises developed I began to see more clearly the pattern in Christ's life and its place in human history—his descent into this world in the Incarnation, his thirty-three years as prophet, king, and priest, his Passion which represents his entry into the lower world of Hell and his triumph over it before reappearing in the material world at his Resurrection, completing the cycle with his ascent to rejoin his Father in the Ascension. While other religions embraced a cyclical vision of history, Christianity saw history as a movement in Time from creation *ex nihilo* to a goal—oneness with Christ-God. The design of the Bible itself—Genesis to Apocalypse—is the design of Christian history.

Most difficult was the daily wrestling with intense and prolonged examination of one's state of mind and one's soul. Purgation or cleansing of sin is the first stage in transcending the world of the flesh. But how does one progress beyond that stage to the path of illumination where one may be granted a vision of a New Jerusalem, a vision granted only to the saint and mystic? Or to a great artist like William Blake. I knew I would never reach that final stage which entailed entering into and suffering the *nox obscura* or dark night of the soul where saints like Saint John of the Cross and Saint Teresa of Ávila had felt abandoned by God and doubted His existence. Even great artists, I learned, who venture too close to the nakedness of Being risk being overwhelmed by it. In a striking passage the poet Wordsworth describes his sensations after a terrifying and existential encounter of this nature:

> *...for many days, my brain*
> *Worked with a dim and undetermined sense*
> *Of unknown modes of being; o'er my thoughts*

> *There hung a darkness, call it solitude*
> *Or blank desertion. No familiar shapes*
> *Remained, no pleasant images of trees,*
> *Of sea, or sky, no colours of green fields;*
> *But huge and mighty forms, that do not live*
> *Like living men, moved slowly through the mind*
> *By day, and were a trouble to my dreams.*

No wonder so many of our probationers fled from the rigours of that thirty-day Retreat to the comfortable material world.

I think I endured because I was so determined to succeed and because I found many aspects of my new life fascinating. Plain chant or Gregorian chant, that beautiful form of Church music, was a comfort to me in its affirmation of the spiritual and I found distraction in exploring the wide range of its musical literature. I also found consolation in the extensive grounds of the Castle and in the beauty of the Castle itself—the former banquet hall was now our chapel and the bedrooms which held three students each had great windows which gave on to prospects of lawn and fields and lakes set against the striking mountains of Wicklow. And inveterate reader that I was I did not feel deprived in the least in my reading for I had discovered a new literature—that of hagiography, the marvelous lives of mystics like Hildegard of Bingen, Meister Eckhart, Saint Catharine of Sienna, Thomas à Kempis. Perhaps I should have been intimidated by their example but I was too fascinated by their extraordinary lives—Saint Francis of Assisi who was so holy he received the gift of the stigmata—the five wounds of Christ—and who could talk to birds and animals as naturally as he talked to people. Or Saint Aloysius of Gonzaga who was so pure that he would not even be alone with his mother, and Saint Teresa of Ávila who had the gift of levitation, shared by many other saints. Nor did I ever have doubts at that time about these miraculous lives or about the miracles they performed. These accounts were sanctioned by the Church and by writers whose reputation was a guarantee of truthful and rigorous scrutiny of their subjects. François Mauriac, a member of the French Academy, included in his *oeuvre* a life of Saint Margaret of Cortona, who raised a dead boy from the grave and healed a multitude of sinners. G.K. Chesterton, who regularly debated writers and scientists like H.G. Wells and Bernard Shaw, wrote a fine book on Saint Thomas Aquinas where he accepts his miracles without hesitation. Then too in our retreat at Humewood Castle we lived in a dimension of faith—not an ignorant faith but one, we felt, that was rooted in reason. If one doubted the miracles of the saints what was to prevent one from doubting the miracles of Christ!

At last the Great Retreat came to an end and we all returned to "normal" life—normal because we had been given back the gift of speech and laughter. But the year continued to be governed by a calendar other than the one which had governed our lives to this point—the calendar of the Liturgical Year. Advent, a period of three weeks before Christmas, was a warming up as it were for the grand event, the birth of Jesus. For the first time I began to realize the importance and significance of this astounding claim that God had decided his Son should take on human flesh in order to redeem the human race. When the twelve days of Christmas were upon us, one of the priests—to my delight—set up a little crèche with Mary and Joseph and the child Jesus and various animals. On the feast of the Epiphany, January 6, they were joined by the Magi, the three wise men representing the Gentiles of the world. As we moved into the new year there followed Lent, a forty-day preparation for Easter, the greatest feast in the Church Calendar, when the crucified man-God rose from the dead and ascended into Heaven. Again I accepted without question this astounding claim which is at the heart of Christianity and which accounts for its growth in the years following Christ's life on earth. Nowhere else in recorded history had such a claim echoed with such resonance—all men and women, this God-man preached, were equal before the eyes of God and no matter how miserable and poor their lives were, they would one day see God face to face and overcome death if they accepted Christ in their lives. Death itself was unimportant since they were assured of resurrection. It was this very message which was the driving force and vision of the Missionary Society of St Patrick, a message I would one day bring to the people of Nigeria.

Such considerations gave new meaning to our preparations for the priesthood. When I served at Mass, I watched the priest dress for the service—every action and movement prescribed more carefully than those of a bull fighter preparing for the *corrida*. First the amice, a linen cloth drawn around the neck, then the alb, a white tunic with sleeves that is bound with a cincture or belt of linen. The maniple is draped over the left arm followed by the stole, a narrow strip of fabric hanging from the neck, then finally the chasuble, a silk garment with a Latin cross on back and front. Its colours varied according to the Liturgical Year—violet in certain days of Holy Week, for example, and a glorious gold for Easter Sunday. The same prescribed preparations governed the saying of Mass wherein the priest exercised his most extraordinary power—that of turning bread and wine into the body of Jesus Christ, not in a symbolic way but in actual fact. Again, I accepted this without question and looked forward to the day, some seven years hence, when I too would exercise this power of transubstantiation.

My life was not spent entirely on matters spiritual. We novices were young and full of energy and so there was also recreation. We had bicycles and at least once a month we rode out into the beautiful Wicklow countryside to places like Glendalough, the Vale of Avoca, Roundwood, and Woodenbridge. We played Gaelic football often and arranged matches with those in the parent seminary about once a month. We did not go home for Christmas or Easter but we kept in touch with our families through letter writing. The months passed prayerfully and the end of the probationary year drew near. We would then go then to the parent seminary for three years of study in philosophy followed by four years of theological training capped by ordination to the priesthood. In 1946, however, the Society decided that education was such an important dimension of its work in Nigeria that selected students should attend University College, Cork, the National University of Ireland, in order to obtain university training in the arts or sciences. I was one of those chosen.

My new home, a large handsome house in the village of Douglas, a few kilometers from the city of Cork, had been owned originally by a merchant named Sutton who imported coal from abroad. Situated in the middle of expansive grounds, it had a French garden and a large orchard. The vegetation and trees were almost Mediterranean in character—there were even palm trees. The largest room in the house was designated as the Chapel, the second largest as the Refectory or dining room. A small library mainly of books of a religious character was established, and our religious life continued as in our novitiate year with Mass in the morning and concluded with evening prayers. But now our religious life was bracketed by our lives as university students which, it was hoped, would prove complementary to our priestly lives. In the first week of our arrival we novices took the oath of obedience to the Society and also an oath to observe a state of perfect chastity. Should I discover that I did not have a vocation to the priesthood or wished to leave the Society for any other reason, I could do so, my decision to be ratified in Rome by the Cardinal responsible for the Society's affairs.

And so I came to know the city of Cork, the second largest city in the Republic of Ireland. I discovered it to be full of churches; on a Sunday morning or during festal occasions such as Easter Week the streets rang with the clamour of a multitude of church bells. It was a city of strong contrasts—great poverty with many beggars and fine houses like the manor house we lived in. It had a reputation as being perhaps the most Republican city of Ireland, having fought the British Army, especially between 1919 and 1921, the years leading up to the south of Ireland achieving independence. The city centre had been largely destroyed by the British military in 1920 and signs of that devastation could still be seen. Stories of the revolutionary days were current and one heard often of the tragic death of Terence MacSwiney, Mayor of Cork, imprisoned by the British, who died after a hunger strike that lasted some three months. Nearer home, the President of the University, Dr. Alfred O'Rahilly, was better known as a revolutionary than as the distinguished mathematical physicist that he was. An outspoken advocate of Irish independence, he had continued to lecture at the university despite being a wanted man. He was finally captured and imprisoned and became a popular hero.

The university in the 1940s was quite small, with about six hundred students in all. The buildings, in Tudor Gothic style, were in a dove grey stone grouped around a quadrangle. All Arts students took courses in common and only after the first year were we separated into pass and honours. For us clerical students, Philosophy was central to our courses, to be read for three years. We were free to select our other four first-year courses. I chose English, Economics, Latin, and Music. Latin came easily since I had a five-year background in the language and its literature. In Philosophy we began with formal Logic which I detested because of its mathematical nature. The differences characterising analogical, inductive, and deductive inferences and the consequent significance of their major, minor, and middle terms (P, S, and M) seemed like exercises in geometry and Aristotle's writings in the area—the *Categories* and the *Sophistical Elenchi*, for example—were hurdles to be overcome before passing on to the greener pastures of Plato's *Republic* and *Symposium* and Aristotle's *Metaphysics*, *Nicomachean Ethics*, and *Poetics*.

My choice of music as a university course was an unconventional one. The professor, Aloys Fleischmann, attempted to dissuade me from taking it, pointing out that I did not have the preconditions that the Calendar called for. When I said that I would work hard he relented and accepted me. The consequence was that I spent more time on this subject that all the others combined. There was only one other first-year student in music that year, a young woman of about eighteen, who helped me with my work when I began to flounder. Fleischmann's emphasis in the first year of the programme was on composition—harmony, counterpoint, canon and fugue, form—and the history of music. And so a completely new area of knowledge was opened to me: Palestrina, Monteverdi, Vivaldi, Bach, Handel, Haydn, Mozart, Bethoven. All the masters. I listened to recordings and read music scores learning how the composers had constructed their work according to accepted patterns and where they developed or modified these patterns. Chaucer's *Canterbury Tales* and Virgil's *Aeneid* jostled for my attention with the language of music—acciaccatura; Dorian, Phrygian, Lydian modes; contrapuntal derivations. The days flew by. Early morning Mass, meditation, ride by bicycle to the university, attend lectures, study in the library, visit the lovely Honan Chapel on campus with its exquisite stained-glass windows, study back in our house at Douglas, evening devotions. Recreation consisted of Gaelic football and rides into the countryside. In my three years at Cork I cycled to such enchanting places as Kinsale where the women still wore cloaks that seemed to be of Spanish origin (relics of the Spanish Armada washing up on the west coast or Ireland perhaps), Youghal, Clonakilty, Blarney with its famous castle and kissing stone, and Cobh, sad gateway for millions who fled Ireland in the famine years of the 1840s. Exploring the city was a pleasure, especially so when I discovered that a number of significant buildings like St Patrick's Bridge, the Berwick Fountain in the Grand Parade, the Shandon Butter Market, and St Vincent's Church in Sunday's Well were designed by Sir John Benson, born in a simple house in Collooney, Sligo. A member of our family!

The year passed rapidly and my music studies continued to be the most interesting and difficult of my first-year courses. Gradually I got to know Professor Fleischmann who began to take a personal interest in me, perhaps because I seemed to him to be an unusual young priest (I wore a clerical collar). He was at pains to inform me that though he had been born in Germany (Dachau, just outside Munich) his parents had long been resident in Ireland. Because he had only eight undergraduate students he was able to undertake numerous other duties—conducting the symphony orchestra which he founded, directing the university choir in such large scale works as Handel's *Judas Macabeus* (in which he insisted I sing), and promoting the Cork Ballet Company which he had formed with a tall red headed woman called Joan Denise Moriarty who impressed me greatly because she played the ancient Irish war pipes with such skill. Fleischmann was also a composer often writing under the Gaelic pen name Muiris O'Rónáin which he felt was better suited to his aim of promoting music in Ireland related to its Irish roots. In his lectures he often made reference to the work of composers who had rebelled against the dominant German and Italian music and returned to their native roots—Mussorgsky, Rimsky-Korsakov, Dvořák, Grieg, and Sibelius. Charles Stanford had done the same with Irish folk materials. Emulating them, Fleischmann wrote the music for two ballets with Gaelic themes—*The Red Petticoat* and a full-length work based on the Gaelic epic *The Táin*—for Moriarty's Irish National Ballet company. His interest in native Irish music greatly influenced his 1949 student, Seán Ó Riada, who in a few years became the most important figure in the revival of traditional native Irish music linked to classical form.

But despite his interest in Irish materials in 1948 Fleischmann was just then completing a ballet with the very non-Gaelic title of *The Golden Bell of Ko* to be performed in the Cork Opera House that year. He told me I must attend and so, although priests and clerical students were generally forbidden by Canon Law to attend public spectacles, I got permission to go. I do not remember much about Fleischmann's ballet because the opener—Ravel's *Boléro* presented as a ballet—had such a powerful effect upon me. The central single musical theme, repeated over and over again with mounting intensity and ever-changing orchestral variation and coloration, was as sensual an experience as any I had experienced in a theatre. It was danced also by young girls with an abandon that increased as the hypnotic music strained towards its climax. The ballerinas with their bared arms and legs and with eyes stylized to match their stylized movements seemed from another world than mine. I understood now why the Church discouraged clerics from attending such fare. This was art, a direct appeal to the intellect by way of the senses. I, in contrast, had dedicated myself to transcending the senses in order to reach the spiritual. It was many weeks before I recovered from that secular vision and again found tranquillity in prayer and meditation. Came the academic year's end and I wrote my examinations. I had been alarmed on learning that my external examiner in music would be Sir Arnold Bax, Master of the Queen's Music, who among other work had written music for Sergei Diaghilev's *Ballets Russes*. I passed.

In our second year of studies I concentrated on Philosophy and English, Honours programme. My professor in philosophy was Dr James O'Mahoney–or Father James as he was better known. He had taken post-doctoral studies at the Catholic University of Louvain, Belgium, where he received the *agrégé en philosophie*—the only other person I knew who had obtained this rare distinction was Father Fulton Sheen of the USA, famous there for his radio broadcasts and for his conversion to Catholicism of Clare Booth Luce, wife of the publisher of *Time* magazine. Father James cut a striking figure with his thin intellectual face and sparse pointed beard, coarse Capuchin robes and open sandals. His looks were complemented by a lecturing style that was highly histrionic being punctured by abrupt laughs, sudden gestures, and a delivery that ranged from a whisper to declamation. He moved easily from the Greek and Roman classics to French, Italian, and German literature and was especially fond of the writings of the Russian Christian existentialist Nicholai Berdyaev and the delicate journals of the Swiss Henri Amiel (*Journal Intime*). For three years this priest led us through our studies in metaphysics, epistemology, ethics, psychology, politics, and esthetics and I never missed a lecture. One of his heroes was Jacques Maritain, the famous French thinker, born a Protestant, whose motto, *Vae mihi si non Thomistizavero* ("Woe is me if I do not preach the doctrine of Thomas Aquinas"), he took as his own. Like Maritain, Father James rooted his teaching and writing in the work of Aristotle and St Thomas Aquinas as reinterpreted and related to twentieth-century thought; it was largely an attempt to counter the forces of contemporary doubt and materialism. The urgency of such an attempt was dramatically illustrated by Maritain's own life—when a student at the Sorbonne he met and fell in love with Raïssa Omansoff, a Russian Jew. So tortured were they by the meaningless of their existence and the crass materiality of contemporary thought that they made a pact to commit suicide within a year if they could not find a spiritual ground for living. Through the intervention of the religious thinker and mystic Leon Bloy they found peace in Catholicism to which they both converted.

Influenced by my study of Maritain's *Art and Scholasticism* I wrote a paper in my second year which I read to the University's Aquinas Society. Titled "The Novelist and his Moral Responsibility," it was an attempt on my part to reconcile the seemingly opposed demands of morality and art. If Leon Bloy was right that the Devil collaborates in every work of art how do Catholic novelists like François Mauriac, Sigrid Undset, and Graham Greene, for example, reconcile their portrayal of sex with Church teaching? I remember invoking Cardinal Newman who wrote that it was a contradiction in terms to attempt a sinless literature of sinful men. But if that was so, how could one justify the Church's *Index Librorum Prohibitorum* which banned so many of the masterpieces of world literature? My paper was really a probe, a series of questions meant to highlight issues central to my thinking at that time and which I assumed were of importance to my audience. Within a few days my Spiritual Director asked me for my paper and some time later—I believe it had been sent to the Mother House in Kiltegan for review—he told me that it would be better not to permit wider publication. He was quite apologetic about the matter but it was plain to me that I would not be permitted to attempt publication. I made no objection because I had taken a vow of absolute obedience to the Society. Why should I object to the very first test of that vow!

But the issue refused to go away and I grappled with it for my remaining time in Cork. I began to have doubts about the Church's teachings concerning human sexuality. As a novice I had accepted unquestioningly the story of Saint Aloysius of Gonzaga who was so pure that he preferred not to be alone with his mother. Such an attitude began to seem perverse to me, not exemplary. And yet it was of a piece with the anti-feminist theology embraced by the Church, a theology rooted in the writings of the Fathers of the Church which I was now reading. For Tertullian, women were the "devil's gateway," a "delicious putridity," Origen, despising marriage, castrated himself, and Jerome spoke of "the filth of marriage." The purpose of Baptism, as a consequence, is to remove the guilt and punishment a newborn infant incurs as a result of this filth. Each question raised another, but one loomed ever larger: was priestly celibacy a precondition of holiness or a symptom of a hatred of women based on a hatred of the human body.

Not long after this an Englishman called Douglas Hyde, a former editor of the communist paper *The Daily Worker*, came to Cork to lecture on his reasons for rejecting Communism and for converting to Catholicism. His was a reasoned, objective account of what had obviously been an extraordinary passage in his life. What was revelatory, however, was the speech of thanks by our university president Alfred O'Rahilly. He immediately launched into an attack on Communism interspersing his words every few minutes with the inflammatory question, "Men of Cork, are you for Marx or Christ?" The effect was extraordinary; the audience, including myself, responded as if we were hypnotized, screaming in answer, "Christ! Christ!" Later that evening I felt a sense of disquiet at having succumbed to such demagoguery that played upon the passions so shamelessly. I learned that O'Rahilly was of a school of thought that distrusted most things modern, even rejecting Darwin's theory of evolution and Einstein's theory of relativity. In his espousal of traditional Church values and his rejection of modern science he represented a threat to intellectual enquiry, a threat which dominated modern Ireland for more than fifty years after it achieved nationhood in 1922.

My English studies were a delight but not because of my professor, Dr Bridgit McCarthy. She was a charming woman, about forty I would have guessed, who had published a two-volume work on women writers of the seventeenth and eighteenth centuries that was very well received and that had won her the Chair of English succeeding the writer Daniel Corkery. What was surprising was that the scholarship so evident in her book was completely absent from her lectures. She read beautifully, and consequently her lectures became a series of readings. Thus we listened as she read from Shakespeare, Milton, Pope, the Romantics, Jane Austen (a favourite with her), Thackeray, Gerard Manley Hopkins, the early W.B. Yeats—the whole spectrum of English-language canonical writers—but without giving us any critical apparatus that might help us understand better these writers. I remember two "lectures" devoted to Shelley's *Adonais* which she read beautifully while concluding each reading with a breathless paraphrase of Wordsworth's lines that the meddling intellect distorts the beauty of things and that mere critics "murder to dissect." The problem was that she did not apply this apothegm to the examinations she set where her students would be asked, for example, to examine in detail *Adonais* in the light of its classical sources and neo-platonic influences.

Lacking a professor I haunted the library where I came under the influence of I.A. Richards and F.R. Leavis then revitalizing critical method. Reading them I was also led to the work of such moderns as Ezra Pound and T.S. Eliot who were not on the English Honours curriculum. Eliot was a revelation—my first encounter with his poetry was like a shock of recognition, an intoxication, an entry into a new grammar of expression. Where Tennyson retold (beautifully) the idylls of the Court of King Arthur, Eliot captured with disgust and a fashionable *ennui* the spiritual bankruptcy of post-World War I Europe in *The Wasteland*.

In my third year my doubts about the authenticity and the depth of my vocation to the priesthood grew even stronger. I sought advice from my spiritual director and he assured me that such doubts were common. I should pray for guidance, hold fast to my purpose, and this phase would pass. But it didn't. I began to see that two forces were at war within me. One was pulling me towards a priestly life, the other—driven by my secular studies—was pulling me towards the profane. I came gradually to recognize that the way of sanctity was reserved for the very few and for a priestly caste to claim it was dangerous. Abraham's willingness to kill his beloved son Isaac is as dangerous as the fear of St Aloysius that his mother arouse his lust. In the spring of that year I was in Dublin on the day that the state was officially declared a Republic. The city was electric with cheering crowds and flags and speakers. As I stood in front of the Gresham Hotel on O'Connell Street an open-air bus drew up, the crowds rushed to it, and a woman, tall and slender with a commanding presence, stood and began to speak. I knew I had seen her before in press photographs and then it came to me. It was the legendary Maude Gonne, widow of Major John McBride who had been executed by the British for his role in the Easter uprising. An ardent nationalist in her own right, twice jailed for her activities, she had long been loved by the poet W.B. Yeats. Her rejection of him as a lover and as a husband had goaded him into writing some of his finest poetry in which he expressed his love and his revulsion, the age-old Catullan *odi et amo*:

> *We sat silent as a stone,*
> *We knew, though she's said not a word,*
> *That even the best of love must die,*
> *And had been savagely undone*

Were it not that Love upon the cry
Of a most ridiculous little bird
Tore from the clouds his marvellous moon.

The sight of Maud Gonne on that Dublin street stayed with me a long time suggesting to me that like Joan of Arc she had achieved a kind of profane sainthood; perhaps the sacred and the profane were not absolutes divorced from each other, I thought. Perhaps salvation could be achieved through art or through sacrifice or through human love.

Came final examinations and I graduated with an honours degree in Philosophy and English. That summer I returned to Belfast where we now had a house but I said nothing to my family about my doubts. In September I returned to the mother house of the Society in Kiltegan, presided over by the Society's Superior General, a remote and austere priest who had spent many years as a missionary in Nigeria. Here in the Kiltegan seminary I commenced my four years of theological training. After one year I would be anointed a sub deacon, in my third year a deacon, in my final year I would reach my goal—ordination as a priest, a priest forever according to the order of Melchizedek. I would be endowed with the awesome powers of baptizing, transforming the bread and wine of the Mass into the actual body of Christ, hearing sins in Confession and forgiving them, performing the marriage service, and administering the last rites to those about to die. My theological training would be rigorous, embracing as it did many areas of theology—hermeneutics (interpretation of the Bible), Patristics (study of the writings of the Fathers of the Church), pastoral and moral theology, and Canon Law, among others. I entered into this new phase of my life with determination, but after the freedom of university life it began to seem stale and enervating. I missed the simple transaction of mingling with people in various walks of life, the sights and sounds of "profane" life with its jazz and films and radio and all the multifarious sensations that constitute its web and woof.

As the weeks went by and as I began to feel more and more alienated from the life of the seminary, I became engaged with a question which I dreaded to explore: was I prepared to live a life in which spiritual values had precedence over every other value? Could I accept a life that so violently opposed the life of the senses or, at the least, asked me to transcend it? Colour, touch, the sounds of music, the voices of women, the sheer thisness of material things made their demands on me, saying with the poet Blake that everything that lives is holy—the lion and the lamb, the spirit and the flesh. "In the hands of my Superior . . . I must consider myself as a corpse which has neither intelligence nor will," Ignatius of Loyola had written, but I now rebelled at the thought. I had intelligence, I was not a corpse, I was twenty-two years old, I was thirsting for more knowledge of myself and of the world. I had read Plotinus and Byron and Hegel and Dostoevsky and I wanted to read all the authors in the libraries of the world, to face, in the words of the Jesuit poet Hopkins, its "ruck and reel". In class that week the professor-priest had lectured on the nature of worship—there were three categories, he told us: *latria*: worship due to God alone; *hyperdulia*: the worship due Our Lady; *dulia*: the worship owed to saints and angels. Furthermore, he went on, the angels were grouped in nine orders of descending importance from seraphim through principalities to mere angels. But now such categorizing seemed to me to be hair splitting, the *odium theologicum*, the craft of priesthood, against which Savonarola and Giordano Bruno had railed so vehemently and for which they had been burned to death on the orders of the Roman Inquisition. *We murder to dissect*. On and on the priest-professor lectured and I asked myself what had this to do with the aspirations of my novitiate year when I had been so inflamed by the writings of visionaries like St John of the Cross and Juliana of Norwich.

In November I developed a painful rash in my groin which forced me to stay in bed for a few days. On the morning of the second day, as I lay alone in the dormitory, the Superior General of the Society entered. He came to my bed, I explained the nature of my illness, he asked to see the rash. I pulled down the bed clothes and my pyjama bottoms covering my genitalia with my hand as he watched me. He left the dormitory abruptly and later that day I was told to see the local doctor who sent me to a specialist in Dublin. Following the treatment he prescribed the rash ceased.

At the time I paid little attention to this incident; I was not shocked by the fact that the priest had so invaded my privacy because I was still naive enough as not to suspect a priest of sexual deviancy, especially one who held so important and sensitive a position. Rather incredibly, this only surfaced fully in my mind and consciousness some fifty years later at which point I began to examine its implications. I did not feel that I had been harmed, that I had been violated in any way; I wondered rather (as I do now) at the power of a sexual obsession that could drive a priest to risk so much, to place his career and reputation so recklessly within my power had I wished to destroy him.

But perhaps I am wrong to say that I had not been harmed by that morning encounter of long ago. A few weeks later, after serious prayer and meditation, I finally decided to leave the priesthood and now in my dreams the ballerinas of Cork came to me dancing to the insistent rhythms of the music of Ravel. When I said goodbye to the seminary at Kiltegan that Christmas, I felt an enormous sense of liberation. But also such a sense of loss—and guilt—that for many years I was not able to speak openly of this part of my life

The Coils of Venus

The Belfast I returned to in 1950 was a city I did not know. Yes, I knew its geography—the Lagan River, the area around Queen's University, the Shankill Road and the Falls Road where Protestant faced Catholic daily in mutual enmity. I knew the Cave Hill above the city and the wedding cake-like City Hall and Royal Avenue with its fine shops and hotels. But I knew little of how the people, especially the young people, lived. Now I was about to enter that world, that secular world so far removed from the world I had known before—the Belfast of Catholic churches that smelled of burning candles and incense, with crucified Christs hanging on crosses on every wall, and Stations of the Cross retracing in bloody detail the passion of Christ, and confessional boxes with queues of weary looking people waiting to be absolved of their sins. And always the smell of the coldness of unheated churches and the presence of black garbed priests. In a famous passage in his *Confessions* St Augustine tells how he was living a life of depravity when one day in a garden in Milan he heard a child's voice speak the words, *Tolle, lege*. He picked up the Bible as commanded and began reading which led to his conversion and rejection of the woman, his mistress, who had borne his child. My epiphany was very different. I wanted to enter the world Augustine had given up, I wanted to leave the enclosed garden in which I had been living since my birth. Augustine had prayed, *Da mihi castitatem et continentiam, sed noli modo* ("Give me chastity and continence, but not yet"); I wanted to taste the fruit of the garden of Paradise. In his transvaluation of symbols Shelley had used the snake as a symbol of good; I wanted ardently to taste the fruits it offered.

Leading me on this new quest was my discovery of money. Until this time I had never earned a penny. But on my return to Belfast I got a position as a substitute teacher for the rest of that school year and each month I began to receive a cheque for what seemed to me at that time to be a substantial sum of money. Very soon I traded my clerical black suit and tie which I had worn for almost five years for a fashionable suit and ties of various colours which my brothers and sisters helped me pick. I now had money to go to movies and to plays and to musical events. I had money to invite girls to accompany me and buy them chocolate. But it was not just the money that was so important to me but what it brought me—independence. Independence of my parents, of the Society of St Patrick, independence to determine the course of my day. Like Caliban I soon discovered the vices of my contemporary world. I began (quite deliberately) to smoke—the movies had made smoking an indispensable part of living. So popular were cigarettes that when Christmas came I bought two-hundred cigarette cartons and gave them to my brothers and sisters—Bernadette, Gerard, and Françoise, and Jackie. They all died of cancer.

To enter totally this new secular world I needed certain skills and one of the most important of these was the ability to dance. I had learned Irish dancing in Donegal's *Gaeltach*—jigs, reels, hornpipes, and so on—but not the waltz or the foxtrot or the tango or "The Moonlight Saunter." My sisters Françoise and Bernadette became my teachers, the kitchen our dance studio, and in a month or so I was ready to venture into the ballrooms of Belfast—the Floral Hall overlooking Belfast Lough, White's Ballroom, Club Orchid, St Malachy's Club, The Orpheus, Fruit Hill Dance Club, and The Plaza. There were dances every night of the week with live bands and singers. Additionally, the various professions—doctors, dentists, teachers, pharmacists—held annual dances, very formal affairs where black tie was *de rigueur* (most men rented their formal wear) and the ladies wore formal gowns and long gloves. All of Belfast was dancing it seemed and I was now ready to join in.

But there is more to dancing than knowing the steps. One must know how to pick a dance partner and how to talk to her and find subjects of conversation that are of mutual interest. Going on about Schopenhauer or points of theology or the imagery in Hopkins' *The Wreck of the Deutschland* was to invite silence or rejection. And picking a dance partner was in itself a task that could be frightening. In those days the women, beautifully dressed and made up according to the current fashion, would congregate opposite the men at the other side of the ballroom. Both sexes would eye the other in a seemingly careless manner until the music for the dance struck up at which point the man crossed the floor to ask the woman of his choice to dance. Crossing that floor was a nerve-wracking experience. Would the woman accept? Would she reject you? And the transaction had to be carried out in full view of one's friends and hundreds of other people! And to enter on this dangerous territory at the virgin age of twenty-two. And so I began my entry from the world of innocence into the world of experience and my only comfort was a literary remembrance from the poet William Blake who assured me that the clash of these two worlds—of innocence and of experience—was prelude to an even higher and richer sphere of existence.

But the truth has always been that women are instinctively kinder than men, more understanding, more tolerant. Yes, there were some who surveyed you as if your asking them to dance was some kind of insult, that never never could they dream of accepting your invitation. But most smiled and said, I'd be delighted to dance, and entered into your arms and talked of all kind of everyday things that seemed interesting and new because her arms were about you, her cheeks was pressed against yours, her eyes were bright and flecked and intoxicating in the semi darkness with the glitter ball high above filling the ballroom with innumerable spots of light reflecting off the walls. In those days a man and a woman did not dance apart from each other but in each other arms. The times were puritan, women were, in general, ferocious about preserving their virginity—not out of a pronounced sense of chastity but because the consequences of pregnancy were so drastic. As if in compensation, other expressions of sexuality were allowed. On the dance floor the girl I had just met a few minutes ago would press herself against me so that I could feel her breasts against me, her thighs, her legs along mine. And then she would be gone, among her girl friends, watching if I would return, playing her part in the cavalcade of the women and men at the dance who had come there seeking human companionship, some degree of undefined sexuality, even—dare one say it?—love. And so the band played on, the singer crooned, and the glitter ball glowed like a radiant planet transforming the ballroom into a place of dreams and hopes.

> *Let's take a chance on love, my love,*
> *Let's see life through.*

You dance with me, I'll dance with you.
Let's take a chance on love.

In September of 1950 I entered Teachers' Training College, Belfast, for a one-year term. The curriculum included courses on child psychology, the history and practice of education, English and Mathematics, and physical education and music. The emphasis was on the practical aspects of these subjects and involved going on extended visits to schools to observe experienced teachers at work and later to actually teaching under the supervision of the School Principal or a qualified teacher. I was particularly struck by the way in which children could be taught to read music at sight (the Solfege method) through the association of each note—do, re, mi, fa, so, la, ti—with a position of the hand, a method I later used myself when training a school choir. After the intellectual excitement of my university years I found these studies boring because they were so practical, but in later life I was pleased to have been exposed to training at the hands of experienced teachers where such simple things as audibility and maintaining eye contact were emphasized. In my university teaching, I saw too many professors who while knowing the subject in which they had invested so much time knew nothing of the art of teaching. They mumbled, they rarely made eye contact with students, and they seemed not to know how to organize their lecture material. On one occasion I attended a fifty-minute lecture where a professor, addressing an audience of eight hundred students, only came to his subject matter thirty minutes into the lecture. As long as professors are rewarded primarily for publication rather than for teaching such malpractice will continue.

In 1952 I got my first full time job—teaching grades one and two. In addition, I taught physical education and music to all eight grades. The school, on the lower Falls Road, in a poor area, was almost Dickensian in character. The area was a hot bed of Nationalist sentiment and when I called the roll each morning in school and a student didn't answer it was probably because someone in his family had been arrested for being a member of the banned IRA. I shared a classroom with another teacher who had about thirty grade three and four children. He was nearing retirement and because he had recently had a severe operation he regularly fell asleep at his desk when I would be forced to shuttle back and forth between his students and mine, swishing my cane (the very symbol of the teacher) to maintain discipline. There were six teachers on the staff and we addressed each other as Miss or Mrs or Mr. To have used first names would have seemed an intolerable intrusion on one's privacy. We all lived in common fear of the Inspector, usually a man, who would arrive unannounced to examine the work being done, and check that we were following the lesson plan that we must have for each day. One of our duties as teachers was to take it in turn to supervise the children's lunch. Sponsored by the Government and entirely free it provided all children with a hot meal—milk, a main dish, bread, and a dessert. I often ate with the children and found the food very good. For some children it was the only nutritious meal they enjoyed daily. I was surprised to discover later that a feature of school life so common in Northern Ireland was not widely duplicated in Canada or the USA.

As soon as my life as a teacher was well established, I spent many evenings going to operas and ballet in Belfast's Grand Opera House which is one of the glories of Victorian architecture, all plush and gilt with fine acoustics. There was no resident company so it acted as a roadhouse for visiting companies like Saddler's Wells Opera and Ballet, the Ram Gopal Ballet, Ballet Rambert, the English National Ballet, and the Carl Rosa Opera. I usually sat in the cheap seats ("the gods") but at intermission I always went to the Premier Bar for a drink. Here the men and women usually wore formal evening clothes for they represented an elite, nearly always from England, who had little contact with or feeling for the province that they governed. I also wrote a play at this time that I submitted to Dublin's Abbey Theatre, hoping to join the ranks of others whose plays had been preformed there—Yeats, Synge, Lady Gregory, O'Casey. My play, *The Crowing of the Cock,* drew on my life as a student for the priesthood. My protagonist falls in love with a woman, an agent of the IRA, who is sleeping with a British officer. Devoured by jealousy he betrays her. I had a polite rejection notice from the Abbey Theatre in which the anonymous reader encouraged me to continue with my writing. Some day, the notice told me cryptically, I might find my true *métier*. In 1953 I heard the poet Louis McNeice reading from his work which led me to read a great deal of his writings including his fine radio play, *Christopher Columbus.* It was at that time also that I began reading, in Latin, the love letters between Heloise and Abelard and finding out as much as I could about these famous lovers who fascinated me. In university I had read some of the writings of Abelard; he was the most brilliant philosopher of the twelfth century, famous throughout Europe, frequently at odds with the Church which ultimately condemned many of his writings. Heloise, the niece of Fulbert, a Canon of the Cathedral of Notre Dame, became Abelard's student, then his lover and the mother of his child. In revenge Fulbert had Abelard castrated and Abelard, jealous that Heloise might be attracted to other men, ordered her to enter a convent without telling her he had been castrated. Their love letters, especially Heloise's, still convey across the centuries the power and the intensity of their doomed relationship. "No more am I ashamed that my passion for you had no limits," writes the nun Heloise from her convent. Attracted to the form of the radio play as exemplified by McNeice's *Christopher Columbus*, I wrote a radio play *Heloise and Abelard* which I sent to the British Broadcasting Corporation (BBC), Northern Ireland. To my surprise I received a letter from one of the producers of its Third Programme inviting me to come and talk about my play with a view to producing it. Since the mandate of the Third Programme was strictly to broadcast the work of such classical writers as Shakespeare, Molière, Ibsen, Strindberg, and Shaw (and classical composers) I felt somewhat intimidated. Within a few days I met two young men, producers at the BBC's Belfast office, both English, who told me how much they liked my work. There was, however, one problem. The castration scene would have to go. They did not wish to censure my work, they understood why it was a part of the action, but the Corporation would never broadcast a work that featured so graphic a scene. Could I omit it? We discussed the matter but I refused to take out the scene—my play (and the historical love story) lost its power and its poignancy if it was omitted. We parted, the BBC did not broadcast it, but I did not forget it and when I left Ireland I took it with me hoping that some day, in some other city, it would get a hearing.

At this time my sister Françoise reminded me that I had made a vow some years before that if I passed my BA with honours I would make a pilgrimage to St Patrick's Purgatory. The pilgrimage, dating from the fifth century, was as famous in mediaeval times as that associated with Santiago de Compostela in Spain or with Canterbury Cathedral. It was a fascinating experience to leave a modern city like Belfast for an island in Lough Derg, Donegal, and to enter on three days of prayer and fasting. Pilgrims got little sleep and we all went about the small island in bare feet as we followed the various Stations of the Cross. I was fascinated by the fact that such a harsh regimen could attract so many people—the majority from the professional classes—and I was also fascinated by the way in which these people in the midst of their devotions made friends, told stories of home, disagreed with each other over small details, and flirted with those of the opposite sex—a high number of young people met on this grim island and later married. Human foibles and traits as depicted in Chaucer's *Canterbury Tales* were no different on this remote island.

On another occasion I holidayed on the Aran Islands off the west coast of Ireland staying on the island of Inishmore. It is rich in ecclesiastical remains such as saints' beds and holy wells and the scenery is stark and striking with cliffs, on the western side of the island, hundreds of feet high. The Gaelic language was universally spoken. It was to these islands that the dramatist J.M. Synge had come some fifty years earlier. Living in Paris, and suffering from what we might call writer's block, he was advised by Yeats to go to there. As Gauguin had fled Paris for Tahiti so Synge fled Paris for the Aran Islands and there among a primitive people and a stark landscape he found the themes that informed his plays *Riders to the Sea*, *The Shadow of the Glen*, and his masterpiece *The Playboy of the Western World*. When I was commissioned years later to write a book on a modern author of my choice I chose Synge.

In the summer of 1953 I set out on a visit to Europe. I decided to hitch hike through England, France, and Germany but not Italy—it offered a very cheap *biglietto circulare* that allowed one to travel by rail anywhere in the country. I decided that I would make Taormina in Sicily my destination before returning to Belfast because I remembered how much D.H. Lawrence loved that area where he had written the wonderfully atavistic poem "Snake":

> *He lifted his head....*
> *And stooped and drank a little more,*
> *Being earth-bound, earth-golden from the burning bowels of the*
>   *earth*
> *On the day of Sicilian July, with Etna smoking.*

Hitch-hiking proved surprisingly easy. Truck drivers and commercial travelers are very often bored from repeated travel on the same routes and generally welcome company. In London I visited some of the usual tourist places—Buckingham Palace, the Tower of London, the British Museum—but the city seemed drab and tired as if the War had drained it of energy. Strict rationing of food and materials was still maintained in the UK, taxes were high, and with the dismantling of the British Empire a sense of loss was evident in every walk of life and in the arts. Osborne's *Look Back in Anger* with its kitchen sink realism and visceral hatred of Britain's class distinction is an index of the times. But France was different and Paris seemed to me to be absolutely beautiful. It had a sense of expansion and freedom I had never seen before. Rationing had long been swept away and food and drink were plentiful, the *cafés* were crowded, there were flowers everywhere it seemed, young men and women embraced openly in the streets as if it were the most natural thing, the great avenues flowed with architectural assurance into the *Place de l'Étoile*, and the Latin Quarter excited the senses with its intoxicating *mélange* of museums, bookshops, art galleries, *bistros*, colleges (*La Sorbonne*), night clubs, *cafés*, and shops.

Then too the city had an added resonance for me because it had been peopled by artists and characters who had for so long nourished my imagination—Rabelais, Voltaire, Balzac, Dumas, Baudelaire, Proust, Gide, Mauriac. To me it was not a foreign city but a place that had shaped my dreams and my longings and the years of my growth. In the Cathedral of Notre Dame I walked where Heloise had prayed as a child and where Victor Hugo's Quasimodo and Frollo, Archdeacon, had loved and died for the beautiful Esmeralda. As I stood in the oddly named *Place de la Concorde* where Louis XVI and Marie Antoinette had been decapitated I remembered again Dickens' *A Tale of Two Cities* and Hugo's *The Hunchback of Notre Dame*, novels whose stories I had told in the dormitory of St Colman's College to ease the young boys into sleep. I found it fascinating also that French philosophic thought in the form of Existentialism had found its way into the fashion of everyday Parisian life—young women patronized the *cafés* of the Latin Quarter dressed in black with hair styled in imitation of the *chanteuse* Juliet Greco, whom the existentialists had adopted, and where Simone de Beauvoir pimped the students of the Sorbonne for her lover, the wall-eyed philosopher Sartre.

At the *Bal Tabarin* nightclub I had my first experience of public nudity when I saw the young female performers dance with bared breasts. My reaction was not so much one of erotic or pornographic interest as surprise at the dancers' apparent enjoyment of what they were doing. Nudity, I began to discover, was a fact of life in France as was the fairly widespread practice of the man keeping a mistress or the woman having a lover. When I bought a newspaper at a kiosk in central Paris the young girl offered to sell me a magazine featuring naked women—again, there was no question of some kind of prurient transaction. Some weeks later when I reached Sicily I became friends with two young Swiss men. One of them boasted to me of how beautiful his girlfriend was and showed me her photograph. She was totally naked! He assured me that many of his friends carried such pictures of their girlfriends—with their approval. In Paris, when I and my friends walked in the Pigalle area of Montmartre at night we were accosted by hundreds of prostitutes offering their services. But there was nothing romantic about the spectacle. These young women, many from the provinces and without education, had flocked to Paris in search of a job, to escape poverty, in pursuit of their dream, only to find that they had nothing to offer but their bodies. Music and literature and painting and sculpture have romanticized France and Paris, but when I visited the Paris Opera I remembered that Guy de Maupassant had died of syphilis contracted from a young ballet dancer there and that the Opera House rented out private spaces where wealthy men seduced the dancers, often as young as twelve; the fourteen-year old child in Degas' famous "The Little Dancer" ended her life in prostitution. I was in Paris when its citizens celebrated Bastille Day, July 14, and while we danced in the streets that night I was unaware that earlier in the day there had been a riot in which six Algerians (Muslims, contemptuously referred to as *Les Bicots*) had been killed and hundreds injured. Their killing signaled the beginning of the war in Algeria when the French, in suppressing the independence movement, killed almost a million Algerians. Paris is a blueprint of human aspiration and fallibility, of extraordinary achievement and of brutal repression, in short, a mirror of human nature. But yet it is a city for which I never lost my first love.

When I crossed into Italy my first impressions were of an intensity of light very different from the muted colours of Ireland and of the beauty of great cities like Turin and Milan and Florence with their striking piazzas, gardens, fountains, statuary—especially equestrian works of art—and a strong sense of a southern Europe where *la dolce vita* was so much at odds with the work ethic of its northern half. I was aware always of the co-existence of a number of civilizations—that of ancient Rome, of the Christian era, and especially, in cities like Florence, of the Renaissance. My studies in Latin provided a commentary on my travels as I followed in the footsteps of Virgil, Catullus, Horace, and Ovid. I spent two days in the Uffizi Gallery and was overwhelmed by the sheer immensity of the artwork displayed and the richness of its holdings—Giotto, Michelangelo, Titian, Tintoretto, Fra Lippo Lippi, da Vinci, Botticelli, Raphael, Titian, Caravaggio, and Rembrandt. There was nothing of such magnificence in Ireland. So overwhelmed and surfeited was I by Florence that I bypassed Rome on my journey south and traveled to Sicily where I reached my most southerly destination—Taormina. It was the perfect place to rest. A small town with a Roman amphitheatre in the hills overlooking the Mediterranean and where, on my first night, I attended a concert given by the Taormina Orchestra of works by Puccini, Brahms, and Bethoven. For some reason there were only strings—no wind, percussion, or brass sections.

Rested after a few days traveling in Sicily I returned to Rome to experience its extraordinary character. Here the co-existence of the past and the present is written on building after building, on church after church, monument after monument. Imperial pagan Rome, the Christianity of the catacombs and the early martyrs, the Renaissance when Michelangelo and Bernini presided over the building of the Basilica of St. Peter, and the *Foro Mussolini*, symbol of twentieth-century Italian fascism. I was at once moved and appalled by my first view of St Peter's Basilica, moved by its vastness—the largest church in Christendom—and appalled by the contrast between the simple and essential message of Christ and what this building represented. I could admire the beauty of Bernini's *baldacchino* above the seat where the Pope sat but it seemed to me to have a kind of barbaric splendour, an outgrowth of Asia rather than of Europe. Because I had studied Church history I was aware of the history of the Papacy at the time the basilica was built. I knew that it was the scandalous practice of the sale of indulgences which financed the building of St. Peter's Basilica and led Luther to nail his ninety-five theses to the door of a church in Wittenberg in 1517 thus precipitating the revolt of northern Europe against a debauched and degenerate Catholic south. But as I looked around me at the marvelous work created by great Renaissance artists I realized again the conflict between art and morality. Had the Popes of the time not plundered Europe in search of funding they could not have financed the miracle that was the art of Renaissance Italy. Evil in their personal lives, in their public lives they touched nothing they did not adorn. And as I watched the throngs of priests and nuns who filled Rome's churches, I could not help reflecting that I too might have been one of them, that I might have been sent by my superiors to take graduate studies in theology at one of the many colleges in the city, that I might one day have become someone of consequence in this great organization.

From Rome I journeyed to Venice and then to Vienna through the Russian zone returning via Munich to Paris. Because the events of the Second World War were fresh in my mind I was surprised to see how prosperous West Germany had become. True, in the cities I visited there were burned out public buildings and churches but already work had begun to restore them. Rationing had been abolished in 1948 and food was plentiful. But I never felt at ease on this part of my journey for just as the Roman classic authors had provided a commentary on my Italian travels, so here in Germany the barbarous practices of the Nazi Party provided a nightmarish quality to the bucolic villages and the *Konditorei* and bars where I ate and drank. Nightmarish, because my adult education and values had been profoundly influenced by German philosophy and music—Kant, Hegel, Schopenhauer, Nietzsche, Bach, Handel, Haydn, Mozart, Bethoven ... the list went on and on. What a shock to discover that Dachau, the scene of the notorious concentration camp, was only a few kilometres outside Munich, and I remembered my teacher Fleishmann who had been born in the village. And I was forced to wrestle with the mystery of how the Austrian and German people I met (they seemed so ordinary) had facilitated and co-operated in the extermination of millions of people. The corruption of values was almost universal, infecting the fields of science, the law, university faculties, the *Wehrmacht*. Nor were the churches guiltless, co-operating as they did so long as the Nazi party respected their jurisdiction. Did the Nazi party, in fact, carry to a logical conclusion the deep distrust, hatred, and prosecution of Jews promoted by Christianity for almost two thousand years? And who could claim not to have been complicit in this barbarity? On Good Fridays I, a student for the priesthood, along with the congregation, had assisted year after year at the service where the officiating clergyman—a priest or bishop—asked us to pray for the conversion of the perfidious Jews: *Oremus et pro perfidis Judaeis.* As the years passed I began to understand that Christianity had been infected from its beginnings by a vicious anti-Semitism that fed on the ur-text of anti Jewish sentiment—the Gospels. Even my revered Thomas Aquinas, a Saint of the Church, had given warrant to confiscating Jewish property on the grounds that Jews practiced usury.

On my return to Belfast I entered my second year of teaching but now I began to feel dissatisfied with my way of life. My brief travels in Europe made me feel more strongly the claustrophobia that marked the northern Irish society in which I lived. The ignorance and intolerance of the poorer Orange Protestant class were matched by that of the poorer Catholic class, and a bigoted and self-serving clergy served only to reinforce the demonized images each class held of the other. The para-military Royal Ulster Constabulary, of which my father was a member, was abetted by a subsidiary police force, the B-Men, universally hated by Catholics. Its function was to maintain a government which ruled by establishing artificially fixed electoral boundaries and by rigging voting. The result was a political and cultural schizophrenia that dominated every aspect of life. This was exacerbated by the fact that the south of Ireland, Eire, was dominated by a Catholic anti-intellectualism that could not but be repugnant to liberal Protestants in the North. Irish politicians openly proclaimed that Ireland was a Catholic nation and that there Rome's writ ran large. An especially ugly manifestation of this triumphalist Catholicism was a Censorship Board which banned such eminent writers as Thomas Mann, F. Scott Fitzgerald, John Steinbeck, Graham Greene, and Evelyn Waugh (the last two Catholics). Eminent Irish writers including Austin Clarke, Frank O'Connor, and Sean O'Faolain were deemed unsuitable authors for Irish readers mainly because they wrote of sexual matters. A particularly galling example of Church control related to the Minister of Health, Dr Noel Browne, who introduced what was known as the Mother and Child Scheme to provide mothers and children with free medical care (including gynecological advice)—southern Ireland had then the highest infant death rate in Europe. The Bishops, ever fearful of outside interference in sexual matters, and the medical profession, sensing intrusion into what they considered their territory, condemned the scheme; it was thrown out, Browne was forced to resign, and Ireland's children continued to die. I followed this debacle with foreboding and it certainly was a factor in my decision to leave Ireland.

A more particular reason was that my School Principal was so pleased with my work that he told me he would recommend me to the Parish Priest as Principal succeeding him. I should, I suppose, have been delighted at such a prospect but it provided a sharp focus in determining my career. I saw myself in the same school, riding on my bicycle through the streets of that impoverished area of Belfast, decade after decade, until came the time for retirement and my pension. I shuddered at the thought, remembering the light on the canals of Venice and the sweeping mountain views outside Udine on the Italian-Austrian border. Then came my liberation. A notice in the *Belfast Telegraph.* "Teachers wanted for Saskatchewan, Canada." I read the details and dismissed the notice. But it would not go away. A few days later, a warm languid day in May, I walked from my school to Royal Avenue and as if driven by an inner compulsion, hardly acknowledged, I entered the office of a building where an official from Saskatchewan talked to me of teaching opportunities in the province. Within thirty minutes I signed the forms he put in front of me and committed myself for the following year. I had only one stipulation—Belfast was a large city and I wanted to teach in a place totally unlike it. The smaller the better. The official, McLeod by name, promised me he would do his best. He proved to be a man of his word.

I had not consulted my parents or my family about my decision to go to Canada and I was surprised that they made no objection. I suspect that because I had lived so long away from the family—since I was thirteen—they trusted my judgement. I remember vividly the last family dinner when my mother, who was avidly against alcohol, drank from a bottle of "Pink Lady" that I had bought for her. We laughed and had a lovely time and I never noticed the way mortality had left tell tale signs on her face. The next morning I left Ireland. At that time—the summer of 1954—as I prepared to leave my father and my mother I gave no thought to their feelings. I was setting out to redefine my existence, to face whatever destiny had in store for me, and the egotism that acted as protection against whatever I might face insulated me to a large degree from others' pain. And so I left my mother and father without regret. It might seem that regret is a less powerful emotion than jealousy or hatred, but because it is so intimately connected with memory it may cause more pain. Over the years—more than sixty since then—I have regretted that I never told my father and mother then how much I loved them, that I never said how much I felt

I had to leave and that I hoped they would not feel too much pain. But there is no armour against pain, especially the pain inflicted on the ones we love, and regret is an emotion of what might have been but can be no more. I did not say any of these things then. We kissed and parted and I left the Old World in search of another life.

Saskatchewan

In 1954 air travel between Europe and North America was still an arduous business and often dangerous. My plane began its flight in London, refueled in Prestwick, Scotland, before setting west across the Atlantic for Reykjavik, Iceland, where it refueled again. Then onwards to Goose Bay, Newfoundland and Labrador (more refueling), before setting down in Montreal, Canada. The passengers were a motley lot—farmers, teachers, nurses, tradesmen, Europeans uprooted by the war now seeking a new life in a strange land, Canadians returning from visits to the tourists places of Europe. Montreal proved a surprise. It was much larger than I had expected with elegant hotels and shops. The hotels featured stores off the lobbies so that an easy flow of people came and went. This was true even of the Ritz-Carlton Hotel on Sherbrooke Street. There was nothing of the snobbery that greeted people who sought to enter like hotels in London—the Dorchester and the Ritz, for example—where doormen surveyed superciliously those not obviously of the better classes.

The evening of my first day in Canada I caught the Canadian Pacific Railway train for the West. It was far larger than any train I had been on in Europe and had much less of the clackety clackety sound of those trains. My mother, bless her, had arranged for me to have a cabinette to myself which contained a pullout bed and a chair and small writing table and a toilet. She had also purchased for me a book of meal tickets to cover the five days I would be traveling. The food in the restaurant car was very good with a wide variety of meats and fish. Portions seemed huge to someone like me used to the rationing still in operation in post-war Britain.

I spend much of my time reading or chatting with other passengers as the train travels through Ontario. Past Kingston to a lengthy stop in Toronto, through Sudbury, and Sault Ste. Marie and ever westwards into the prairies to Winnipeg, Manitoba. Day by day we push deeper and deeper into the interior of this vast country where I try to get my bearings on a map and day by day it grows hotter and hotter and the nights chillier (it is mid August). The business suit, tie and white shirts of the East are replaced by check shirts, jeans, larger hats, browner faces, more casual conversation. We enter Saskatchewan and stop in Regina where I change trains and travel north to Saskatoon. The landscape changes. Hills now, a welcome relief after the thousand miles of surreal flat prairie country. Great forests of fir and spruce and maple, and the smell of lakes and red ochre dirt roads in the distance, the quality of the light electric. Change again at a small town, Prince Albert, and by slow train to Canwood, my destination. I survey the village from the railway platform—one long drab street and a few side streets that straggle off miserably into weedy uncultivated areas. Lawns are scorched and brown. I had asked not to be assigned to a school in a large town and my wishes have certainly been met. But Canwood is not my destination. A car drives up to the railway station and the driver introduces himself and his wife as Mr and Mrs Skafte. There has been a change—I am to teach in Blue Heron where they live.

We get into their car—how huge these North American cars are—and again we drive north, about ten miles. As we chat they display an obvious anxiety, glancing frequently at the sky and commenting on the weather. Soon it begins to rain and then I notice that the road is not metalled, that its mud surface soon begins to disintegrate, and that we ride in the ruts of cars that have preceded us. If we move out of the rut, Mr Skafte tells me, we will slide into the ditch. At last we come to where four roads or rather tracks meet and I see a small building to my left which I am told is the school where I will teach, a small store to my right, and then what looks like a barn but which I soon discover is Blue Heron Hall. A few minutes later we arrive at a very modern house overlooking a lake, Blue Heron Lake, and I am home at last. On the Skafte farm. I will be boarding with the Skaftes, have all my meals in this house, live here until the end of the school year. The nearest hotel is in Canwood and should I want to live elsewhere it will have to be on a farmhouse just like this. Later, after a meal, I go out and wander about. The lake is placid and quite beautiful and the landscape is pretty with bushes and trees. But it is hot and in the shade. I make the acquaintance of mosquitoes, far bigger and fiercer than the midges of Ireland. As I gaze about me I begin to realize that there is not another dwelling of any kind in sight, that Blue Heron is not a town, it's not a village, it's a name that embraces an area that happens to include a number of farms and a school. From where I stand facing north to the vast reaches of the Arctic there are no cities or towns or opera houses or art galleries or book stores or cinemas or pubs. No phones. Curiously I am not frightened; I am exhilarated. I look forward to what the year will bring.

The next morning—it is a Saturday—Mr Skafte suggests that I meet the members of the School Board beginning with the Chairman of the Board, Jens Christiansen, a tanned farmer in denim overalls. He answers my questions. When does the school open? Monday morning. How many children will I be teaching? Twenty-two. I comment that this is quite a good teacher-student ratio—I had taught thirty-two in Ireland. Could I meet some of my fellow teachers? No. Why not? I am the only teacher. How many classes? I ask. Grades one to ten, excluding grade seven. There are no students for that class. We shake hands and then drive off to meet other Board members, all farmers, all Scandinavians it turns out, all working on their farms. We drive by the school room then, a one-storey wooden building about 27 feet by 27 feet, with a pot-bellied stove and a washroom or toilet. There is a hitching post outside the building. I pick up various materials that had been sent to me by the Education authorities in Regina and then I inspect the store opposite. The shopkeeper, Walter Odegaard, another Scandinavian, shows me around but there isn't much to see beyond canned food, winter clothes and boots, and tobacco and cigarettes. That evening the Skaftes are astonished to discover that I am a Catholic—there is no other in the entire area. But they quickly arrange to take me to church in a small town called Shellbrook about twenty miles away. The next morning, as I kneel in the smallest and poorest church I've ever been in, I am pleased to discover that the language of the Mystery transcends the boundaries of continents, making Canada and my Ireland one. *Introibo ad altare Dei. Ad Deum qui laetificat juventutem meum*—"I will go into unto the altar of the Lord. To the Lord who gives joy unto my youth."

I met my twenty-two children next morning. They ranged in age from seventeen to five years old, nearly all of Scandinavian stock, excited, chattering, older sisters looking after younger sisters and brothers, eager to meet their new school teacher from a far away country named Ireland.

I call the roll: Marie, Joan, Joyce, Ivy, Richard, Sheila, Jimmy, Dagmar, Kurt . . . and wonder how to begin my teaching. I have not been trained for this. Is there a manual somewhere that tells me how to teach nine different grades? Is there anyone I can turn to for help? Somehow I muddle through the first day and by the end of the week I have begun to see how I should proceed. The five girls in grades nine and ten have distance-education texts that lead them assignment by assignment through the year's work. Once I have set them to work on an assignment they need only occasional supervision or help which usually totals not more than thirty minutes a day. I am surprised at how well these girls work so independently among themselves. In the evenings I grade their work and write long comments to compensate for lack of detailed attention. I have given these senior girls complete freedom—they may talk at any time, leave the room when they want, compare notes, and help each other. I also call upon them to help teach the children in grades six through eight, which they love to do. The only restriction I have placed on them is the necessity to follow a regular program each day—bookkeeping, Social Studies, English, chemistry, Home Economics, mathematics.

It is the younger children who need the most attention especially when they are learning a new step such as adding fractions. Once they have mastered it, they polish off the attendant questions easily. Again I encourage them to seek help from the older students and since there are many brothers and sisters in the school they have no hesitation in doing so. These family relations also extend to me in regard to the children in grades one and two. They refuse to stand beside me when I gather them around me to teach them reading and they push and nuzzle their way under my arms so that they can sit on my knees the way they would do with their parents in their homes.

If the children are learning so am I. There is, naturally, emphasis on Canadian history about which I have only the sketchiest knowledge. Now I encounter new names and events—de Maisonneuve, Champlain, the *couriers de bois*, Cartier, Tupper, Mackenzie King, the War of 1812, E.J. Pratt, Stephen Leacock, Bliss Carmen, Mazo de la Roche. And I have to work extra hard on double entry bookkeeping. Depreciation of office effects. What column does that go in? Home economics is also a new area for me with terms such as back stitch, running stitch, slipstitch, French seam, flat felled seam. I leaf further through the assignments and discover that the girls in grades nine and ten must make a dress incorporating what they have learned during the course and that I, their teacher, will forward my grading of their work to Regina at year's end. I try not to panic. Something will turn up to help me. Sufficient for the day is the evil thereof.

There is a lake below the Skafte home and shortly after I come to Blue Heron I ask if is safe to swim in it. The Skaftes do not know nor does anyone else. No one has ever swum in the lake; why would they, the people ask, incredulous. It is the end of August, very hot, and I tell the Skaftes that I intend to try out the water tomorrow. They are surprised—but I am not—farm people very seldom go swimming. They watch as I set out for the far lake shore, about a half mile away, I guess. There is mud where I venture in and reeds, but a little way out the water is clean and clear and cool. I take my time because it is a lovely evening, inviting after a day in the hot classroom. The swim takes longer than I had guessed, about a half hour. I rest on the far shore, then start back again. In the distance I see small figures which gradually become the Skaftes, the Jensens, the Odegaards, many of my school children, especially the older boys. I reach land and the crowd disperses. In the days that follow there is a subtle change in the parents' attitude towards me—I cannot tell if it is an increased respect because I have bested the lake or the kind of resignation one extends to pumped up adolescents or naïve newcomers.

A few weeks after my arrival in Blue Heron I met the Lutheran Pastor, David Riley. I had been told that he wanted to meet me but although he was reported as visiting Mrs Gruening a few miles away, that he'd been in the Blue Heron store but had not had time to come by. After a while I began to think of this Lutheran pastor as a lion or tiger skulking on the outskirts of my bivouac area and the local people as scouts bringing me word that the game had been seen, now here, now there. But then one evening there he was—tall, blonde, very good looking, voluble, American, and continually, it seemed, on the move. It was the beginning of a life-long friendship. He was not yet an ordained pastor but had volunteered for service in this remote part of a country foreign to him. He was university trained and could speak well on a variety of subjects, but was, of course, especially interested in philosophical and theological topics. He often invited me to his services and out of a sense of friendship I attended and once, when the regular organist was sick, I took her place. I remember an occasion when he chose marriage as the topic of his sermon. I was somewhat surprised at the choice since most of the women in his congregation were in their fifties and married for many years with children. But they did not seem to mind David's thoughts on marriage and after the service they spoke admiringly of his good looks and his charm and what a lucky girl she would be who could catch the pastor.

David seemed very different from the Catholic priests I knew. When not conducting church services he wore jeans and sweaters and did not seek special privileges; he was continually falling in love which shocked me at first since all my life I had associated priesthood with celibacy. He lived life to the full, like a clerical Zorba, visiting the sick in the hospital in Prince Albert, driving all over his extensive parish to call upon his parishioners, organizing picnics and hayrides, burying the dead, joining in a multitude of activities ranging from birthdays to weddings, at which he loved to dance. After a few weeks he offered to drive me to a Catholic church should he be free. I learned from him how to live life more fully but more importantly I learned a tolerance I did not have before. When I quoted to him the Latin saying, *Extra ecclesiam nulla salus* ("Outside the Church there is no salvation") he was shocked by such an exclusionary doctrine arguing with me that surely the people among whom I lived, devout Lutherans all, deserved more than a Hell devised by Catholic theologians. He had no time for the Virgin birth of Mary nor for papal claims to infallibility. In our long and often heated arguments I was forced to re-examine doctrines and ideas that were a part of my Catholic and Irish life. It was, in fact, the beginning of another quest that I began to undertake, a quest to understand other systems of belief and, indeed, to question the nature of belief itself.

And so the days go by. Addition, subtraction, multiplication, division, fractions. Conversion of Centigrade to Fahrenheit. The capital of British Columbia is Vancouver. Sorry, make that Victoria. What is the chemical formula for hydrogen? For oxygen? Who are the members of the Group of Seven? The time passes quickly. August is gone, and September, and October. A hint of frost in the air, the night skies sparkling and more vivid than ever, the wheat cut and stored for shipment to the markets of the world. Some days now the stove is lit in the school and occasionally the older students come to school on horseback. This delights me. And sometimes in the evenings I see my senior girls at work in the fields mounted on tractors. I am overcome with admiration. This morning that girl of the rich red hair, Joan, sat, pen in hand, grappling awkwardly with the symbols of a chemical equation; now in her familiar element she manoeuvres the huge tractor with ease. In this world of ploughing and sowing and reaping, of instinctual feeling for weather and soil and animals, I am inferior to any farmer's child of fourteen years. These young adults know plumb line and axe—by sixteen most of the boys go north in winter to work in uranium mines or in the bush. Their knowledge is survival. It is knowledge I do not have.

There are distractions, incidents that divert me. I am at the blackboard illustrating a problem when I hear the children talking excitedly. The cause of it is hulking just outside one of the schoolhouse windows—a great black and brown bear busily occupied eating berries. I panic and rush to lock the door. But the children reassure me, they've grown up living with these bears, just don't get between the mother and her cubs. The bear ambles off. We return to our work. A School Inspector, Mr Kenneth Hensbee, turns up one morning without notice. He is not much older than I. "Call me Ken", he says and tells me to carry on as usual. At lunch time he dismisses the students. "Let's go fishing, Gene" he says. "I know a good place." So we go fishing calling each other by our first names. Unimaginable in Ireland where we teachers always addressed each other as Mr or Mrs or Miss and where School Inspectors, usually failed novelists or painters, looked down upon Primary School teachers with condescension or boredom.

In my third week I become a teacher of music. Just like my old Professor Fleischmann. I was visiting one of the Jensens when I began to amuse myself on their piano—nearly every farmer had a piano. That was Mrs Jensen's cue. She asked me to give Gary, her ten-year old son, lessons. I protested that I wasn't really qualified to give lessons, it would be like having a ten-year-old teach a five-year-old to read. "And isn't that the way most of the children learn to read?" she replied. So I ended up giving Gary basic piano lessons, and then Dagmar and then . . . Since I wouldn't take any payment the parents insisted on me staying for dinner and when it got late—which was nearly always—I stayed over at night and went straight from there to school.

The music I hear, broadcast from local stations, introduces me to a new literature—that of country and western music. Mozart and Brahms and Gilbert and Sullivan give way to singers like Kitty Wells, Patsy Cline, and Hank Snow. I notice too that their songs like "Your cheatin' heart" are nearly all about unrequited love. In contrast, the Irish songs I know are nearly all about the pain associated with emigration and the loss of loved ones to America:

> . . . *whisperings come over the sea.*
> *Come back, Paddy Reilly, to Ballyjamesduff,*
> *Come home, Paddy Riley, to me.*

I am pleased with the children's work and progress. With one exception. Danny Isaacksen in grade two. He was most definitely failing. I check his marks for last year; they are very poor. Did the teacher pass him because he was so young? I give Danny special attention, the weeks pass, but his grades do not improve. And then I find the solution. I ask him and Sharon Howitt to come up to my desk, Sharon comes up, Danny doesn't. I call again in the same tone of voice. No movement from Danny. That's it, I thought. After school I detain Danny and ask him to do a few simple exercises for me. He sits at his desk, back to me, while I sit at mine and ask him to repeat what I say. What he repeats is too often garbled. I send for his mother and tell her I think Danny has a hearing problem. She is a little offended at first—who is this stranger to tell her about her own child!—but she does take him to see a doctor. Danny does indeed have a problem in one ear which is solved with a fairly simple operation. He returns and his grades rapidly improve. I am pleased.

The state of my children's teeth leads me into a protracted correspondence with the Board of Health in Regina—one of my senior girls is already wearing false teeth. I am informed that the problem is due to the lack of calcium in the water in this area. I ask for a dentist or trained dental nurse to investigate our problem but there are no funds available for that I am told. And so the children's teeth continue to rot.

The first flurries of snow have fallen, intimations of the fierce winter I have heard so much about but of whose savagery I have no comprehension. This climate continually surprises and delights me. Since I have arrived there has been little rain, day after day the skies have been blue, the quality of light clean and lucid unlike anything I had ever known in the Fall of the year. In Ireland the Fall is wet and damp and warm, always with a hint of mist. It is a beautiful season but it is a beauty of dim colours, soft rain, the smell of wet woods and streets, subdued lights. But this Saskatchewan Fall is bold and brilliant, the daylight assertive and strong, the nightfall sudden and dramatic. The foliage does not linger; yesterday the trees were in the blossom of summer, it seemed, but with the first blast of November frosts all that summer beauty has shattered into a sudden moment of shocked red, orange, blue, ice-green. Suspended between the fire of summer and the ice of winter for a moment the trees are suddenly bared of leaves, except where the fir stand electric blue against the more intense light of winter skies. There are occasional slivers of ice on the lake. One evening the Skaftes call me from my reading to see the lights in the sky—it is the *aurora borealis*. Above me in the vast sky, deeply tinged with green, lights flash as in a cosmic dance. The immensity of the spectacle hints at worlds that reach on and on into infinity and I have an existential sense of the utter insignificance of human living in the face of such cosmic forces. The Prince Albert radio the next days refers to the belief of the Cree native people that the enormous patterns of light are really the spirits of those who had fallen from the pre-birth world of light into the trap of time and space and the flesh and that their ecstatic celestial dance is one of joy and a reminder to those left behind that they too may one day join them above.

About the beginning of November I became aware of talk about the Christmas Concert. On enquiries I discovered that I was expected to offer an evening illustrating the various talents of the students. As to what format the concert should take, when it would be held, how many people to expect I got little help. The school concert had always been associated with the school and the schoolteacher; I was the schoolteacher and therefore I must know. It soon became clear that The Christmas Concert was among the most important social events of the year. The problem was that in my school in Belfast I had never had anything to do with school concerts. So there was nothing for it but to rely on my own instincts and design my own program. There would be singing and dancing and recitations and I would have an orchestra—the Blue Heron School Orchestra with all twenty-two students as instrumentalists. Soon we had rounded up three guitars, an old drum, three recorders, one tin whistle, a piano accordion, a harmonica, and a cheap xylophone. Dagmar brought along a seven stringed instrument that no one knew how to play. I decided the percussion section would fall to the youngest children. We used matchboxes with stones in some and gravel in others. Every Monday, Wednesday, and Friday we practiced in the afternoon.

I decided that the dances had to be group dances. I ransacked neighbouring homes and discovered a book of Danish dances. I decided to use two of them using eight students per dance. I added two Irish set dances, "The Rakes of Mallow" and "The Walls of Limerick," that involved all the students. The senior children had no trouble learning the steps but the youngest ones did. Take the schottische, for example, with its tricky rhythms. Even the terms "right foot" "left foot" do not mean much to five-year-olds and I wasted a lot of time on it. Eventually I gave up and used my chalk to mark the numbers 1 and 2 on their shoes. One, two, three, hop . . . and away they danced.

The schoolhouse during that November and December hummed with activity. Reading, writing, reading, arithmetic, spelling, home economics, social studies, chemistry, algebra, bookkeeping, singing practice, dancing practice, elocution lessons, rehearsals of The Blue Heron School Orchestra. The nights got longer and as the thermometer began to drop below zero I opened school at nine-thirty. I had discovered a provincial regulation which permitted a Principal to do that if weather conditions seemed risky.

And then in December, at the very height of our activities, came a telegram from Belfast, from my brother Charlie. "Mother died yesterday. Letter following." I remember putting on my winter clothes and boots and leaving the Skafte home, walking very fast and crying aloud as I had only once cried before on the day I heard of Philomena's death. And I remembered the day when my mother and I sat in the dingy railway station in Newry as she told me of Philomena's death, when I first noticed the white in her hair and the deep lines in her face, the shadow of her own death twelve years later. I don't know how long I walked but it was the extreme cold that brought me back to the present. And then I was afraid for I had lost my way. Was I right to go back on this track or had I strayed off it at some point? As I began to run flakes of snow fell in the near darkness of early evening. I don't know how long it was before I saw the lights of a car in the distance. "I thought you might get lost," the pastor said. David. Friend.

The next day a tiny nosegay of flowers lay on my desk, my children's tribute to her death and my sorrow.

When I look back on that day I am struck by the intensity of the pain I suffered on learning of my mother's death. It was like an amputation, sudden, primitive, not to be restrained. Many years later when my father died I felt no such pain despite the fact that I loved and admired him deeply. But my mother's death seemed of a different nature as if our sundering exposed me to an existential aloneness that would be with me all my life. She had given me life and now she had showed me death.

Came the night of The Christmas Concert when I drove with the Skaftes to the community hall. Already the parking area is filling up with cars and trucks. The hall is warm because the senior girls had started a fire in the afternoon. The women are unpacking the food they have brought—hams, turkey, potato salads, pies, pastries. There is no alcohol—the men sit outside in their cars and trucks and drink before making their appearance. David Riley appears in a flurry of fur coat and hat, heavy boots, a powder of snow, his entry a sign we can begin. The hall is packed. Jens Christiansen, the chairman of the school board, opens with a very few words followed by the Pastor. The Christmas Concert begins—dance, song, poetry recitations, the Blue Heron School Orchestra. I watch the rapt faces of the parents in the audience. Only thirty years ago they had sailed from Oslo, Copenhagen, Narvik, Helsinki seeking a better life, the women, young then, following their men to a place where there were no roads, no schools, no hospitals, no shops, only their dreams. Had it been worth it? The loss of friends and family left behind, learning an alien tongue so that they might speak with their children who had abandoned their mother tongue in favour of English, their children now dancing on the bright stage before them.

The concert is coming to the end. A Danish song, *Det gamle trae* ("The Old Tree") and on to the Christmas songs. "Silent Night. Holy Night,," "O Little Town of Bethlehem,," leading into our final song, "O Canada, our home and native land . . .." Time for food and I am congratulated. I have passed an important communal test. Soon the dance begins and everyone joins in. Various farmers play fiddle and guitar, they are replaced throughout the evening by anyone who can play an instrument and wants to join in. Foxtrot, schottische, reel, quick step, polka, waltz, Swedish *hambo*. The hours fly and the young children fall asleep and are bundled up and placed in sleeping bags. I walk home before the dance is over; I fall asleep and my dreams are full of children's voices and memories of my mother.

Winter is upon us now. The temperatures are consistently below zero, one morning the mercury drops to minus forty-seven Fahrenheit. The farmers bring in the batteries from their cars every night so that they will not freeze. The snowdrifts in some places are as high as thirty feet and the glare from the snow and ice under the blue, blue skies and the dazzling sunshine is so strong that most of us wear dark glasses. When a blizzard blows all outdoor activity ceases. I have been warned not to go outside at these times and always the farmers keep tuned to the radio for weather reports. Sometimes the parents come to the school for their children and I soon learn that this means the end of the school day even though the time might be 11 am. To be caught in a blizzard can mean death. Already this winter an Inspector with the Royal Canadian Mounted Police was been found frozen in his car in northern Alberta. Some of the farmers run guide ropes from the house to the outlying barns; in a blizzard one can lose all sense of direction even fifty feet from one's own home.

Many of the school children now come to school on horseback or by horse drawn sled. Gary Anderson in Grade Five with his horse, a spirited four-year old mare—and sled—a simple wooden platform on polished steel runners—picks me up but within a week I take the reins. The road to the school is about a mile long and it is my delight. A touch of the whip and the mare is off across the packed snow. When I think later of Blue Heron it is that scene that comes oftenest to me—the bright blue bowl of the sky, the smoke of our breath like plumes at our lips, the vast ice-blue landscape of snow and ice, the flying horse, Gary and I braced on that sled hissing across the snow road, and the immense silences of Saskatchewan north.

Despite the severity of the winter these hardy people have achieved a very comfortable existence. The houses are well heated with wood stoves, the roads between farms are kept clear because of an unspoken rule that each farmer looks after this, families get together on a regular basis for card-playing sessions from about nine in the evening followed by generous suppers at midnight. Each winter the farmers drive their tractors on to Blue Heron Lake and clear a large area for an ice skating rink for the young people. Even large bonfires on the lake make no impression on its frozen depths.

When any of David's parishioners are in the hospital in Prince Albert we drive the seventy miles to visit them—David insists that it is God's will that I go! In the hospital we soon become known as Pastor Riley and

Father Benson. But it is a sad experience because the great majority of the patients are from the area's aboriginal peoples who are scourged by tuberculosis and respiratory diseases. In winter these trips can be risky. Twice David's car slides off the ice-slicked roads at night but soon a tractor appears to pull us out of the ditch. No money is exchanged—again there is an unwritten rule that neighbour helps neighbour in such emergencies. This is not charity. It is survival.

Four or five evenings a week I am at my desk until midnight marking papers, reading, preparing for the next week's classes, writing letters, playing on Mrs Skafte's harmonium from her *Book of Danish Songs*. The radio is my link with the world beyond Blue Heron and Canwood. Not the stations in Canwood or Prince Albert which play only country and western music (which I like), but the Canadian Broadcasting Company. As important as the railways, the CBC programmes are the chain linking the Canadian people from British Columbia to the shores of the Atlantic Ocean. From studios in Montreal and Toronto and Vancouver these ghostly radio impulses bring me plays, opera, interviews with celebrities, international news (West Germany joins NATO, anti-French rioting in Algeria, the US Senate condemns red-baiting Senator Joe McCarthy), and national news (the politics of Prime Minister Louis Saint Laurent and those of Tommy Douglas, Premier of Saskatchewan). From time to time, almost subconsciously, I begin to think of what I will do and where I will go at the end of the school year.

Gradually winter's grip lessens, in late March the temperature rises to thirty-two degrees Fahrenheit, and soon one hears, hour by hour, the slow drip drip of melting ice. Then one day in April the delicate balance of Spring and Winter is broken and Spring explodes upon us. The sun shines with a warmth hardly remembered and there is the sound of running water everywhere. The hedgerows and drains are tumultuous with the swollen waters from the snow banks, the fields and roads are awash in mud. The farmers eye their fields impatiently, the beaver and the bear are abroad, the earth awaits the seed, the spring burgeons. On the seventeenth of March the Skaftes arrange a St Patrick's Day celebration. I am reminded that my year is running out. April, May, June. I will soon have to let Ken Hensbee, the School Inspector, know whether I am leaving or staying.

When we resume school after the brief Easter break there are changes. Marie in Grade Ten is engaged to be married to a local farmer and her engagement ring is the envy of all the other girls. Her sister Joan has written to Saskatoon about becoming a teacher when she finishes high school. Richard has decided he wants to join the Royal Canadian Air Force. There are new faces also for we are joined by six five-year-old children—kindergarten. Now I have ten classes instead of nine.

I have made my decision to leave Blue Heron. When the people hear of it, they draw up a petition asking me to stay because "you are a good teacher and especially because of your sociability." I treasure their estimate of me but I have made up my mind. In mid June my senior students complete the twenty assignments in each of their eight subjects. The air is heavy with heat and drowsy with the drone of bees and other insects. In the fields the farmers, dressed in tight clothing with face and neck under fine webbing against huge swarms of mosquitoes, are seeding the ground. Now the senior girls write the final examinations which I will mark and send off the results to Regina. But I must grade the work they have done on making those dresses called for in assignment 15. I tell the girls to bring their dresses to school, parade before their fellow students, and I will award my grade in response to the volume of applause. They agree and so one afternoon, like models, they show us their work each one making an entrance to applause. I have not time to take in whether the hem lines are level or what kind of stitching they have used—I am in admiration. They are young women, beautiful. For a time I even fancy myself in love with one of them. The question of a grade becomes academic. I give my five girls the highest grade possible—independent work should be rewarded!

At last my time is up. It is a Friday afternoon. I say goodbye to my students, Marie thanks me on their behalf, and they rush from the schoolroom to the freedom of summer. I clean the blackboard, collect my books, pull down the flag and put it away. That night at a party to mark my departure there is already speculation about the autumn crop for the sowing has been a good one. As I move among the people I become aware that that I have again become a stranger. They are still as kind as ever, but I have stepped outside this circle of friends, this family. They have not banished me from their community; I have chosen to go. To go west again, to British Columbia. I do not know what I will do. I have no job, no family or friends there. But as inevitably as birds fly south at winter's end, I must leave Blue Heron and play out a new chapter in my life in another place.

The next day David drives me to Prince Albert where I will catch the train south to Saskatoon and Regina, and board the Continental Express that runs west through the Rocky Mountains to Vancouver and the Pacific shore. I shake hands with David and I watch his old car disappear in the dust and the sunlight and then the train came.

THE PEOPLE OF THE SUN

Vancouver, embraced by the Pacific Ocean and mountains to the north, is one of the most beautiful cities in the world. In the 1950s it was also known as being among the most free-wheeling of cities whose stock market was regarded as a joke, unregulated as it was and open to blatant manipulation. Come the end of winter and loggers by the thousands make their way south from the vast forests of northern British Columbia to the fleshpots of Vancouver. When I arrived in the city and booked into a hotel, I was offered a room, a bottle of hard liquor at an inflated price and—for the first time in my life when signing into a hotel—a woman, probably at an inflated price.

   Like so many other young people, I stayed at the YMCA but later, in September, when I had made friends I rented an apartment with two of them, Kai Malthe, a Dane, and Jacques Bouvier, an Englishman, both about my age. Jacques was a product of Eton, one of England's most exclusive public (read private) schools. He had a quite wonderful accent that could caress a word or phrase in the most compelling way. One might have expected him to be something of a snob, given his background, but he was the most delightful of friends who took an enormous joy in living. We all worked at various part time jobs while looking for something more permanent. At one point we were canvassers for the Vancouver *Province* newspaper. Here Jacques was the star outselling every other marketer—his accent made him and his selling pitch irresistible. After that I took a job selling encyclopedias. The pitch or sales line here was remarkable in its psychology. In the brief training session that we were given as prospective salesmen our supervisor emphasized that we must always follow the script which asked questions that would elicit a positive answer, "yes." "If you were given the *Encyclopedia Britannica* free, would you accept it?" How could one refuse? And it was, in fact, given free. The catch was that one had to buy the Supplement which was not free.

The supervisor took us out on our first night in his car and dropped us off at designated points where we would try to sell our product door to door. I was admitted to the very first house I tried and met a young couple, both immigrants from Italy with children. The ideal family! I began my pitch and very soon they were handling the beautiful specimen volume of the *Encyclopedia*, and saying yes to all my questions. Even when I came to the part about the Supplement they were not put off so thoroughly had I indoctrinated them. But as I neared the conclusion to my pitch I began to have scruples: it was obvious from the furnishings of their home that this young couple was living on a modest income; their two children—five years old and seven years old—were highly unlikely to use my product for many years; the young couple didn't really understand that the *Encyclopedia* was not free. I decided quickly that I had to persuade them not to buy my product but found that I had done such a sound job that it proved almost impossible. Eventually I escaped, *Encyclopedia* unsold. That night I resigned my position.

But if this was my first taste of the business world I was not put off. I had come to the conclusion that I wanted to make money—many of my friends were earning a lot of money as engineers, doctors, real estate salesmen, advertising executives. I had put teaching behind me—I would be as successful as they were.

My opportunity came in September when I applied for a job with Remington Rand which was then a pioneer in the new field of computing science. It was well known, of course, for its typewriters and office equipment. I was interviewed by the Area Manager for western Canada, an American, and was later asked to write an intelligence test. I must have done well because I was selected as a trainee in the computer division. I was also informed that the company expected a high standard of work since the Chairman of the Board was none other than the famed five-star General Douglas MacArthur. And so I began a new life which was immediately dominated by a huge machine, the Remington Rand UNIVAC that lived on a diet of punch cards fed to it daily in enormous quantities. My boss, Norm—Mr Cotrell to me—was my mentor whom I followed everywhere. I soon learned that the punch card was the key to my work. A thin piece of stiff paper, it contained 45 columns with 12 punch locations each, two characters to each column. It would be my job to get the information that would be punched into these cards which would then be read by the UNIVAC—the digital material on the cards was represented by the presence or absence of holes in predefined areas, all calculations based on one and zero—the binary code. If payroll information, for example, entered on punch cards, was fed to the UNIVAC it speeded up immensely work that formerly took days.

And so I entered a period when I had to wear a business suit (Mr Cotrell would approve what I wore or suggest what I should not wear), I had to observe strict office hours, I had to learn the workings of factories, companies, municipalities that might want to computerize their taxation notices or gas bills, for example. Soon I was given partial responsibility in preparing a proposal to computerize the operations of the Canadian Pacific Steamship Company and day after day I trudged into their offices exploring how their payroll was set out or how they handled stock control. As I remember that period it always seemed to be raining so that I seldom saw the mountains that beckoned to me in the distance and I rarely got out for a walk at the beach on English Bay or to Stanley Park. Only at night did I sometimes escape the demands of the UNIVAC. Then Jacques and Kai and I would go to out for a drink and the talk would be all of books and films and travel. Never a word about the UNIVAC or selling encyclopedias or about money. Gradually I began to have doubts about the kind of work I was doing—I missed the interaction with people that had characterized my work as a teacher. I seemed to spend all my time with organizational charts and with computer manuals. But I was determined to succeed. A colleague at Remington Rand who had just computerized the payroll of the city of Edmonton told me that if I wasn't making $20,000 within five years the firm would have no use for me. That was a great incentive to brave the rains of winter and continue feeding the UNIVAC.

And then everything changed. In December. A Tempter in the shape of a Lutheran candidate for the ministry phoned me. David Riley. Why was I doing this, he demanded. I had spoken to him often about writing a novel. Now was the time to do it. He also wanted to write a novel and he had decided we should both go to Mexico as soon as possible. It was the will of God. I rejected his offer outright. I could not, I explained. Remington Rand had gone to great trouble interviewing me, selecting me from a large number of candidates, I was indebted to Mr Cotrell, I couldn't let him down. I couldn't bear to think of going into his office to tell him I was going to Mexico to write a novel that I hadn't yet planned. Could Mr Cotrell sue me for misrepresentation? No, I told David. I am not going to Mexico. It is not the will of God.

But in the days that followed my work with Remington Rand seemed to become more depressing and David's idea more attractive. But still I resisted. I am trying to escape responsibility, I told myself. Of course it would be pleasant to live in Mexico for a while writing a novel but what will I do when my money runs out. With my small savings I could maybe live there for six months provided living was cheap in Mexico. No, it's impossible. Why then was I looking at maps of Mexico rejoicing in wonderful names that seemed to offer pleasures unknown to the UNIVAC—San Miguel de Allende, Guanajuato, Zaachila, Durango, San Cristobal de las Casas. And so while rehearsing all the obvious and sound reasons why I should remain at my job I found myself in Mr Cotrell's office telling him I wanted to leave. He took it well until he asked me why. I said it was really my fault, that it had nothing to do with the company which had treated me well, it was just that I was not happy in my work. At the work "happy" he got very angry and ordered me out of his office. It was only that night after I had talked it over with my friends that I began to understand Mr Cotrell's anger. I had introduced a forbidden word—"happy"—into the rationality of the business world, a word that spoke of family and love and personal values and contact with people where money simply did not count. But what did I know of Mr Cotrell's life and ambitions and aspirations? Perhaps he too was chained to the UNIVAC, condemned to ever higher quotas and business returns by Head Office in New York. Maybe he dreamed of writing a novel or sailing a boat around the world but didn't because he had a wife and children who were attending expensive colleges, because he had a mortgage, because he had obligations to old parents. The next afternoon I saw Mr Cotrell and explained that I felt I would have to wait too long to get to know the business and so make the kind of money I hoped for. Hence my decision to leave. Immediately Cotrell was solicitous, saying he understood, offering to write a letter of commendation and to facilitate my departure which he deeply regretted. And so we parted on good terms. I saw him once more, three years later, at the airport in Toronto. He said he remembered me right away as the trainee who was in search of happiness.

And so I found myself on a Greyhound bus on New Year's Day 1956 bound for Mexico on a journey that took me ten days before I found my next home, all my possessions in two cases and a knapsack. Southwards through Washington and Oregon to northern California where the rain ceased and the weather became warmer. San Francisco where I stopped over for a day at the Hotel Odeon and did what tourists usually did—visit Cliff House, Fisherman's Wharf, Chinatown, ride the cable cars—before traveling south. Much warmer now. Los Angeles with its palm trees and architecture in pale pastel colours. I had no wish to sightsee here but spent the day wandering around a landscape shaped by memories of Hollywood and its film stars—Chaplin, Flynn, Gable, Bergman, Hepburn, Tracy, Bogart—so many who had given me great pleasure through the years and the plots of whose films I recited in the dormitory of St Coleman's College as I lulled the boys to sleep. The headlines in the Los Angeles papers scream that Merle Travis, a guitar player known to aficionados for his "Travis picking style" and author of the song "Sixteen Tons," has just been arrested for assaulting his wife and holding off the police with a rifle. I caught a midnight bus for El Paso, Texas, on another twenty-two-hour odyssey.

I am not at all exhausted or bored by these long trips. I curl up at night and usually manage to sleep well. And I am never lonely. I meet soldiers and sailors and airmen and housewives and students and drunks and salesmen and even one woman who is traveling all the way to San Salvador, on a far longer journey than mine. But she will stop over in Mexico, in the town of Cuautla, with a cousin for a couple of days, she says, in order to get a rest. Here on these huge Greyhound buses is the whole human variety and these people are glad to tell me their stories to pass the time and to hear mine. I meet a middle-aged man who has given up his job in Sacramento to go to Mexico where he will meet a guru whose transcendentalism offers him solace in a world he wants to abandon. I meet a Customs official, a former soldier who had been stationed in Richfield, Northern Ireland, during the war. He waxed nostalgic about an Irish girl to whom he had proposed marriage. She had turned him down, afraid, he said, of going to a foreign land. Although he was now married with children he confessed that he still loved her and had vowed one day to go back and see her. His memories of Ireland were principally of her long red hair and of the greenness of the country which was in such contrast to the land around El Paso. And of course I never traveled without books. I was reading simultaneously Christopher Isherwood's *World in the Evening* (a portrait of a world weary traveler Stephen Monk who is trying to come to terms with life in America) and Diaz's *The Discovery and Conquest of Mexico*. It was fascinating and tragic to read how despite the fact that Montezuma's spies reported in detail the march of Cortés and his few hundred *conquistadores* from the Yucatan peninsula to *Tenochtitlan* (Mexico City) that the Emperor with his thousands of warriors hesitated to strike. Like a rabbit paralyzed by the anaconda that will devour it. A paralysis that allowed Cortés to destroy the city—and Aztec civilization.

The El Paso leg of the journey is over and I stay for the night at the Knox Hotel and sleep until the afternoon preparing for the next leg—thirty-eight hours—which will take me through to Mexico City. The predominant language is now Spanish and when we make our first Mexican stop at Durango I order a glass of tequila in halting Spanish phrases (*Una tequila con hielo, por favor*) and I have my first Mexican meal—*pollo con queso. Bravo!* I shall survive. And so to the last lap—Chihuahua, Torreón, Durango where I change buses, on to Zacatecas, Aguascalientes, Salamanca, and then Mexico City. On the way from Los Angeles someone had given me the address of a hotel on the *Plaza Buenavista* and since that was the name of the terrace in Larne where I was born I made my way to the Hotel Oxford. It was in the centre of the city, in the Tabacalera area not far from the leading thoroughfare the *Paseo de la Reforma*, and close to Sanborns the large American owned store which had a wonderful café. After I had checked in I got a map of Mexico for I had already made up my mind that I would not stay in Mexico City—too large, too expensive. I would bypass the city as I had bypassed Rome in 1953 and sightsee at a later time. But where to go for the months ahead? I was aware that Taxco and Cuernavaca were popular tourist venues but for that very reason I ruled them out. As I pored over the map one name began to emerge—Cuautla—and I remembered my traveling companion on her way to San Salvador. She had spoken of it warmly. I would go there. I next sent a telegram to David advising him of my whereabouts and plans and some time later received a reply stating that he must cancel his visit to Mexico, he had just met a woman called Daisy, she was so beautiful, so loving, I would understand. It was God's will. So there I was, friendless, in a strange city, unable to speak Spanish, and with only English, Latin, Greek, and Gaelic (the last three very dead languages) to assist me in finding my way around.

On the following day I headed over to the White Star terminal and boarded a second-class bus for the three-hour journey south. There were no other tourists I guessed; these were Mexicans one and all with their packages and bundles and children and food and drink. In the distance were the soaring twin peaks of the volcanic mountains Popocatépetl and Iztaccihuatl. When we finally got to Cuautla I was glad that they still could easily be seen, beautiful, aloof, disdainful of the fury and the mire of human passions. That night I went to sleep in the *Hotel España* (room *con alimento* fifteen pesos per day) and the next afternoon I began writing.

On the bus trip from Vancouver I had thought a great deal about the subject of my novel and had sketched out a rough framework. I knew that many novelists used autobiographical material as a springboard and I decided to do the same. The story would be about Ireland and about the fictionalized "me" but I would complement that with the story of the struggle being conducted by the Irish Republican Army. At some point the personal tale of my alter ego would link with that of revolutionary politics. I would rewrite in novelistic terms my play "The Crowing of the Cock" and its theme of love and betrayal.

But writing in the confines of a small room in a crowded and noisy cheap hotel was difficult and so I was continually alert to the possibility of moving to some place more congenial. On my fourth day in Cuautla I went to the upscale *Hotel Vasco* for a swim (three pesos charge) and afterwards as I was having a *cerveza* at the bar I saw a pink Cadillac draw up and a well dressed middle aged man accompanied by a beautiful young woman get out and come into the bar. He ordered drinks and soon we fell into talk. He introduced himself as Carlos Tornel and immediately began enquiring, in very good but accented English, who I was, what was I doing in Cuautla, how long would I be staying. It was a veritable interrogation and not once did the young woman speak nor did Señor Tornel introduce her—she sat prettily sipping her cocktail, smiling when I looked at her, crossing her elegant legs and tossing her hair. I concluded she must be a relative—a daughter or niece perhaps. Somewhere in that one-sided conversation Señor Tornel decided he liked me, that I was a young man of talent who should not be asked to write a work of importance in such a cheap hotel as the *Hotel España*, that he had the very place in mind for me, a room in one of his properties that I could share with an American who had been looking for someone share the rent. The rent would be very reasonable because he, Señor Tornel, believed in treating artists properly. When we had finished our drinks we could go and see Jimmy, the American. He was a little peculiar, Señor Tornel said, like all gringos. Overwhelmed I got into the pink Cadillac—the *señorita* delegated to the back seat—and drove off to see (hopefully) what would be my new home.

The street was disappointing—unpaved, small adobe houses undistinguished in character, jacaranda and papyrus trees growing wild. Tornel's house could not be seen from the outside being hidden away, like many upper class Mexican homes, behind a high wall. But when we entered what a vision! A large gateway opened into a beautiful garden with an immaculate lawn and with masses of different coloured shrubs and flowers—hibiscus, bougainvillea, trumpet vine—clinging to the walls. There was a gardener's cottage at the entrance where Juan and his wife lived, a large bungalow at the end of the garden where Tornel lived, and a smaller bungalow, immediately to the right as one entered, where Jimmy the American lived. We were introduced and Carlos and the young woman went off to the larger bungalow. Jimmy was about six feet three inches tall, mid thirties I guessed. He held one arm in a way that seemed to indicate it had been injured at one time. After a chat over rum and coke (another interrogation) Jimmy agreed that I could share the bungalow with him and told me what my share of the rent would be and how much I would pay Cypriana, the gardener's wife, who was the cook. The large bed sitting room had two beds which were at right angles to each other and separated by a night table. That evening as I sat on the patio in front of my bungalow chatting with Jimmy I rejoiced at my good luck in finding such a beautiful setting and at a price I could afford. There was even a dog called Byron of whom I grew very fond.

And so I made my home for the next four months at Number 79 Calle Gabriel Tepepa and I began to feel at home in Cuautla. I got to know its dusty streets and its noisy, fly-ridden market where I sometimes went shopping with Cypriana. On the first visit I was appalled at the flies that infested all the uncovered food for sale. When the butcher wanted to show Cypriana a piece of meat he swept the flies off it with his hands, but one only had a momentary glance before the flies covered it again. I understood now why our meat always seemed so hard—Cypriana quite rightly over cooked it to prevent food poisoning. Jimmy and I made our own breakfast and lunch and here I discovered that although Cypriana was supposed to keep our bungalow clean she did not. I opened one of the shelves above the stove to discover cockroaches and on further investigation discovered that all the shelves in the kitchen were infested by a mass of cockroaches. Cypriana promised a cleanup *mañana* but when *mañana* turned into a week I finally got bug spray and began my own war. I finally got the kitchen cleaned up but I never could get rid of two huge cockroaches that lurked inside our radio and appeared spectrally in a faint green colour when I switched it on. At the end of my sojourn in Cuautla they were still there, immured eternally it seemed on the dial, between Mexico City and Guatemala City.

Jimmy proved a congenial enough companion but I learned very little about his background. He was always polite, fastidious about bills that we shared for food and maid service, helpful in giving me useful information such as how to rent a postal box. In the second week, however, I met a very different Jimmy from the one I thought I knew. We had gone to bed about our usual time, midnight, and I quickly fell asleep only to be awakened by loud screams that filled the room. I started up and saw Jimmy, eyes bulging from his head and arms outstretched as if to choke something, sitting up in his bed and screaming at the top of his voice in a language I could not understand. I cowered in my bed, afraid that if I came within his line of vision he would harm me. In a few minutes Jimmy fell silent and went back to sleep. The next day I wondered if I should bring up the topic but decided not to. A week or so later the same thing happened— the same screaming in a language unintelligible to me. I told Carlos about what had happened (he now insisted that I call him by his first name in the crazy Americano fashion), but he merely said that something had happened to Jimmy in the war and that he was living cheaply in Mexico on a disability pension. In the following months I did learn a few more things about Jimmy from various Americans living in Cuautla—he was a native of Los Angeles, he had been a sergeant in the US Marine Corps, he had been wounded in hand to hand combat on the island of Iwo Jima where he had been posted after attending an American military school learning Japanese. Jimmy spoke to me only once about his past and that was to tell me that he'd heard crooner Bing Crosby sing in the Paul Whiteman band when he was a boy.

I now had a fairly predictable schedule. Breakfast about 9 a.m. followed by reading, followed by lunch after which I began writing (in long hand). This would continue until late in the afternoon. Generally speaking I did not write after dinner. By the end of my first month in Cuautla I had written about one hundred and twenty pages of my novel now titled *Minute after Noon*, a phrase from a poem by the metaphysical poet John Donne: "*Love is a burning or full constant light/ And his first minute after noon is night.*" By the end of my first month I had also got to know some of the few English-speaking people who had come to Cuautla either to retire or to work in various artistic areas. Nick Sceso, for example, is an artist who has been living here for three years and swears he will never return to the USA. He's middle aged, unmarried. After we get to know each other he invites me to his studio to see his work of three years—thirty-nine paintings of Popocatépetl and Iztaccihuatl, twin volcanic beauties. I ask him about other paintings with other subjects but he had none. There was no reason to paint anything else, he says, the mountains contained everything he had ever wanted to paint, every shadow and highlight, every hue and tint, a daily invitation into the mystery of being that seems to him inexhaustible. He seems not to belong to any school or to acknowledge any mentor whether classical or contemporary. We meet often and discuss his newest painting as it grows and develops. I have no idea whether he is a good artist or merely an amateur but I am pleased to have him train my eye to see the subtleties of landscape and light.

Then there is Jack Grove. He's fairly young, claims to have had the largest car dealership in Los Angeles before he sold it to come to Mexico to settle down and find a wife. He tells me in no uncertain terms of his contempt for modern American women who he claims have taken over the country and emasculated their husbands and spoiled their children. His wife is a good-looking Mexican woman with only a limited command of English and she is a wonderful cook which is one reason, Nick claims, that he married her. Jack knows all the gossip about the small American group in Cuautla but he does not socialize much with them. Adrian Glass, another middle aged American and would-be writer, tells me he once lived on a Pacific island for a year after reading Somerset Maugham's novel *The Moon and Sixpence* which was based on the life of Paul Gauguin. He claims that when he met Maugham in his home in the south of France he was reading one of his own novels. Because I go to Mass on Sundays I meet a German priest, Father Herman, who says his parish is all of Mexico since he travels throughout the country to its scattered German Catholic communities. He is in Cuautla for three weeks. Every time we meet he brings up the subject of Thérèse Neumann, a woman living in Bavaria, Germany, who claims to have the stigmata and not to have eaten or drunk anything since 1922. I am skeptical about such claims but years later I read in Indian yogi Paramahansa Yogananda's autobiography of a visit he made to Thérèse and of his belief in her claims.

   One evening I am invited by Carlos to a dinner which includes a local retired judge, an actor and his wife, and Bob Quigley, an American radio and screen writer—Carlos' mistress, Patricia or Patti as we call her, is not present but hovers prettily into view now and then. It is a very pleasant affair with much of the conversation in English—partly out of deference to me and also because educated Mexicans love to practice their usually limited English with native speakers. The judge is a distinguished looking man, about seventy years old, with a fund of interesting anecdotes which he tells with wit and humour. The actor is a handsome man named Victor Manuel Mendoza who, I learn, is something of a matinee idol in Central and South America. I discover that he has worked in many films including some directed by Luis Buñuel, the Spanish director who left Spain vowing never to work there again while Generalissimo Franco and the Fascists were in power. He talked interestingly of such actors as Gérard Philipe, Michèle Morgan, Gary Cooper, Susan Hayward, and others with whom he has worked. His wife, a tall woman who I believe had herself been an actress, said little. The next morning Carlos descended on me wanting to know if I had enjoyed his dinner and who of his guests did I find most interesting. When I told him I had been most impressed by the judge, he roared with laughter. You have very good taste, he told me. The man is a murderer. It seems that the judge, married to a much younger wife as is so often the custom in Mexico, came home unexpectedly to find his wife and her lover in bed whereupon he took his pistol and shot them both to death. He then phoned Carlos who advised him to get out of Mexico for a year which he did spending it in Spain. On his return he was charged but acquitted on the grounds that it was a *crime passionnel*, that any gentleman would be duty bound to defend the honour of his family. I was shocked by this story but could believe it since I had experienced in a different way this kind of violence. Pedro, a Mexican friend of Jimmy's, came by one evening for a game of cards. As we drank tequila and played I remarked on what a fine watch Pedro was wearing. Immediately he took off his watch and gave it to me as a present. I told him I could not possible accept such a valuable gift at which he pulled out a pistol, cocked it, and said I had insulted him. I put the watch on my wrist and we continued playing with the cocked loaded pistol facing me for the rest of the evening as Pedro got slowly drunk. The next morning I sent the watch back and when I saw Pedro again he did not bring up the matter of his honour which I had impugned.

I also wondered whether Carlos' story of the judge was a subtle reminder to me that Patti was his property. He was a man nearing sixty I guessed and she was probably about twenty-three years old and I was twenty seven. Many afternoons when Carlos was having his siesta Patti would wander over to our bungalow. She did not speak any English but I knew enough Spanish by this time to allow for communication. And sometimes when the radio broadcast a particularly popular dance tune we would dance—she even taught me the cha-cha-cha, then the rage. I gradually pieced together some fragments of her life. She had been born dirt poor in Mexico City to a large family, because of her looks she had got a job as a cigarette girl in a nightclub when only fifteen, she had met Carlos just a year ago, he was kind and generous, life was good, who knew what tomorrow would bring. I told her she must elope with me to Canada and she laughed and said she would willingly come as soon as she had learned English. I must repay her for her dancing lessons by tutoring her in English. And so we danced on many afternoons, and I was quite intoxicated by her closeness and her beauty. And when Carlos came over to our bungalow after his siesta he seemed not to mind our intimacy. He was wise enough to know that Patti needed young company and that I would understand the parable of his friend the judge.

And then there was Rebecca. A letter had been wrongly delivered to our address and when I took it to an address not far from Calle Gabriel Tepepa I met her. The house was not as large as Carlos' but it also was surrounded by a wall so high that when a young woman opened the gate the garden was in shade. She was a woman in her early twenties, slim, dark, with enormous expressive eyes. I gave her the letter and we chatted for a few minutes—her English was quite fluent and charmingly accented. I hoped we might meet again. A week later when I we met her at the market with her maid she invited me to her house. We sat in the living room overlooking the garden drinking lemonade and then I was introduced to her parents who left us after only a few minutes. When I mentioned the baby grand piano in the room she said that she had once hoped to be a concert pianist and thus see the world but that had not worked out. She played a number of études by Chopin for me before she led me out of her house into the busy street outside. And so we began a relationship that lasted until I left Cuautla. I would come to her house, usually in the early evening, and we would talk or she would play the piano. Sometimes I read parts of my novel to her or from a volume of poetry or I told of my year teaching in northern Saskatchewan and of how some nights I had seen the *aurora borealis* when the colours of the sky danced in green and red and black across a vast cosmic space—a dance that the Cree natives called the "Dance of the Spirits," reminding those left at death of their enduring presence. She loved that story and made me tell it again and again.

   I rarely met her parents who existed somewhere vaguely in the background, like insubstantial figures from another era. I gradually learned that Rebecca was Jewish, born in Dresden, Germany, and taken to Mexico in 1938 by her parents after the family business had been confiscated by the Nazis. There were a number of fading photographs on the wall and once I asked her about them. Her family, she said. All gone now. *Der Massenmord*. The Holocaust. But she said little about herself and I did not press her. She represented a kind of serenity for me, a pastel shading in the tempestuous palette that was the teeming town of Cuautla with its flaming bougainvilleas, jacaranda trees, hibiscus, azaleas, and sinuous cacti and *burros* and dogs and chicken and babies and my own imagination forever at work on my novel and the business of living. So one or two evenings a week I sat with her as the evening shadows closed in on the garden and she played the music she loved, the nocturnes of John Field, Chopin, and Scriabin. Then a kiss on the cheek and I would make my way home, back to the ever present music of mariachi and marimba bands and the popular songs of Beny Moré of Cuba. My time with Rebecca was special. It was as if we lived in a secret place and in a timeless condition.

   Cuautla is well known for its sulphur baths and I regularly go swimming with my friends. There is also a river nearby where the ice cold water from the mountains meets the warm water of the Cuautla aquifer. As I swim there in the sunlight I can see in the distance the twin volcanic mountains and on the far shore Mexican women, naked from the waist up, washing their clothes and themselves. I talk to a young boy of fourteen who is tending sheep and he tells me his ambition is to join his cousin in the USA, in El Paso, where he can get a job in a factory. I wish him good luck but can only wonder will he end up years later regretting the paradise of his youth. *Et in Arcadia ego.*

I also do some sightseeing—Cuernavaca and Taxco—and am glad I chose Cuautla. Both are full of tourists with a large expatriate group mainly Americans with some Canadians, British, and Germans. In Cuernavaca I am astounded by the 1930s murals by Diego Rivera in the *Palacio de Cortés*—he is a quite extraordinary artist. Taxco interests me especially for the work of its silversmiths who use wonderfully arcane pre-Hispanic forms and motifs, chiefly plumed serpents, jaguar heads, and fierce-eyed eagles, and, occasionally, monkeys. These artists achieve remarkable effects in wedding silver with turquoise, lapis lazuli, mother-of-pearl, malachite, abalone shell, obsidian, onyx, and diverse jadeites of the most tremulous colours.

Meanwhile my novel grow day by day and takes new directions and surprises me by its turns of narrative and even of tone. The action of the novel is set in Ireland but soon I follow my alter ego to European locales where his fascination with their cultures is gradually given a newer and darker dimension as he learns more of Europe's blood-drenched history. Perhaps it is the influence of Rebecca that leads my protagonist, my *alter ego*, to Germany where, inadvertently, he betrays a Jewish family to the Nazis and to death because of his sexual obsession with a German woman. And so gradually the writing of my novel forced me to look at life beyond the walls of Carlos' home. Outside these beautiful grounds is poverty of an appalling nature, families living on a dollar a day, a political system based on corruption and a legal system easily manipulated by those with money. There are millions living in Mexico City on the edge of starvation and yet when I visit the city I discover hotels and nightclubs more extravagant than any I have seen in London or Montreal or San Francisco. Carlos had became my friend, someone whom I admired for the sheer extravagance of his character and his zest for living, but like the majority of those tracing their lineage to Spain he despised the native peoples of Mexico. They were mere "Indians," dirty, uneducated, without ambition or drive. He refused to believe the story Nick Sceso told us of a woman, unmarried, who supported herself and her four children by making tortillas or of a woman in Cuautla who, in the final hours of her pregnancy, bleeding profusely, was refused medical help because she had no money. When the baby was born dead at midnight it was hung in a bucket high in a tree to keep it from the cats—the father was too drunk to make a wooden box for its burial. Sometimes my novel and what I am doing seem inconsequential, a futile shoring up of shards of memory and I am reminded of the poet Matthew Arnold's lines:

> *. . . we are here as on a darkling plain*
> *Swept with confused alarms of struggle and flight,*
> *Where ignorant armies clash by night.*

I am fascinated by Mexico, by its sense of urgency of life and by its colour and its landscape that arouses in me a sense of a primeval prelapsarian world, but I am appalled by the voraciousness of the rich who pay few taxes, by the poverty of the native peoples, and by the violence that lurks everywhere like a cancer.

I try to discuss these matters with Bob Quigley and Jack Grove and Nick Cseco but they are impatient with me. What can anyone do? The country has always been like this. Life is short and brutal for some, for others relatively pleasant. Shut your eyes, enjoy what you have, you have earned it. And so we go from day to day, Nick painting his mountains, Bob writing his screen plays, I typing away on my novel. What else can we do? We are outsiders here. *Gringos.*

I read a great deal in Cuautla. FitzGerald's *Tender is the Night,* Hemingway's *For Whom the Bell Tolls*, Louis Bromfield's *Night in Bombay*, Robert Graves' *Antigua, Penny, Puce*, Salinger's *For Esmé with Love and Squalor*, Michener's *Tales of the South Pacific*, Thomas Merton's *Seven Storey Mountain*, and Tom Lea's *The Brave Bulls*, among others. After reading *The Brave Bulls* I decided I must visit a bull fight and Bon Quigley, who has written on bullfighting, arranged to meet me in Mexico City and Carlos told me I could stay in his house there. It's quite central and I found it easily—Number 6, Calle Artes. It's large, with a master bedroom and two other bedrooms, a dining room and a drawing room, a kitchen and servants' quarters. And a parrot who talks loudly in Spanish and two cats. There is a large photograph of a José Tornel, perhaps the father of Carlos, as a student at Stonyhurst College, the private and elite school in England run by the Jesuits. The house is full of statues and Spanish *objets d'art* and paintings.

The next day I went to the *plaza de toros*, the largest bullfighting arena in the world holding about 45, 000 spectators. Quigley and I had good seats in the shade where we watched the plaza fill rapidly as hawkers sold posters of bullfighters, cold drinks, brandy, postcards, and fruit. Opposite us the people in the sun wearing glasses against the sun looked like row upon row of the blind. At four o'clock boys entered the arena riding horses at a slow walk. The horses were heavily padded and their eyes were bandaged, some on both eyes, others on one eye only. They've been ridden that way since early morning, Quigley said. The more exhausted they are the better. They won't panic so easily at the smell of the bulls.

At four thirty the President's Box began to fill and when the President entered the band commenced playing and the stewards came out on well fed horses to lead the *paseo*: first the matadors in the suits of light, then the *banderilleros* followed by the *picadores* on their blinded horses. Soon the trumpet sounded and the red gate was opened and the first bull, powerful and terrified, came charging into the arena. And so I sat for the next three hours while every thirty minutes a bull was let loose in the arena and was killed according to a ritual as prescribed and inflexible as that governing the celebration of the Catholic Mass. First the matador "tames" the bull with his large yellow and magenta *capote* or cape, large because at this early stage he wants to show off such passes as the *veronica* but primarily because he does not want to go too close to the bull. The main function of this taming is also to exhaust the bull. At this point the *picador* enters and entices the bull to charge the horse while he pierces the neck muscles with the steel-tipped lance. This is where most bulls are ruined, Quigley told me. Some matadors let their *picadores* butcher their animals so badly they have little power left.

The second act commences with the placing of the *banderillas*, short barbed harpoons which further weaken the bull. By this time he is sweating and covered with blood and it is now that many bulls are so weakened and shocked that they will refuse to fight. The third act in the ritual is the *faena* when the matador changes his *capote* for the much smaller red *muleta* and with his ceremonial sword further tames the bull. Finally, as a hush descends on the crowd, he takes his real killing sword and prepares for the moment of truth, the slaughter of the animal, which is meant to be done by leaning in over the horns and piercing the bull between its shoulder blades. This is a delicate and dangerous procedure and its botchery is usually what makes a crowd angry and scream threats against a matador who because of cowardice stabs the bull at random and against the strict ritual which endows the killing with a kind of sacramental risk. It is as if the man has broken a covenant with the bull, a covenant which, in some inscrutable way, justifies its death.

There were three matadors this day and six bulls. Two of the matadors were mere butchers who drove the crowd to a frenzy of protest so threatening that police in full riot gear moved into view. The third, a matador named Humberto Moro, drew the crowd's approval. He made long sweeping *veronicas* that seduced the bull ever closer and when he stabbed the bull over the horns its life was extinguished as if one had switched off a light. He gave some credence to those who held that the bullfight was misnamed, that it was a religious performance where the man and bull were merely players in a ritual as old as time itself—even in Crete, centuries before the encounter of man and beast is documented in Spain, bare-breasted girls embraced the bulls in a perilous duet where they soared over the bulls that raced to gore them and where no blood was meant ever to be shed.

The next day on the bus back to Cuautla Quigley and I talked about the bullfights which were still so vividly in our minds. I once visited a Mexican ranch, Quigley told me, where I saw the bulls grazing among the steers that they serviced. I was struck, he said, by the peaceful nature of the bulls which can be driven even through the streets of a town provided they are in the company of steers. I realized then, he said, the demonic side of man's nature that could so transform a peaceful animal into a beast that must spend the last twenty minutes of its life fighting in the bullring. He had the same feeling as when he read in Melville's *Moby-Dick* of the slaughter by humans of the great mother whales of the Pacific Ocean even as they suckled their calves.

That evening I went to Rebecca's house and as we sat in the dim living room with the shadows slowly deepening I told her of what I had seen, of my conflicting emotions. She brought lemonade then and afterwards she played some pieces of Chopin for me that she knew I liked. When I went to bed that night I fell quickly asleep and the blood and sand of the arena in Mexico City which I feared left me. But for years after they came back and they stayed with me until I finally exorcised them in a novel I wrote in fascist Spain called *The Bulls of Ronda.* Its themes were also those of love and betrayal.

The first draft of my novel is almost finished and my money is running low. I have been here over three months and have paid my rent until the end of April when I must leave. But there are certain places I must visit for I do not know if I shall return. And so I traveled to Mexico City where I saw some of the work of the great Mexican muralists Rivera, Orozco, and Siqueiros. Their magnificent murals on the walls of the Library at the National Autonomous University of Mexico, the *Palacio de Bellas Artes*, and the *Palacio National* evoked in me as much admiration and awe as that I had experienced when first seeing St Peter's Basilica in Rome. Rivera's recreation of his famous "Man at the Crossroads" in the *Palacio de Bellas Artes* was his *riposte* to the philistines who ordered the original mural in New York destroyed because it contained a portrait of Vladmir Lenin. I also visited the Basilica of Guadalupe with its renowned icon of the Virgin of Guadalupe where worshippers cross its vast square or atrium on their knees.

On the advice of Carlos I visited Acapulco—it's the playground of very rich South Americans and *gringos* like John Wayne and Rita Hayworth, he told me, but worth visiting. And so I rode a bus all night from Mexico City and came over the mountains at Chilpancingo at dawn and there before me was the most beautiful curved beach I had ever seen, framed by jungle and mountain. Paradise! But Paradise has always had its immemorial snake and it this case it was someone who robbed me of my wallet as I lay asleep on Acapulco's golden sand. At the Police Station they said they could not help. I should report my loss to the police in Mexico City. As I left the Station the wives and mistresses and whores of the prisoners in the jail next door were being let out—sexual privileges, I learned, have always been afforded those in prison. The next day in Mexico City I went to the British Embassy in order to get a loan to get me to Canada but they referred me to the British Society on Calle de Carranza where a harassed looking Englishman said the Society did have a fund "for the relief of distressed gentlemen and ladies" but that the fund only amounted to seventy-two American dollars. He gave me the money and off I went to Police Headquarters where I reported my loss—I needed to do this in order to have my Bank in Canada pay me for a draft order for $100 that had been in my stolen wallet. The square outside the Police Station was packed with scruffy looking men whom I took to be criminals but a police officer told me irritably that they were policemen. The next day was Labour Day, May 1, and any signs of dissatisfaction with the government would be suppressed with the utmost brutality by these men. Afterwards I bought a bus ticket to San Antonio, Texas. My business in Mexico City concluded,

I took the bus to Cuautla and made preparations to leave. It was more difficult than I thought. I had grown to think of Cuautla as my home. I knew its streets, gaudy at nights with its many shops, its churches, its spas, the wonderful views of Popocatépetl and Iztaccihuatl I had come to love. I said my goodbyes to Juan and Cypriana and Jack Grove and Adrian Glass and others whom I had come to know. Nick Cseco was in his studio still at work on the painting I had seen four months before. It's almost finished, he told me. Perhaps next month. In truth, I could see no significant difference. Patti came over in the afternoon when Carlos is having his siesta and we danced as we had so often done. When she left she hugged me closely and kissed me for the first time on the mouth. Later Carlos came over and upbraided me for leaving and offered to let me stay as long as I want free of rent. In the evening I went to Rebecca's house. She asked me what my plans were and I told her I would go straight through to New Orleans via San Antonio where I would stop over for two days to sightsee and have coffee in the restaurant known as "Antoine's"—I had recently read Francis Parkinson Keyes' novel *Dinner at Antoine's*. After that I would go north to Toronto, Canada, stopping to see the blue grass country of Kentucky which had always fascinated me. But Rebecca didn't really want to know my travel plans. She wanted to know what I hoped to do in the future, what I intended to do with my life. Was I not afraid of the unknown? No, I told her. Perhaps I am limited in my imagination, maybe even irresponsible in not making plans to live a safe life, to settle down, to make life-long commitments. An inner compulsion drove me to explore life every day, to visit new places, to imagine that everything would turn out well. That I had luck on my side.

When I asked her about her plans (which I had never done before) she said she had none. She could not leave her parents who were getting old. In Cuautla she saw little of her Mexican neighbours and there were only two other Jewish families. She had a second cousin in Mexico City whom her parents sometimes mentioned vaguely as a possible husband. But how could she marry a man she did not love. When you sell your novel and become rich and famous, she said, promise me that you will come back and take me to Canada so that I can see the great lights dancing in the northern skies. I'll come back, I told her, in a Cadillac even grander than that of Señor Tornel and I will sweep you off and we will live happily ever after. She sat down at the piano then and as on so many evenings in the past four months she played for me. But the music was different, music I had not heard before. When I left she cried on my shoulder and she kissed me again and again before she ran off leaving me alone. It was many years later that I learned the name of the music she played that night—Ravel's *Pavane pour une infante défunte*.

The next day I left Cuautla and traveled north as I had told Rebecca I would. Through New Orleans to Tallahassee, Florida, Atlanta, Georgia, Knoxville, Tennessee, Springfield, Ohio (where I visited with David Riley for five days), then across the border at Niagara Falls, and finally to Toronto. Twelve days, a hundred cities, a thousand faces, a continent traveled. A new horizon.

The Rain in Spain and NATO Pilots

When I arrived in Toronto from Mexico in the third week of May 1956 I had neither the time nor the money to explore the city. I soon found lodgings on Brunswick Avenue not far from the intersection of Bloor Street West and Avenue Road, a central location. It was a small boarding house owned and operated by a large Polish woman who rented by the week. The floors were covered with linoleum, the walls painted a sickly green, and a smell of boiled cabbage permeated the house from dawn to dusk. The four rented rooms were spartan with a small fridge in each. Toilet facilities were shared. There was a pay phone in the hallway. An unattractive place, but cheap.

My first priority was to get a job of some sort since I had very little money left after I paid my first week's rent. A fellow boarder suggested trying Fran's Restaurant at Yonge Street and Eglinton Avenue where he worked as a waiter. I went there and was hired on the spot as a dish washer working the night shift which meant I was on duty from 10 p.m. until 6 in the morning. To bed then and up at noon to look for a job. I registered at the Unemployment Office where a sharp faced lady took down details of my educational background and said I should drop in every day in case she had something for me. After a week or so the lady told me a large insurance company was advertising for an adjuster and I might fit the bill. I told her I knew nothing of insurance or of what an adjuster did, but she assured me that there would be on-the-job training. I duly reported the next day to an insurance company on University Avenue where an official not much older than I ("call me Bob") instructed me to fill in a Personnel Form and write an Aptitude Test. I returned in a couple of days when I learned that

I had failed. I protested that there must be a mistake, I had never failed an exam in my life, I would write the tests again. No, Bob told me, I could not rewrite the Test. You did extremely well on the Aptitude Test, he explained. I've seen few better. But your Personnel Form! He opened it. Utterly damning. You don't have a bank account. You don't have a credit card. You don't even have a car, he went on reproachfully. No phone, no apartment. You don't belong to a club of any sort. You don't have any relatives in Canada. No wife. No children. No life insurance. You gave up a job with Remington Rand that had very promising prospects to idle away your time in Mexico. And look here. Under "Present Occupation." A dish washer! Yes, definitely a failure, the worst I've ever seen. There was nothing I could say and so I left, thoroughly chastened, but not before Bob asked me, rather wistfully I thought, how I had managed not to get married and how it had been in Mexico.

I decided that it might be a good idea to find a job that required writing skills and so I approached *Maclean's Magazine* because I had happened on a copy of the magazine one night at Fran's. I was interviewed by an editor who took me to lunch—he told me he wanted any excuse to get away from his desk. It was an interesting meal because the editor spent most of the time telling me what a rotten job it was, that only a few journalists like Pierre Berton and June Callwood and Clyde Gilmore got a decent salary. He said his work at *Maclean's* had given him a fibrillating heart and at least three times during the meal he took my hand (to my embarrassment) and placed it on his heart to prove his point. After lunch he promised to get in touch but I don't know how that would have been possible since he did not have my address or my phone number.

A week later I got luckier. My sharp faced lady told me there was a teaching job being offered by the Canadian Department of Defence and that I should report the next day to an address on University Avenue right beside the American Consulate. In the waiting room there were at least ten other young men and women, candidates for the solitary job being offered about which I knew nothing. Soon my time for interview came where I was faced by a committee of three, a Squadron Leader in the RCAF by the name FitzPatrick, an Army Colonel, and a civilian representing the Department of Defence. I was questioned at length about my background and my education. I dreaded any question about my present employment but when it inevitably came I said that I was working as a dish washer in Fran's Restaurant. At the interview's end I was told to come back in a couple of hours because the decision to hire someone would be made that day. When I returned I was delighted, and surprised, to discover that I had been hired to teach at the NATO Language School, the RCAF base, London, Ontario. I should report there for work the following Monday, I was handed a military voucher for a first-class rail ticket, and a form authorizing me to live in Officers' Quarters. The committee wished me good luck and sent me on my way.

The RCAF base was just a couple of miles from London, in south western Ontario. Officers' Quarters turned out to be wooden buildings that proved to be very comfortable, each person having his own room with bed, wardrobe for clothes, a wash basin, a table and chairs, and some book shelves, There were ample shower facilities and a laundry room in the building. Meals were provided in the Officers' Mess which had a large lounge that served also as a ball room on occasion, a billiards room, and a bar where the drinks were at least 50 percent cheaper that they were off base. Sandwiches, milk, and juices were available from early morning until midnight.

The next day I discovered that my future students included would-be flying crew—among them officers and non-commissioned officers—from a number of NATO countries who had been sent to Canada for training as pilots or navigators and who had to become proficient in English because English was the international language of flying as, for example, French was the international language of diplomacy. These students came from Norway, Italy, the Netherlands, Denmark, Belgium, Portugal, West Germany, and Turkey. With the exception of the Turkish officers, they took three months of instruction in English before being sent for flight training at the nearby Centralia air station on what were known as the "Chipmunk" trainer and on the Harvard trainer before been sent out to Alberta to train on the T-33 jet trainer aircraft known colloquially as the T-Bird. Turkish students took an extra eight weeks of language training because of the vast cultural differences between their country and western European countries and because the linguistic differences from most western European languages were so extreme. I would not teach for the first three weeks but would go from one classroom to another as an observer. There was an unwritten understanding that we civilian teachers ranked above the highest rank of any officer in the class we were teaching—at one point I reached the *pro forma* rank of lieutenant colonel.

The basic textbooks were those written by two professors, Charles Fries and Robert Lado, for use during the Second World War by the US military which had established a number of schools for the teaching of languages, including Japanese. The significance of the work of Fries and Lado was its emphasis on actually speaking the language—what came to be known as the Michigan Oral Approach. Just as a manual could be written to detail how a machine gun could be assembled and disassembled in the fastest and most efficient manner so could a manual be written that would teach a language quickly and efficiently, it was postulated. The title of their book *English Sentence Patterns and English Pattern Practices* succinctly describes their technique—identify the basic patterns of English speech and devise a pedagogical method for teaching these patterns, a method which depends on oral repetition complemented by audio-lingual aids. Related to this was the teaching of vocabulary geared to the frequency of its use in everyday speech. There would be no point in teaching a student the word "frequency" since it was not part of the basic vocabulary identified by Fries and Lado as necessary for a student to know in the course of his twelve-week language course. Key words learned in the first three weeks of English language training would be supplemented in the second phase by scientifically determined vocabulary and that in turn would be supplemented in phases three and four. By the end of the twelve-week period the student would have a vocabulary that would be sufficiently large to enable him to take up technical lessons in English as a pilot or navigator. And so in my first three weeks I went from classroom to classroom watching Portuguese officers in their first three weeks practicing the most basic of English sentences while in another classroom I saw Portuguese officers in their final weeks debating in fluent English. No reference was made to novels or plays or poems. This was boot camp where efficiency—and the officer's life—depended on understanding a functional English and not in savouring the subtleties of Shakespeare or John Dryden.

Came time for me to teach—a first-phase group, Italian officers, talkative, animated, eager, ten in all so that each be given the opportunity for individual attention. We worked on the basic sentence patterns prescribed for that day followed by pronunciation of key English words. Then followed laboratory work where each student puts on ear phones and repeats sentences. I sat at a master console where I could plug into each student's work and guide him. Before lunch we watched a film whose language and situations have been carefully matched with that day's work. After lunch back to the same basic sentence patterns and vocabulary. There followed a period where students practiced on the many audio-lingual aides that we had—machines into which they can insert cards and hear the sentences we have been working on repeated by trained English speakers. They also watched short films illustrating the actions of the various sentences such as jumping, walking, eating, and so on. We had a richness of supplementary aids that few civilian language schools could afford. And we teachers had some freedom which we often exercised in staging debates or impromptu speaking which were judged by the students. Very soon I incorporated a Broadway musical—*My Fair Lady*—into my various classes as much for relief as for instruction. My students loved it since they identified with poor Eliza Doolittle suffering at the hands of her English language teacher Professor Higgins. They especially loved the wonderful scene where Eliza finally manages to pronounce perfectly the lines, "The rain in Spain falls mainly in the plain" and "How kind of you to come to tea," when they would burst into applause at Eliza's impeccable diction. Years after I left the NATO language school the occasional NATO officer would visit me and as we chatted about those days it was not uncommon for them to burst into song, singing "The Rain in Spain" in an impeccable Turkish or Dutch or Danish accent.

In July come the girls of summer, invading the base with their beauty and charm and zest for living, young women from universities all across Canada enrolled in Reserve Officer programs. In their crisp Air Force uniforms they look smart and especially alluring as they drill on the square in front of the Officers' Mess—who can resist a uniform?—and in the evenings what transformations into the latest fashions in clothes, hair, and cosmetics! Infatuations and love affairs multiply and our military base is electric with hormonal overdrive. I fall for a red-haired girl from British Columbia, then a Gaelic speaker from Nova Scotia , before falling irrevocably in love with Louisette from Montreal. It is high summer and Louisette and I play tennis, see movies at the drive-ins, go to Niagara Falls for sightseeing and sometimes to the village of St Mary's where we swim in the quarry. The quarry is also a favourite haunt for actors like Christopher Plummer and William Shatner who are playing at the nearby Stratford Shakespeare Festival under a huge tent. Louisette and I see a memorable production of *Henry V*, featuring Plummer as King Henry with Gratien Gélinas as the French King, his court members played by actors from

Montreal's *Théâtre du Nouveau Monde*. It was obvious even then that Plummer was marked for greatness. He had a kind of edge, a dangerous quality that I associate with actors like Marlon Brando and Richard Burton. If the play was memorable because of its production values and acting it was also memorable for me because it was raining heavily when we saw it and so when the actors turned away from our area of the theatre the rain on the tent's roof made such a noise that we would hear half a sentence and miss the rest. The next year the tent was replaced by the present structure. My favourite play from that year was *Twelfth Night* with Plummer as Sir Andrew Aguecheek and a luminous Siobhan McKenna as Viola. In Stratford in that same year I heard Billie Holiday sing. She came burdened by musical greatness and a lurid life that included being raped as a child and two prison terms. That night when she sang "Lady sings the blues" she had less than two years to live but the voice, raddled by drink and drugs and abuse, was still enormously moving.

Louisette introduced me to the politics of Quebec and its literature, but I soon realized that far more important influences on her education and background were those coming from France. Her Quebec was as much a victim of French colonialism, it seemed to me, as English-speaking Canada was a victim of English colonialism. The contemporary writers she quoted were all French (Anouilh, Sartre, Claudel) and the songs she sang were by French artists including Charles Trenet (*La Mer*), Georges Brassens (*Les amoureaux des bancs publics*), and Edith Piaf (*L'hymne à l'amour*).

And so the golden weeks of summer flew as did the golden girls back to their universities across Canada. In the Language School I was busy and in the course of the next twelve months I taught airmen from all the nations represented at our School. The contrast in the conduct of these groups of officers was quite vivid. The Italians were voluble and excitable and gave generously of themselves. The Norwegians were much more reserved and it was very hard to establish a close relationship with them. If the homework I assigned was fairly heavy the Italians groaned and complained histrionically whereas the Norwegians took it on with remarkable stoicism. But when it came time for the Norwegians to graduate they showed another side at the Mess party given to send them off. Then they got uproariously drunk as the other officers rarely did and they flirted outrageously with their female language teachers and backslapped the male teachers. The Turkish officers were distinct in that they were the most literal minded. Debates in class were commonplace in our teaching and I remember on one occasion giving the Turkish officers as the subject of debate the proposition—"Communism is superior to Democracy." The class absolutely refused the debate and I was unable to convince them that such a debate was merely an exercise. They said that the motion made no sense. Later I learned that they were also extremely sensitive to anything that might be interpreted as less than total obedience to the political regime in Turkey which professed democracy while practicing a form of feudal absolutism.

Life on the air base sometimes took a tragic turn. A young Belgian officer took a bus to Detroit and hanged himself there in the YMCA. He had been my student. When I learned that the air base Chaplain had denied him the benefit of a Catholic service, I made enquiries and learned that none of the usual reasons—gambling, drugs, a sexual affair—could be found to explain the suicide. I immediately got in touch with a priest whom I knew, assistant to the Bishop, and argued that the young Belgian officer's act was not deliberate, that he must have acted irrationally. The upshot was that the young pilot was given a Catholic service before being shipped back to Belgium and to his family.

Bu in general life was held rather cheaply on the air base. The main cause of fatalities was not flying, as might be expected. It was driving. These young men were highly specialized, gung ho, with lighting fast reflexes. They bought or rented fast cars, they drank when they went off base to the pubs and to parties, and when they returned late at night too often they made mistakes on the last mile that led into the base. At the bar we would raise a glass to the chap who had "bought" it—our fatalism and our gallows humour were born of a deeply ingrained attitude that was a hangover from the Second World War. This fatalism extended even to security matters which the aircrew despised and consequently ignored. One evening I was drinking in the Officers' Mess with a young Englishman called Tommy Hunter, a pilot trained in the RAF but now enrolled in the RCAF. When I told him I had never been in a military aircraft he insisted that I come with him to his aircraft, a P 51 jet if I remember correctly. I climbed up and into the cockpit and sat facing an array of buttons that controlled the plane's weapons system. Most terrifying of all was a red-flagged lever that read, "Eject." A false move and I would be flying in the air over RCAF base, London. We were interrupted by a jeep that raced up to disgorge a very angry Duty Officer who marched both Tommy and me to his office where he threatened to have us court martialled—not only was I as a civilian forbidden from entering a military aircraft but Tommy had allowed it. We were very lucky that Flight Lieutenant Baril let us go with a very firm warning. Many years later I did board a military aircraft when the public was invited—a B-17 landed in Cape Cod, Massachusetts, and I crawled through its belly imagining what it must have been like to ride in one of these machines over Germany in 1943 when casualties in both the German and Allied air forces were so brutal.

Our base was also home to the Junior Officers Administration Course for promising young officers who came to London for a five-week specialized training program. These included military nurses, doctors, accountants, lawyers, and so on. At weekends and especially at graduation from the course they liked to party in the Officers' Mess and very often I was the pianist as they sang all the old songs, many from the Second World War. "I've got sixpence," "Roll me over in the Clover," "The Whiffenpoof Song":

> *Gentlemen songsters off on a spree*
> *Damned from here to eternity.*
> *God have mercy on such as we!*
> *Bah. Bah, bah.*

One night I accompanied on the piano a West German officer as he sang a haunting ballad, "*Lili Marleen*", shared by both German and Allied soldiers as they fought and killed each other just a few years earlier.

The months went by, Russian armies invaded Hungary to suppress a people's revolution, British, French, and Israeli armies attacked Egypt to reclaim the Suez Canal, and on the air base I followed closely these acts of international terrorism. I took evening conversational French lessons and listened to French-language tapes alongside my NATO students, I bought my first car, I met lots of attractive women, and life was very good. But I knew that eventually I would leave the NATO Language School, that I must leave it. I had begun to grow tired of a pedagogy which was so prescribed, so bound day-by-day to a routine that even though it secured quite remarkably successful results ultimately began to pall on me. And I realized that my teaching had only one purpose—to give my students, not much older than I, knowledge of the English language so that they could fly planes that were in essence weapons of mass destruction. And I had got to know the city which was *de facto* the capital of south western Ontario. It was far enough from Toronto to have its own character and to create a thriving business, social and artistic life. It was the home of Canada's largest insurance companies; it had a good theatre, the Grand Theatre under an ambitious Artistic Director Peter Dearing; the University of Western Ontario provided an academic milieu sympathetic to and supportive of the local arts scene which included painters Jack Chambers, Philip Aziz, and Greg Curnoe. And there was a satisfying night life. In one of my favourite bars, the Brass Rail, wizard Peter Appleyard performed nightly on the xylophone and there were dances at the various frat and sorority houses. I soon decided that I would apply to enter the MA program in English at the University of Western Ontario.

I have to confess that I had inherited the prejudice—based on ignorance—that all education in North America was second rate, that degrees earned in the UK had real merit while those granted in Canada and the USA were suspect. I was soon to learn a very different reality. The end of the Second World War saw the return of many soldiers, usually officers, who entered graduate programs and later joined university departments. One of these soldiers was Brandon Conron, a tank commander with the rank of Captain who was with the First Hussars on D-Day when his regiment proved to be the only unit in the Allied forces to reach its objective that first day. Wounded, decorated, and promoted to Major, he returned to Canada on demobilization, got himself an MA and then went on to Harvard on scholarship to take a PhD He returned to Western, took over as Head of the English Department, and married a Miss Spencer, the very rich daughter of the Commanding Officer of his regiment. He was succeeded as Head of Department by M.H.M. MacKinnon (known to his friends as Murdo), who had been a Squadron Leader in the RCAF. Both Conron and MacKinnon were keen to build up a first-class Department and they set about hiring a number of very good young faculty. They were also on the lookout for good graduate material.

My interview with MacKinnon was very informal. Once he had established that I had an honours BA degree, and that I actually had studied Greek for five years—which delighted him—he accepted me into the program. So informal was the meeting that I do not remember even signing a form. I would take four courses, write a MA comprehensive examination, and a thesis. Squadron Leader FitzPatrick at the Language School was very accommodating about the whole matter, even arranging for a teacher to cover for me when I had to attend a weekly seminar at the university during the day. I took a course in modern English poetry (Yeats, Pound, Eliot, Auden) from a Professor Ron Bates, a published poet, who during the course of the year agreed to be my MA thesis supervisor. My other course on the poetry of Shelley was taught by Professor Ross Woodman. He was to be the most important influence on my intellectual development at this time combining as he did scholarship of the highest order with an artistic temperament that complemented in the most attractive way the spiritual and the aesthetic. He was then working on his magisterial study of Shelley whom Matthew Arnold had characterized as an "ineffectual angel, beating in the void his luminous wings in vain"; Woodman's lectures (and book) demonstrated the bankruptcy of such criticism which depended on a fine turn of phrase rather than on an understanding of the depths of Shelley's poetic genius and its philosophic underpinnings.

The way Woodman conducted his MA course was most unusual in that he invited fellow members of the English faculty to attend and ask questions and he had his MA students write critiques of his lectures. It was with some trepidation that I critiqued his lectures on *Queen Mab* and *The Triumph of Life*. And for the first time in my life I was working with a professor who demanded the highest standards of scholarship. No more "as the critic Coleridge says somewhere" but rather exact references to the works cited, including the edition, page number, year of publication—in other words, detailed bibliographical reference. Students were given a bibliography of publications relevant to Shelleyan research which they were expected to read and use in their assignments. And so in the course of the year's study Woodman led us through Shelley's writings from *The Revolt of Islam* to the great odes to his masterpiece *Prometheus Unbound* and the unfinished *Triumph of Life*. Woodman also related Shelley's vision through allusion and example to the writings of Wordsworth, Keats, and especially William Blake so that by the end of the course we had been introduced in a most meaningful way to such important Romantic texts as *The Prelude, Hyperion, The Four Zoas, Milton,* and *Jerusalem.* What gave meaning and experiential relevance to this academic course was the Romantic belief, expounded so powerfully by Woodman himself, that by

"Transforming enlargements of the imagination" artists were the "unacknowledged legislators of the world" bringing to humanity moments wherein the eternal is made manifest. Under Woodman's guidance I came to accept as my own personal *credo* what the poet John Keats wrote, "I am certain of nothing except the holiness of the Heart's affections and the truth of the Imagination."

Woodman was of medium height, about thirty-four years old (six years older than I) and he lived in a beautifully appointed rented house within walking distance from the university. Very soon he was not only my teacher but my friend, someone with whom I went on long walks, with whom I listened to music, and with whom I dined very often. He made the perfect martini and he won my admiration when I discovered he could actually make Baked Alaska Pie. He had a girlfriend called Marion Boa, a high school teacher, my age, who even then showed the kind of enquiring mind that one day would make her one of the most influential exponents of Jungian analysis in Catholic priest with a view to becoming a Catholic since, like so many intellectuals, he was attracted to the rituals of the Church. Nominally he was of the Bahá'í religion and I was astonished to learn that he had often gone to New York as the guest of a rich lady, also of the Bahá'í persuasion, who put him up in a hotel overlooking Park Avenue and gave him a hundred dollars each day as long as he was in the city. Woodman's interest in a possible conversion to Catholicism came to nothing and as the years went by his faith in the Bahá'í religion became paramount in his life. Other key influences on his life and thought were the work of Freud and Jung (probably influenced here by Marion). He had a great interest in art and had already begun to collect paintings and sculpture that he and Marion would gift to London's McIntosh Gallery making it one of the finest in Canada. Now and then I invited Woodman to dine with me in the Officers' Mess. On those occasions he came to my quarters before dinner where he would lie on the floor for up to twenty minutes meditating. I was surprised by this but later concluded that it was his way of preparing himself, because of a deeply ingrained reserve, to meet the many strangers who would be in the Officers' Mess. It may also have been due to the fact that being once again on a RCAF air base reminded him of the past when he had been a rear gunner in the air force. But he loved congenial company and often he and Marion and I and my date of the day would go to some night club where we danced the night away.

In September of 1957 I resigned from my work as a teacher in the language school and enrolled fulltime at the University. I got an apartment on Dufferin Street so close to St Peter's Catholic Church that its bells rang me awake on Sunday mornings and I settled down to work on my two courses—one on the modern British novel, the other on Shakespearean criticism offered by Erik Atkinson whom the writer Alice Munro praised as being the finest teacher she encountered at Western. I also began work on my MA thesis which became a study of *Chamber Music*, a number of short poems by James Joyce. My argument was that these slight poems contained the genesis of Joyce's break with the Church in that they present a struggle between the lover and the rival-priest for the soul of the loved one. I argued, ambitiously, that Joyce's last work *Finnegans Wake* was merely the magnification of the thirty-six slides that constitute *Chamber Music*. Much of my research was related to the new scholasticism expounded by Jacques Maritain in his *Art and Scholasticism* and to the ideas developed in Wyndham Lewis' famous attack on Joyce in his *Time and Western Man*. Later I was to see that Joyce's examination and rejection of Catholicism prefigured, in some ways, my own.

There was a quiet reserved professor at Western whom I got to know rather well even though I never studied with him. His name was Carl Klinck—a shy retiring man, he seemed to me. Ultimately he would prove to be the most influential member of the Department because of his academic interest—Canadian literature. At that time the concept of a distinct Canadian national literature was regarded in Canadian universities with suspicion. For example, it was possible for Canadian students to take a degree in English and French literature without ever studying a Canadian author and students in high school rarely studied a Canadian novel or play. To take a PhD in Canadian literature was rare and was regarded generally as a sign of eccentricity. But Klinck, with the authority of a PhD from Columbia University behind him, began writing and publishing on such figures as W.W. Campbell, "Tiger" Dunlop, and Susanna Moodie; more importantly, he joined forces with Professor Reginald Watters at the University of British Columbia to publish their ground-breaking *Canadian Anthology*. This work established a canon of short fiction, essays, and poetry that slowly began to leaven the canonical texts of British and American literature with a Canadian flavour that led ultimately to the documentation of the origins of a Canadian national literature and the birth of a Canadian modern literature.

The students I got to know at the University of Western Ontario were a motley lot ranging from my fellow MA students to undergraduates. The MA students included Wally Ryerson, Paul Fleck (and his wife Polly), Patricia Robinson, who introduced me to Klinck for whom she was writing her MA thesis. Among the undergrad students I came to know well were Jeff Smith and Graeme Gibson. I first saw Jeff in a play at the Grand Theatre—something by Anouilh, I think—and I was immediately so impressed by his acting and extraordinary speaking voice that I went backstage to congratulate him. I discovered he was a first-year arts student and in the course of the year I also discovered that he didn't really like his studies, that he was getting B grades mostly because he was uninterested, and that acting was his passion. We had a long talk one evening before the academic year ended when I told him that I thought that rather than graduating with a mere pass mark he should think of becoming a professional actor. Two years later when I was taking my Ph.D, at the University of Toronto he phoned me and invited me to his apartment for dinner. There I discovered that his very attractive Swedish girl had advised him that numerologically speaking his name Jeff Smith did not promise a bright career. Accordingly, Jeff Smith was now Colin Fox, the name under which he later appeared in a number of films and on stages throughout Canada, including stints at The Stratford Festival.

Paul Fleck, a man with` a great liking for theatricals, was also a very good amateur actor besides being a first-rate student. In his MA year he became interested in doing advanced work on the poet Lord Byron. I was pleased and somewhat surprised to discover that he intended going to Belfast, Northern Ireland, for his doctorate in that area having discovered a professor at Queen's University, a specialist in Byron, who would act as his supervisor and mentor. On his return to Canada Paul became a professor at his *alma mater* and then Chair of the English Department all the while continuing his favourite pastime—amateur theatricals. Later he became the President of the Ontario College of Art, and ultimately President of the Banff Centre, Alberta, during the 1980s. He died prematurely at the age of fifty-eight; it was the perfect gesture when the Fleck family arranged to have the marquee of the Stratford Festival Theatre named in his memory.

Wally Ryerson had two great loves in his life—his girlfriend in nearby

Stratford and Ernest Hemingway on whom he was writing his MA thesis. I have met a number of actors in my life who attempt to identify completely with the character they are playing and so it was with Wally. He talked as he imagined Hemingway talked, he read voluminously on bullfighting and fly fishing, he even attempted to duplicate his hero in eating and drinking. When he got his paycheck from the university he would throw a dinner featuring the kind of Spanish fare he imagined Hemingway enjoyed. There would be *manchego* cheese, and *jamón Serrano*, tinned *gazpacho*, *paella,* dark bread, a wine from Rioja and perhaps a Spanish brandy like *Fundador* to finish off. The next dinner would be based on Hemingway's life in the 1920s Quarter of Paris and if we weren't particularly taken by the *escargots* and duck *confit* (tinned), Wally's *Pernod*, a drink I had never tasted before, washed away misgivings. By the third week of the month he was usually broke and then he would live on scraps—or on his friends—while dreaming up another Hemingway event. And every week he made the trip to Stratford to see his girlfriend. We never thought Wally's behaviour strange—after all, one of the philosophy students who sometimes came to our parties was a pyromaniac.

Graeme Gibson was the most memorable of the students I met at Western. An undergraduate in his final year, he was a striking man, about six feet four inches in height, with a beard that outdid Hemingway's. He was the son of a much-decorated war officer, Brigadier Gibson, then the Commanding Officer of Wolseley Barracks in London—Graeme himself had been an infantry officer before entering university. His mother was a very beautiful Australian with a great interest in the arts which may have accounted for Graeme deserting a military career for what turned out to be a life time spent in promoting Canadian writing and publishing. I had never met anyone so interested in ideas—he was continually discovering new authors, new music, new ways of living life—and I had rarely met anyone with his zest for living. In my own mind I christened him the Prince of Enthusiasms and was always delighted to be caught up in his newest fervour over a book or a piece of music or a newly-made friend. We acted in theatrical pieces together—Pirandello's *Henry 1V* and Ben Jonson's *The Alchemist* where we played the two Puritan preachers, Graeme as Tribulation Wholesome and I as Ananias (what wonderful names). Graeme read parts of the novel I had written in Mexico; it was typical of his enthusiasm and encouragement that he did not attempt to criticize any aspect of my novel but rather expressed admiration that I had taken time out of my life to actually write a book. He had never met a writer before and he sometimes told me that he wished he had the courage to lock himself away for a year and write a book. But, he said, he lacked a theme.

During the summer of 1958 I got a job doing market research which is a fancy name for saying I drove all over south western Ontario (to places like St Thomas, Strathroy, Tillsonburg) with a check sheet to discover if the pharmacies in those places stocked things like Gillette razor blades and various brands of mouth washes, tooth pastes, and deodorants. My boss was a young man from the USA, an MBA at Harvard. He stayed in a hotel near my apartment and when I discovered that he knew no one in London I invited him to join me and my circle of friends. He was grateful, so grateful in fact that he took it on himself to alter the detailed and totally honest expense claims I turned over to him for food and gas. So it was that my hundred and fifty miles became two hundred and fifty miles and my food bill doubled. When I first protested (lightly), he rebuked me by pointing out that he was the boss, that his MBA gave him the experience to make such decisions, and that his own bosses would look askance at someone who only drove one hundred and fifty miles. They would conclude that I was not working hard enough and he would be blamed. We became very good friends for that summer although he never did convert me entirely to his way of doing business.

On another occasion Ross Woodman rang me and asked if I could introduce Bruce Boa, the brother of Marion, to my student friends. Bruce was an actor it seemed, home for a few days from England with time on his hands. Of course he was welcome and the following evening he joined Graeme Gibson, Wally Ryerson, and Jeffrey Smith and me for drinks in a local beer parlour. Bruce made his entrance about a half hour after the time we had agreed to meet—and an entrance it was. Assured, histrionic, commanding attention which was reinforced by his throwing a twenty dollar bill on the table as soon as he had removed his coat. Bruce did nothing by half measures. We felt privileged to be in the company of such a figure, one who was rich enough to stand a few rounds.

We sat drinking our beer—at ten cents a glass—and Bruce in his marvelous actor's voice that later he used to such good effect as General Rieekan in the movie *The Empire Strikes Back* and in many other such movies regaled us with scandalous stories of leading figures in English society whom he had met—or claimed to have met. He talked and talked, wonderfully, and all the evening the twenty dollar bill lay tantalizingly on the table. When we rose to leave Bruce swept it into his pocket and our party broke up. I had read somewhere that Byron was regarded as the most entertaining talker of his time; I felt that Bruce was the most entertaining talker I had yet met and I did not begrudge paying for such an extravagant diversion.

The academic year flew by—I was also teaching a section of introductory English with attendant heavy marking—and the graduate exams were upon me and then the final preparations of my MA thesis and its defence. All went well and almost without conscious planning I had applied to enter the PhD program at the University of Toronto in September and was accepted.

A few months after I left London Wally Ryerson was killed in a hit and run accident when on his way to visit his sweetheart in Stratford. Wally's immediate circle was immensely saddened by his death; so powerful was Graeme Gibson's sense of loss that he gave up all interest in academic work and dropped out of the MA program in English. I did not see him again until a year later when he visited me in Toronto and we had drinks on the rooftop bar of the Park Plaza Hotel. He was now married—Shirley was blonde and very intelligent and very cheerful because she had just come into a small inheritance—and he was off to England to write a novel. He had found his theme but like most writers he did not want to talk about it. I asked him to keep in touch about the novel and he did. I received the first pages of his novel a year later; they told of the funeral of a young man killed in a hit and run accident near Stratford. The novel was later published under the title *Five Legs*.

Cold Bacon and Doctoral Studies

During the Second World War the writer and painter Wyndham Lewis lived in Toronto and later published a novel, *Self Condemned*, a withering indictment of a city that he termed "a vast mining camp." In the late 1950s it was still a city dominated by commerce and by a WASP culture with a strong strain of Northern Ireland's Orange Lodge culture–some forty of Toronto's past mayors were members of the Orange Lodge. But change was in the air. The election in 1957 of a Jew, Nathan Phillips, as mayor was herald of a new era. Emigration, especially from southern Europe, was altering the ethnic and religious character of the city—some 350,000 Italians arrived in the late 1950s to swell that ethnic group to about half a million people. Immediately after the end of World War Two large numbers of Dutch, English, Irish, Greek, and Portuguese emigrants arrived—even Germans were accepted with little checking because northern Europeans were considered to be superior to those of southern Europe (despite the fact that many of the Germans were former Nazi). Restrictions on Jews were eased somewhat to permit them entry. In 1956, following the Hungarian Revolution against the Russians, about 50,000 Hungarians fled to Canada, most settling in Toronto, although about 50 percent of the forestry department of Hungary's University of Sopron decamped to the University of British Columbia where they were of enormous benefit to that province's forestry industry. There were other signs that Toronto was ever so gradually becoming a cosmopolitan city—the Canadian Ballet Company, founded in 1951 by Celia Franca, an English woman, began offering work of a fine professional calibre. Nicholas Goldschmidt, an Austrian, Herman Geiger-Torel, a German, and Ettore Mazzoleni, a Swiss, founded the Canadian Opera Company, and in 1958 the design for a new and architecturally exciting City Hall was won by Viljo Revell, a Finn. At this time engineers were also dreaming of erecting the highest building in the world in Toronto to house an advanced communications centre and work had commenced on building the longest highway in the world, the trans-Canada highway from the Atlantic to the Pacific.

Inevitably, but surely, the ethos of this new and diverse emigration ate away at the restrictions of Ontario's Puritanical laws. Archaic liquor laws were gradually amended and the dreadful men's only beer drinking saloons gave way to more pleasant bars. Outdoor cafés, despite the best efforts of bureaucrats to ban them, sprang up everywhere. Expresso coffee made its appearance and poets like Milton Acorn, Margaret Atwood, Gwendolyn McEwen, and Dennis Lee read their poetry in the Bohemian Embassy, a grubby café, where audiences persuaded themselves that this was the next best thing to the *boîtes* of Montmartre. Art galleries made their appearances and small professional theatres like the Crest Theatre and Toronto Workshop Productions offered plays from the international repertory and even, rarely, Canadian plays. Glen Gould, at the height of his eccentric powers as a pianist, brought the breath of the international scene to the city. Toronto was on the verge of being transformed into a new and exciting place where multiculturalism replaced the old Wasp mono-culture and the colonialism that had so strangled native artistic values was finally being replaced by a nascent Canadian nationalism.

In September of 1958 I came to this city to begin PhD studies at the University of Toronto. My first few days were spent combing the city, newspaper in hand, seeking a place to live, checking out the many rooms and apartments directed at students. It was a dispiriting business. Most were single rooms so badly insulated that one heard noises from the other rooms that smelled of cooking. Eventually I found a notice advertising a place on Playter Boulevard, just east of Broadview Avenue, off Danforth Avenue. It turned out to be a single house, two storied, obviously belonging to people of some means. When I entered I was greeted by an elderly lady called Mitchell who told me that she wanted to rent to a student because her husband was dead and she feared to live alone. She showed me the rooms she had to let—a large bedroom, a separate bathroom, and, joy of joy, her husband's study, a spacious room with bookcases and a fine desk. A student's dream at a modest rent! I took it immediately.

My next task was to pick what courses I would take in the coming two years as I worked towards my doctorate and so I made my way to the University of Toronto where I browsed through the University Calendar. I already knew a good deal about the university since it offered the only PhD program in English in Canada and it included some internationally acclaimed professors. The university was patterned after the English colleges system such as that at Cambridge University. Toronto's colleges were also associated with religious affiliations—Trinity College was Anglican, St Michael's College was Catholic, Victoria College was United Church. University College was for those not readily identifiable with any religious group and for Jews. At the graduate level students took courses associated with their own special interests or because of the professors offering them and University College was the administrative centre. I soon settled on my two first-year courses: a seminar on Milton offered by the Head of the Department, A.S.P. Woodhouse, and "Principles of Literary Criticism" offered by Northrop Frye. I chose these courses because these were areas that would be critical when it came time to write the dreaded General Examinations which covered the entire range of literatures in English. In addition to selecting courses there was the very important matter of selecting and getting a Dissertation Director. My first choice was Marshall McLuhan, a professor at St Michael's who was then making a name for himself exploring the relationship between oral and print cultures and communications. In his book *The Mechanical Bride* and in *Explorations*, a journal co-founded with the anthropologist Edmund Carpenter, he conducted his research that would in the early 1960s make him the most famous and controversial professor of English in the world.

Students in the PhD program had to submit a prospectus or summary of their doctoral dissertation to the department for approval. My dissertation topic, which was accepted, was grandly titled "Myth and Religion as Source of Tension in the writings of James Joyce." It would be an extension of my MA thesis intended to cover Joyce's entire *oeuvre* including *Ulysses* and *Finnegans Wake*. When I tried to set up a meeting with McLuhan I was directed to first see Edmund Carpenter then preparing to leave Toronto for the USA. Accordingly I sought out Carpenter a little bewildered as to why I should be seeing someone in a field about which I had only a passing acquaintance. He was a man in his mid thirties well known for his field work among the Inuit and for his explorations of the anthropology of visual media which made him an ideal colleague of Mc-

Luhan with whom he sometimes co-taught a course. I had no sooner introduced myself to Carpenter when he handed me what was obviously a wood carving, about eighteen inches high, of an Inuit woman. "Notice anything unusual about that," he questioned me. I examined it but, unable to find anything unusual about it, I said no. "Put it on the table," he told me. I tried to do so but was unable because there was no base. I even tried to place the carving on its head but to no avail. I told him there would be nothing unusual about the carving if the sculptor had given it a base. "Concepts of space mean different things to oral peoples. That's why it has no base," he retorted, telling me the interview was over and that I could now go and see McLuhan. I sensed that I had failed a hermetic test of some kind, a test whose nature I did not understand.

McLuhan looked more like a British officer than a professor. He was handsome, lanky, about six feet tall, with a military type mustache. "Professor Carpenter called me," he said. "We both think you would be better off with Frye—if he will take you." I was not sure if he meant that Frye was used to taking on PhD students who could find no one else but I walked over to Victoria College where Frye taught and where I was lucky enough to catch him. He asked me to tell him about my proposed dissertation and when I was finished he agreed to supervise my dissertation. As I walked back to the main campus I reflected on my day's business. I was delighted to have Frye as my supervisor—I had just begun to read his *Anatomy of Criticism* which Ross Woodman swore was the finest critical work in English of the twentieth century. When I reflected on my interview with Carpenter I came to the opinion that he (and McLuhan) wanted disciples rather than students; I had shown doubt when Carpenter had offered his gnomic wisdom about an Inuit carving and that doubt had disqualified me. Some weeks later I learned that McLuhan had indicated to the Secretary of the Graduate School that he would be willing to sit on the Committee that would examine me when I came to defend my completed dissertation; I hoped that future encounters with McLuhan would be more auspicious than the first.

Some time later that day I called on A.S.P. Woodhouse, who headed the Graduate Department of English and whose course on the poet and polemical writer Milton I would take. Woodhouse's major publications had to do with the Puritan debates of the seventeenth century which found voice in his *Puritanism and Liberty*, a landmark work in its field. Because he presided over the country's only PhD programme in English Woodhouse dominated the world of English scholarship in Canada, placing students as they graduated from the doctoral program in universities from coast to coast. When I saw him conduct meetings in the next two years or preside over lectures given by visiting professors it was evident that even such stars as McLuhan and Frye deferred to him. This was the formidable man I met him in his office in University College after I had safely negotiated my way past his ever-vigilant secretary, Miss Stevenson. He was sitting under a portrait of the great Dr Samuel Johnson, whom he revered, drinking tea and smoking a cigarette and holding it in a peculiar way as if to shade it from being blown out. A large-framed man with a high domed forehead, he had a kind of ironic assurance that I think came from his sense of power and control. His first question to me when he had glanced at my file was to enquire if I had read Spenser's *The Present Discontent in Ireland.* I had not and I told him so. Round one to Professor Woodhouse. But there was no intention on his part to put me in my place. I was Irish and here was a book that possibly he could discuss with me. I told him how I had secured a dissertation supervisor and when he heard that McLuhan had turned me down he declared that I was lucky to get Frye. I discovered later that he had opposed hiring McLuhan and thought that his ideas were dangerous in that McLuhanism meant the substitution of dubious cultural studies in place of the canonical English courses over which he, Woodhouse, presided. That evening as I went home I began to realize that the two years ahead of me were bound to be challenging. There were six doctoral students in my year, drawn from the best MA students across Canada and from a number of other non-Canadian universities such as Harvard and Cambridge. Within the month we would write a comprehensive examination in English Literature to make sure we had the right stuff and at the end of our course work there would be the General Examinations. During my two years residence there would be examinations in the courses I was taking plus a course in Philosophy and also examinations to prove competence in two foreign languages, one modern—in my case French—and Latin. In addition I had to teach a first and fourth year undergraduate class of engineers composition and selected English texts to make sure they could write competent reports and essays. The regimen of studies I was about to undertake was as demanding as any offered in doctoral studies in North America and more demanding than any offered in Europe.

And so my daily life began—preparations for my teaching, interviewing my students, marking their papers, attending lectures by Frye and Woodhouse, preparing papers to be read in Woodhouse's PhD seminars. And all the time reading as widely as I could with a view to the General Examinations which I would write when I felt ready to do so. Because I knew there would be a special examination devoted to Anglo-Saxon and Middle English I audited a course on the epic poem *Beowulf* given by a Professor Bessinger. It was in complete contrast to the similar course I had taken at university in Ireland where the emphasis, aping German scholarship, was primarily philological in nature. The result was (for me) the kind of study I detested. Bessinger did not neglect philology, but he treated the texts he offered as works of art, as literature. It was a genuine pleasure to hear him read *Beowulf* in Anglo-Saxon (he recorded the Caedmon version of the poem) as he led us to an understanding of the sweeping architectonics of this great epic while relating it to its individual elements.

The contrast between the way Northrop Frye and A.S.P Woodhouse taught their graduate classes could not have been greater. Frye's "Principles of Literary Criticism" was open to all graduate students in any discipline and was enormously popular given his fame. *Fearful Symmetry*, his magisterial study of the poetry of William Blake, and his *Anatomy of Criticism* further cemented his reputation. I expected some degree of flamboyance from such a renowned scholar but there was none. When Frye entered the classroom he did so quietly, glancing almost shyly round the room as if to determine the nature of his audience. Of average height, undistinguished in appearance, he could have passed for a small-town clergyman and he was, in fact, an ordained United Church minister. He began his lectures without any preparatory remarks, launching directly into his material and seamlessly taking up where his previous lecture had ended. He spoke in a rather flat, even boring, monotone, and I often wondered whether he deliberately rejected rhetorical flourishes and any hint of histrionics in order not to detract from the substance of what he was saying or whether, in fact, he lacked the fire that sometimes will overtake a lecturer in full flight. He did not use notes nor did he ever address any of us by name, but he did invite questions from time to time. Although the class was made up largely of students specializing in many different fields of English, Frye, when questioned, never hesitated or said that he would need to look the matter up. A question on Icelandic sagas was answered with the same certainty as a one about seventeenth-century publishing in England. And while he had a command of Latin and Greek literatures (as was common with most scholars in the Humanities then) he also displayed a surprisingly deep knowledge of French and German literatures. About three months after I attended his class Jack Robson, a professor and Frye's colleague at Victoria College, told me that Frye had complained to him that our class lacked humour. I found the remark interesting because Frye's own humour was so disguised in a deprecating irony that it was never apparent. But I was amused when a fellow student in the PhD program told me that when she had complained to Frye that she was at a disadvantage in following his many references to the Bible and especially to the New Testament because she was Jewish, Frye reassured her with the remark that it was all in the *Kabbalah*. On the very few occasions when I spoke to him about my dissertation, he never resorted to a file or asked for a reminder but seemed to remember instantly my concerns and the substance of our previous brief talks. Nor did he ever ask to read my dissertation as it developed. He said that he would only read and judge the completed work; this was flattering in that it suggested he trusted me to work independently, but it was also intimidating in that if I did not measure up to his standards I would have thrown years of research away. In our few conversations we never had any small talk and this continued in later years when I would meet him at academic conferences. I always made a point of greeting him but at the first opportunity I escaped since we were soon reduced to a mutual silence by his inability to indulge in small talk or by an innate reserve. Most of the professors I knew experienced the same difficulty in trying to converse with him. Surprisingly, the only person whom I saw chatting comfortably on a number of occasions with Frye, who obviously enjoyed his company, was the poet Al Purdy, a gangly man lacking a university education who had spent most of his early years working as a labourer and riding the rails.

Woodhouse's seminar on Milton and Spenser drew only a small number of students—about eight in my year—because it was confined to PhD students in English and also because Woodhouse lacked Frye's star quality. He was, however, a fine teacher thoroughly grounded in the major figures of the period 1600 to 1800 and in Victorian literature. He began the year's work by lecturing for the first few weeks on general concepts relating to his authors while we, his students, prepared a seminar topic for each of the two semesters in the academic year. As we read our seminar papers to him and our fellow students, he sat hunched over his cup of tea, smoking interminably on a cigarette from which the ash, it seemed to me, always threatened to fall into his tea cup. Fellow students commented on the paper just presented, offering criticism that was sometimes quite severe. If it was ill-founded, Woodhouse redressed the bias, offering his own critique or running commentary which was always, I thought, comprehensive, lucid, and remarkably informed. I remember presenting my first seminar paper on Book 1 of Milton's *Paradise Lost*, when I quoted from an obscure sixteenth-century Latin source. Woodhouse immediately stopped me and asked me whether I had consulted this book in the library. I said that I was reporting at second hand, that I had taken the quotation from a study of Milton by the eminent scholar E.T.M. Tillyard. "I didn't think we had that volume in our library," Woodhouse said, revealing to me how well he knew the Library's resources in his area of expertise and reminding me gently that I should acknowledge quotations taken second hand. These seminars were very useful in their give-and-take and they also served to reveal to us (and to Woodhouse) the strengths and weaknesses of our training to date. When I quoted from Latin sources in my own seminars, Woodhouse seemed amused by my pronunciation, influenced by the ecclesiastical Latin with which I was so familiar and further flavoured with an Irish accent. When he wanted a Latin passage read aloud, he would say, "Let us hear Benson read this in his inimitable Latin." In the course of the next two years I developed a strangely warm relationship with Woodhouse. We were never friends—our differences in age and position precluded that—but I sensed that behind his carapace of academic authority he was a lonely man. A misogynist, the two most important people in his life were his secretary, Miss Stevenson, and his mother to whom he was devoted.

My own teaching was, in general, uneventful—except for the initial occasion when I met my first-year students. I had been warned that Engineering students could be troublesome since they resented having to take an English course which seemed totally unrelated to their interests. On this occasion one student was especially troublesome. He refused to sit down and shouted so loudly and incoherently that I was sure he was drunk. Eventually I managed to get him out of the lecture room when I began my lecture. Two days later, when I again came to meet my class, I saw my wayward student waiting for me. He immediately began to apologise explaining that he suffered severely from diabetics and that because his surroundings were so new to him and there were so many strange customs such as hazing to go through he had neglected to take his medication. It was my turn to apologise and reinstate him in my class.

But there was more than teaching and books to my life. I had many friends, some, including Douglas Spettigue, from among my fellow PhD students. I was impressed by the fact that he had written (and had published) a history of the RCMP and I was even more impressed when in our first year he sold a short story called "Carnival of the Animals" to an American journal—it may have been *The Atlantic Monthly*—for the then very large sum of $750. When I first was invited to his home for dinner, there sitting on the mantlepiece was the family carnival of animals, small figurines made from glass. On another occasion when I was visiting, his wife Jill was very disturbed. She had received a phone call that afternoon from Helen Frye, wife of Professor Frye, inviting her to the annual tea party she gave for new faculty wives and the wives of first year PhD students. Mrs Frye had said that following the tea there would be a *conversazione* on the theme "Turkey." Jill was understandably upset because Mrs Frye had not specified whether the talk was on the country Turkey or on the bird and she was spending a great deal of time reading up on both subjects. Some years after leaving Toronto to join the faculty of Queen's University, Spettigue turned literary sleuth and in the course of his research uncovered startling evidence that the revered Canadian novelist F.P. Grove was in fact a convicted German con man by the name of Felix Paul Greve who had faked his suicide in 1909 before hightailing it out for the USA and Canada where he finally settled. Had all this been known in his life time it is doubtful that he would ever have been admitted to the Royal Society of Canada, and criticism of his work—hitherto so often characterized as *echt* Canadian—would have taken a very different tack.

Other students with whom I became friends were William Keith a Cambridge University graduate, Roland Frean a young man from New Zealand who had recently taken his A.M. from Harvard and who became full professor at the age of thirty four when he returned home, Oreste Rudzik who, after taking his PhD, combined teaching part time at the university with a very busy law practice, and Clara Thomas. Clara had wonderful red hair and an unusual interest in Canadian literature (her mentor had been

Carl Klinck) in which she became an authority. Most of my fellow students went on to staff departments of English throughout the country and to take up positions as Chairs of Departments, Deans, and Presidents. I had other friends who included actors and musicians and many beginning their careers in the various professions.

My own weekly pattern was soon established. I usually rose after eight, breakfasted at a nearby restaurant (I did not have cooking privileges), on to the university where I would perhaps catch up on the day's news in Hart House and where I usually had lunch. Hart House was my salvation in that it was a social, cultural, and recreational centre with a restaurant that offered good food. In Hart House one could listen to music, attend very good theatre or recitals in the Great Hall that doubled as dining room and concert/theatre space. Interestingly, no women were allowed into its hallowed precincts until the 1970s—the Puritan ethic of Toronto was also tainted by a widely practiced misogyny. My mornings and afternoons were spent lecturing, or being lectured to, or in seminars, or in the library. Evenings I had dinner at cheap places like Fran's or Murray's restaurants before returning to work at Playter Boulevard until about 11 p.m. At weekends I would go to a movie or perhaps to a musical event in Massey Hall—there was always plenty of music available even in puritan Toronto—or drop into the Bohemian Embassy. I dated a great deal but during my two years of Ph. D. study I did not have a permanent relationship with any woman—I was too busy to cultivate such a relationship. Because I nearly always appeared with different women at dinners or parties given by fellow students I got the reputation of being a man about town, a dilettante who somehow got top grades without effort. But in fact I worked very hard and led a limited social life confined to weekends. Every few weeks I treated myself to dinner at the Hungarian Village, a restaurant on Bay St operated and staffed by Hungarians who had fled their country after the 1956 Revolution. It was a cosy place with a bar and good food. It also featured a violinist who played wonderful Hungarian music—with one eye covered by a black patch he looked like a revolutionary transplanted to the safer shores of Canada.

I got into trouble occasionally with my landlady Mrs. Mitchell because I was working so hard. In the first weeks in her home I usually had a little chat with her when I returned at night before going up to my study. She would tell me stories of her youth (she must have been born in the 1890s), of how she would go roaming in the fields just a block or two away from Playter Boulevard, now part of a densely sprawling and ever growing metropolis; of the Great Fire of 1919 when much of downtown Toronto was destroyed. That was the same year, she recalled, when the viaduct linking Bloor St and Danforth Avenue was completed. And she attributed her good life with her husband to the fact that she had been present at the unveiling of the statue of Timothy Eaton in the Queen St Eaton store when she joined others in rubbing his left toe to bring her good luck. She and her husband had long been season ticket holders for the Leafs, Toronto's hockey team, and the further she went back in memory—to just after the first World War when they both supported the Blueshirts—the sharper her memory seemed to become. Andy Blair, Turk Broda, Hap Day, King Clancy, Joe Primeau—she knew them all. She still loved to watch hockey on television and very often she invited me to join her for the games. I have always been rather hyperactive when watching sports but Mrs Mitchell was even more so. She hated the *Montreal Canadiens* with a passion (partly because they were from Quebec which she also hated) and would sometimes apologise after a game for being so outspoken. But because I was becoming more preoccupied with my work I often came home quite tired and went straight to my room without stopping to chat. One morning she asked if she could speak to me on a serious matter and after she had led me into her living room and sat me down she asked me what she had done wrong that made me treat her so coldly. I immediately apologized and explained that it was my work which made me seem so ill mannered and not any thing she had done. And so we made up and became friends again. But every so often I would forget and we would go through the same scene—accusation, explanation, reconciliation. When I look back at it now I realize how lonely my landlady was, how in need of someone—anyone really—to talk to. As a reward for my company she invited me once a month to have Sunday breakfast with her, a breakfast I came to fear intensely. It consisted of juice, coffee, bacon and eggs, and toast. The problem was that she did not have very good sight and so the bacon invariably came to me barely cooked and quite cold—a recipe for all sorts of diseases, I imagined, if the bacon also happened to be old. At my first breakfast I watched until she went out to the kitchen for more coffee when I literally stuck the bacon, unwrapped, in my pocket. Thereafter when I breakfasted with Mrs Mitchell I took a large napkin with me and managed surreptitiously to wrap the bacon in it. I had no intention of dying ignobly in Toronto of such a prosaic disease as trichinosis.

And so the weeks flew by. Christmas in Boston with my sister Françoise and her family, then back to Toronto where I take a half course on advanced bibliographic method with Professor Endicott. Half a dozen of us meet each week in his office and we write simple assignments–how to discover on what day T.S. Eliot's *Four Quartets* was published, where one would search to discover which libraries are richest in first editions and holograph materials relating to Byron and Shelley. Endicott was in some ways the stereotype of the professor—absent minded, encyclopaedic in his own field of scholarship, a poor lecturer. My own name for him was "Unfinished Endicott." He would begin a sentence, "Let's start with Burton's *Anatomy of Melancholy* . . . " before a book on his shelves caught his eye. Taking it down, he would say, "If you examine this eighteenth-century colophon . . . " A dozen or so such digressions and the class was over. I returned my first assignment to him and heard nothing more from him with the result that I didn't bother turning in any more. At the end of the course the Registrar notified me that I had passed this course–on what basis I will never know. I have no idea whether Endicott ever read or marked any of our assignments—I suspect that every time he sat down to do so another volume on his shelf caught his attention and led him off to greener pastures than that offered by his students. But then Marshall McLuhan was also notorious for his grading methods—he would flip through a Ph.D dissertation, reading a paragraph here and there, before pronouncing his verdict.

In the Spring I sat for the French examination—a simple test in translation—which I passed. Came the end of the academic year and examination in the courses offered by Woodhouse and Frye. Woodhouse's examination was the standard test lasting three hours with a choice of questions, no literary materials allowed. Frye's examination, on the other hand, was as freely structured as one could ask for—take as long as you want, bring in an encyclopedia and a raft of books if you so desired, leave off the finished paper in his office. I took one book with me—Frye's *Anatomy of Criticism*—and finished in two and a half hours—I heard later that one student spent eight hours answering the two prescribed questions. I now had one last hurdle to complete in that year. Our PhD regulations called for a two-hour oral examination in the candidate's special field–in my case modern

English literature. Woodhouse presided and in attendance as examiners were McLuhan (friendly and expansive), Frye, Professors Jack Robson and Robert Greene. It was a gruelling business, but fair. By the end of that year I had obtained A standing in all the work I had taken except for those courses where a Pass/Failure system was in place.

That summer of 1959 I got a job teaching a six-week Summer School course at the fledgling University of Sudbury. I met the assistant Dean of the university in Hart House for an interview—he was younger than I—which lasted all of twenty minutes before he and I went off to the King Cole Room in the basement of the Park Avenue Hotel for a beer. Thus did Paul Scanlon and I begin a friendship that was to add richness to the rest of my life and made the time I spent in Sudbury tolerable. The city itself was a shock to me. It was a mining town that owed its existence to INCO, one of the largest nickel-producing companies on the planet. The smoke pouring from its great stacks polluted the country for miles around so that trees, plants, flowers, grass even, shrivelled and died. These adjacent areas with their huge slag heaps, especially around Copper Cliff and Falconbridge, reminded me of Milton's Hell as described in *Paradise Lost*. These scenes of desolation were further fouled by a recurrent sulphuric miasma seeping from huge sulphur deposits in the ground.

In the 1950s the city was racked by labour disputes with rival unions seeking control of the work force. I now understood why my MA supervisor Ron Bates, whose wife came from the area, told me that he always sat with his back to the wall when he went into a bar. Interestingly, despite the fact that the population of Sudbury was about thirty per cent French speaking, there was no anti-French feeling. The university itself had no formal buildings but housed its administration and classrooms in rented spaces. For example, I lectured in what had been the embalming room of a former funeral parlour where I imagined I still detected the smell of chemicals like formaldehyde and glutaraldehyde. There were no bookstores in the city and its library offered mostly light fiction. But there was no lack of determination and idealism among the students who were excited at the prospect of a university education in a way that I had not seen before.

Again my time was spent teaching, ordering books and journals for the small library, marking papers, and endless hours spent preparing for my General Examinations—Baugh's 1600-page *Literary History of England* was always on my desk as well as the Harvard University prescribed reading list for PhD students which had been adopted by Toronto. It included thousands of English-language novels, plays, volumes of poetry, works of criticism, and related materials and also a large selection (in translation) of the masterpieces of French, German, Russian, Scandinavian, and Italian literatures. There were only one or two Canadian titles on this magisterial and canonical list.

On my return to Toronto to begin my second year I met with Woodhouse who told me that I would offer an English class to final-year engineering students. The course had been set up following a request from the Dean of Engineering who discovered that many of those graduating hesitated to take on important office positions because they felt uncertain of their command of written English. I would also offer a few lectures on basic bibliographic practice to final year dental students and help them organize their final short theses. This was a plumb assignment which paid very well.

The PhD Final Examinations consisted of four three-hour papers covering four fields or areas of English literature. They were Old and Middle English which included most notably *Beowulf*, Caedmon and his school, Langland, Chaucer, *Piers Plowman*; the period 1570 to 1660 which included such important literary figures as Marlowe, Shakespeare, Ben Jonson, Donne, and Milton; the period 1660 to 1830 which included Dryden, Swift and Pope, Congreve, Johnson, Goldsmith, and the major Romantic poets; 1830 to the present (1950) which embraced great novelist like the Brontës, Dickens, Thackeray, Melville, Hawthorne, poets Browning, Arnold, and Tennyson, the Irish Literary Renaissance, and so on to the major figures of the twentieth century. Four weeks or so before the Finals I indulged in a rare pleasure—I bought myself two bottles of Irish whisky. At day's end, about ten-thirty, I poured myself a small glass of whisky and listened to tapes I had made of Anglo-Saxon grammar. In this way I strengthened an area of knowledge in which I felt weak and squeezed out an extra period of work. Later in life when I sometimes needed to work despite being tired I learned how to use hypnosis in order to finish urgent tasks.

The two days during which I wrote the Finals remain a blur. There were seven of us in a large room in the English Department wing of University College—a supervisor made an occasional appearance. A detail does however remain in my memory. One of the candidates—a woman—who sat opposite me at a large table went through a lengthy routine before putting pen to paper. She meticulously arranged various items from her purse on the table, items which included a great many cookies and chocolate bars and proceeded to eat her way through her collected booty all the while writing slowly and with great deliberation. I never did learn whether she passed or failed.

   I have no doubt that these academic trials were meant to test us and to weed out the weak, but they also were capable of doing severe damage. A year after I wrote these exams a close friend also attempted them but was sent to hospital when the examination supervisor noticed that he was mechanically writing only his name on page after page. He was subsequently exposed to electroconvulsive shock therapy which involved sending currents of electricity through his brain. On his release from the hospital he seemed to have such a totally different personality that I felt I was in the presence of a stranger. He never did finish his PhD I did not escape untouched. When in the Fall of 1959 the actor Errol Flynn died of a heart attack I was surprised at the depth of my melancholy that lasted for days. For many years I had admired his zest for living, his seeming inexhaustible virility and energy, his life of action. And then to die, so young, on the floor of a Vancouver apartment. I came to suspect that Flynn's death at the age of fifty reminded me of my own mortality. I was thirty-one years of age, alone, working at full stretch, closer perhaps than I knew to breaking point.

   I now had only two courses to complete in my second obligatory year of residence, one of which was "Chaucer and his Age" and the other a graduate philosophy course. Dr Shook of St Michael's College, a Catholic priest of the Basilian order, was the professor in the Chaucer course. A small man of great charm and with a Harvard PhD in mediaeval studies, he was Director of the Pontifical Institute for Mediaeval Studies which had been granted its pontifical charter by Rome largely due to the efforts of the eminent French scholar Étienne Gilson who lectured in Toronto in the 1930s and who took up full time teaching and writing at the Institute in the early 1950s. Dr Shook gave little indication of the busy life he led—teaching, publishing, translating works from Latin and from French, supervising theses at the MA and PhD levels while at the same time celebrating mass, hearing confessions, and tending to the sick and to his parishioners. His course was a delight as he guided us through texts that he illustrated with reference to Greek, Latin, French, German, Anglo-Saxon, and Italian literatures.

My course in philosophy was taught by Professor Larry Lynch also from St Michael's College. Since all the students in his graduate course in Existentialism and Phenomenology that year were Philosophy majors, Lynch took pity on me and allowed me to write on topics related to his course that had a literary bent. It was in his class that I became very interested in the philosophy of Martin Heidegger which led me some years later to investigate his life. I was astonished to discover that he had been an ardent supporter of the Nazi party, betraying some of his university colleagues, and that he had taken a young Jewish woman as his mistress despite being married with a family. The woman, Hannah Arendt, escaped to America before the war began where she became a distinguished political theorist in her own right and famously covered the trial of Adolph Eichmann in Jerusalem. What astonished me was the fact that after the war she returned to Germany and resumed her affair with Heidegger. How strange and tortuous the equations of human love and lust.

My life now resumed a more reasonable pace. I went to many concerts in Massey Hall and I saw as many plays as I could manage at the Royal Alex, Hart House Theatre, and the Crest Theatre which offered international plays along with some Canadian plays by such writers as Robertson Davies and Bernard Slade. In April 1960 I attended the premiere of James Reaney's play *A One-Man Masque* in tandem with *Night-Blooming Cereus*, a chamber opera for which he wrote the libretto and John Beckwith the music. The *Masque* was a most extraordinary performance. Reaney, no actor, played the various parts that linked a series of poems that constituted the "play." His libretto seemed to me to be extraordinary because of the banality of its lyrics. Because my appraisal of Reaney's work was contradicted by the warmth of the audience's applause I began to think about the state of criticism in Canada, especially in relation to Canadian work. In what tradition was Reaney working? Was he influenced by other Canadian writers? What theatres were offering Canadian drama? Was critical taste being influenced or biased from an understandable desire to find some one who would write the Great Canadian Play complementing the search for the Great Canadian Novel? And why weren't Canadian novels and plays and poems being studied at the university level? I had never taken a course in Canadian literature and yet I had an MA and was close to having a PhD Was there indeed such a thing as a Canadian literature and if so why was it ignored by the entire higher educational establishment? These were matters that exercised me then and would continue to exercise me later in my career.

In the meantime more mundane matters held my attention. My work with the dental students and final year engineering students was *pro forma* and going very well except for a small number of the engineers to whom I was forced to give failing grades. I called in some of these students and in the course of our talks discovered a common factor—they were all of Hungarian origin and they had been engineering students in their home country before fleeing with their families following the abortive 1956 Revolution against the Soviets. I sympathised with their plight but I could do nothing for them—it would have been entirely unethical and against every precept I knew were I to inflate their marks to allow them to graduate.

About this time Professor Woodhouse told me that the Royal Military College of Canada had contacted him about a replacement for a professor who had recently drowned in a boating accident. He had nominated me for the now vacant position and I should proceed immediately to Kingston, Ontario, for interview. I did so and after a lunch in the Officers' Mess I was interviewed by Colonel Sawyer, Director of Studies, Professor George Stanley (whose design for the Canadian flag was adapted four years later), and by the Head of the English Department, Walter Avis. I got the job. Back in Toronto Woodhouse filled me in on the background of the professor I was replacing. His name was Peter Fisher, aged forty, a young Captain of Artillery in the Second World War who had been decorated for gallantry under fire in the Italian campaign, and who had returned to the University of Toronto to take his PhD under Northrop Frye with a dissertation on the visionary William Blake. Fisher had been by all accounts a brilliant man of intellect and action.

Came April and examination time. I did very well and had now discharged all requirements except for the writing of my dissertation. But my Hungarian students did not do well. The group represented about twelve per cent of the class and they failed with the result that they could not graduate. Not prepared to let the matter rest there, I went to see Woodhouse. After I had outlined the case he said, "You do have a solution, don't you, Benson?" I said that in view of the fact that these fourth-year students had been burdened with a condition *post facto* concerning English proficiency it would probably not be enforceable in law. "The Dean would certainly not want lawyers interfering in our affairs," Woodhouse said, hunched over his cigarette and his cup of tea. "Are you suggesting that I go over your head and change your marks?" I said no, that he did not have that authority (the cheek of me!). However, I would not object if he left my grading unaltered but used his considerable influence (flattery!) to see that my grades did not appear on the Hungarian students' transcripts, but rather a P for pass. I left him to mull over the matter and when the results were finally posted by the Registrar I was pleased to see that all my Hungarians had graduated and received the iron ring that indicated to the world that they were *bona fide* engineers.

It only remained to store my possessions, make plans for a summer holiday and study in Europe, partake of a celebratory and farewell breakfast with my landlady (including the obligatory bacon), and say goodbye to friends and to Toronto.

The Wandering Scholar

The Royal Military College of Canada, Kingston, enjoys a beautiful site on Point Frederick, a small peninsula jutting into Lake Ontario. In 1959 it received a university charter allowing it to grant degrees in the arts, science, and engineering at the undergraduate and graduate levels. Unlike its USA counterpart, the Military Academy of the United States—better known as West Point Academy—RMC gave preference to its academic program rather than to its military program. This was a decision carefully arrived at and greatly influenced by its Director of Studies, Colonel Sawyer. The main building which housed the administration and the academic programs was the Mackenzie Building that overlooked the Parade Square. In The Officers' Club huge windows gave a fine view on Lake Ontario and the jetties where RMC recreational boats and yachts lay at anchor. The faculty consisted mainly of non-military professors but there were, of course, a number of officers who managed the students' military training. The student enrollment in 1960 was some five hundred young men known as Gentlemen Cadets (there were no women in the program). They were housed in buildings on campus called forts and they wore scarlet uniforms with pillbox hats. The attrition rate in the first year was very high because of the demands made on students which included carrying out all activities on the run—walking at any time was forbidden. For many students this traditional treatment was not a problem but some broke under the constant hazing. For those who endured, the rewards were an indoctrination that served well under conditions of warfare and stress. For all cadets the hours were long stretching from 6 a.m. to 11 p.m.

The Chair of the English Department, Wally Avis, assigned me my teaching duties—Modern English literature; the key Romantic poets; an introductory English survey. I would also offer a class in debating and public speaking once a week. I protested that I knew nothing of debating, but was told that the junior member of faculty always was awarded this class since more senior members disliked an 8 a.m. start on Monday mornings. And so I settled into my new job, I got myself an apartment in Kingston, and quickly became involved in RMC life which centered on the class room and the Officers' Club. On the occasion of my first evening visit to the Club's bar I was joined by a portly man with a highly flushed face, nattily dressed, and carrying an umbrella over his arm. He ordered a drink and introduced himself as John Spurr. I rejoiced for here was a talker of rare talent. Before twenty minutes had passed he waved loftily to the barman for writing paper and began drawing a plan of the palace of Versailles. Then followed a virtuoso performance as he proceeded to tell me the history of the various significant rooms in the palace such as the *enfilade* of seven royal rooms named after Roman deities—the *Salon de Diane*, the *Salon de Mercure*, and so on—peopling them with the dozens of historical characters associated with them. That was the first of many wonderful evenings with John Spurr, RMC's librarian, former Intelligence officer during the Second World War, and *raconteur* par excellence.

The Department of English was small. Wally Avis became a linguist and lexicographer after visiting a Chicago store where he was directed to the cigar counter when he asked where he might find chesterfields. He discovered that "blinds" were "shades" to Americans , "taps" were "faucets," "braces" "suspenders, and "serviettes" "napkins." Eventually what seemed like a hobby metamorphosed into a special dictionary of Canadian usage as distinguished from British and American usage. Another professor I got to know well was Michael Booth. He was an expert in eighteenth and nineteenth century melodrama who in his writings and lectures did much to restore the reputation of a genre that had in the twentieth century fallen into disrepute. Born in India, Booth possessed the plumiest of English accents and a stutter. I soon discovered that the stutter was an affectation to draw attention to himself. We acted together in a play, *The Reluctant Debutante* by William Douglas-Home, where his stutter never once appeared. I am not sure if the RCM authorities were aware that Douglas-Home who had been a tank commander in World War Two had been court martialled and jailed for refusing to join in the attack on the

French city of Le Havre because he feared massive civilian casualties—he was right since over 2000 civilians died and eighty five per cent of the city was razed.

And then there was sad, lonely, and beautiful Pierre Dumont, a young lecturer in the French Department. He hovered around my existence so that when I look back across the years I reproach myself that I did not offer him more help or friendship. I was too busy with my teaching and marking and my plays and my debating team to ever truly know him. When I call him "beautiful" it was in the sense that Marcello Mastroianni is beautiful in the movie *La Dolce Vita*—Pierre was beautiful in his looks and in his bearing that spoke of deracination and of loss, beautiful in his culture and breeding and good manners in a world where these things seemed to him at risk. It was many months before I discovered that he was homosexual, that he sought me out because although we never spoke of it he trusted me and found solace of a sort in my company. We talked often, listened to music, swam together, and he envied me for what he called my optimism and hope. At the end of the academic year Pierre went to Europe during the summer to attend a lecture series at the Sorbonne and to travel in Europe. But his postcards to me from Paris and Amalfi and Rome and Prague and Berlin spoke only of loneliness and of an enduring *ennui*. During the next academic year at RMC he met a young professor at Queen's University and they fell in love. When the authorities at RMC found out about this they fired Pierre immediately and he vanished from my ken in Montreal from where he had come.

I also learned more about Peter Fisher, the professor I succeeded. Appointed Head of the English Department in 1955 he had won the position over formidable competition from Roy Daniells and the poet Earle Birney. Fisher's death was still mourned because of the impact he had made in his few years at RMC. He fitted into the College's military milieu easily because he was a former soldier of distinction, but he was also valued because of other gifts. He had been a brilliant teacher and a student of many languages including Sanskrit. He had, incongruously, combined a deep interest in various forms of Western and Oriental mysticisms with a love of many women and a huge capacity for drinking that had won the admiration and envy of his former teacher Northrop Frye who saw Fisher as the intellectual and man of action that he wanted to be. Frye's heavy consumption of beer was, I believe, an attempt to emulate Fisher's prowess as a drinker. Frye's *homage* to his former student and hero was a remarkable one—he took Fisher's unfinished papers and sketches for a volume on the poet Blake and shaped them into the book *The Valley of Vision: Blake as Prophet and Revolutionary*.

I think I must have been in need of a break from intensive study and research for I did little or no work on my PhD dissertation during that year at RMC. Perhaps it was the very relaxed lifestyle of the faculty—both military and civilian—that influenced me. The Officers' Mess was popular in the evenings because alcohol and food were very cheap. Then too there were the military balls held every few weeks which were very striking. Because the three services were represented at RMC and because the officers' dress uniforms were so very colourful and different, the scene at these balls was one where the officers' formal wear outdid the evening dresses of the ladies and the white tie with tails that we civilian professors wore. At formal dinners throughout the year fresh lobster was flown in from the RCAF base in Nova Scotia—the pilots' obligatory flights were re-scheduled to land at Trenton airbase just a few miles away so that they coincided with these dinners! And as at the air base in London, drinks—including champagne—were often free.

Not long after I joined the faculty at RMC Graeme Gibson sent me two chapters of the novel he had gone to Europe to write. After a brief spell at Oxford he and Shirley had been loaned a house in Antibes in the south of France where he began to write a novel that took as its *point de départ* the hit-and-run death of Wally Ryerson. I wrote him a twenty-page handwritten letter detailing my reaction to the material he sent me. When I read that critique now, I am embarrassed by its frankness and by its prescriptive tone and it is a mark of Graeme's tolerance and friendship that he did not take my criticism amiss. In fact, in later years when he introduced me to various people he very often remarked that I was the person who had most influenced him to become a writer. The key thing about my response, he told me, was that in my letter I had taken him seriously.

Despite the early hour at which I taught debating and public speaking I began to enjoy the work and I discovered that, properly handled, the cadets also enjoyed it and some made good progress. The debating team had about twelve members and I soon selected a core team of four that included two particularly good debaters—Fred Webster and Brian MacDonald. Webster's style of debating was graceful, light, and colourful in language;

MacDonald's was rather heavy in the manner of a politician. But I knew that many judges would favour this manner of debate mistaking his pomposity for *gravitas* and that it would balance Webster's lightness of touch. Throughout the year we debated teams from various universities in the province and quite often won. The real test came in the second academic semester which featured the annual contest with the United States Military Academy at West Point, New York in two areas—ice hockey and debating. I began to get some idea of the earnestness with which West Point approached this event when I received a letter from one of the officers there asking me for my physical measurements—height and weight—and age. There was to be the inevitable military ball and the Academy needed these measurements to pair me with a suitable dancing partner whom they would provide.

The weekend at West Point was a full one. On the Friday evening the Americans held a cocktail party for the RMC officers and professors attending. I remember at one point standing with three generals and five full colonels discussing our respective military academies while black army sergeants hovered over us with cocktails. Most senior of the generals was the Superintendent, William Westmoreland, filling a role taken before him at West Point by such military luminaries as General Robert E. Lee and General Douglas MacArthur. Westmoreland had been the most brilliant graduate of his year at West Point—he won the Pershing Sword—and went on to high command in the Second World War and then to Vietnam four years after I met him. There he was fated to meet a Vietnamese general, General Giáp, who had never been to a military academy but who defeated the finest products of French military academies in his stunning victory at Dien Bien Phu. His will to victory was undoubtedly reinforced by the fact that the French had tortured and executed his wife, sister, father, and sister-in-law for seeking independence from France. Some years later, despite being faced with overwhelming American forces who had total air superiority, Giáp out-generalled Westmoreland and drove his forces out of Vietnam. It is an ironic commentary on military science that an actress, Jane Fonda, read correctly the dynamics of American society and Vietnamese resolve which Westmoreland and his generals failed to do. But as we drank cocktails that evening in 1961 with our genial host, General Westmoreland, no one could have foreseen such an encounter and how it would forever cast a shadow on the reputation of a soldier who had presided over the deaths of some four million Vietnamese soldiers and civilians as against a loss of less than sixty-five thousand Americans .

The next morning I met some of my academic counterparts at West Point (all military officers) who taught such subjects as American literature, psychology, and history. They told me that each lesson was carefully set out in detail and written down so that should they be transferred to active duty a replacement professor-officer could pick up exactly where they had left off. This differed radically from RCM practice. True, I did have a course outline which I followed but if, for example, I decided to spend more time on Jane Austen than I had allotted I would do so. Nor did I have detailed notes but rather half a dozen points per lecture that would not have been very helpful to someone brought in to replace me.

In the afternoon came our debate which we won. Our American hosts assumed, incorrectly, that most Canadians were bilingual—English and French. Playing on this assumption, I had instructed our two cadets MacDonald and Webster to introduce a number of statements in French into their opening remarks and also to use some French in their rebuttals. I hoped that neither of the two West Point cadets would speak or understand French. Thus Webster would say, "As I pointed out in my opening remarks in French" or throw in phrases in French that need not have a lot to do with the actual subject under debate. The ruse worked and we won the cup. Rather, we won a replica of a military cannon—I still have a picture of my two cadets, myself, and Brigadier General Anderson of RMC posing with our cannon. That evening after the ice hockey game—we lost—there was a splendid ball where I met my date, Lucinda, an army brat. She was tall and willowy and desirable and a lot of fun and I like to think we made a fine couple—she in her silver backless evening dress and I in my white tie and tails. The ballroom was a riot of colour with so many Canadian and American uniforms and the military band played until midnight. On our return to Kingston I and my debating team were a two-day wonder because we had defeated the Americans.

In March of 1961 Wally Avis informed me that my contract for the following year would not be renewed—I had always been viewed as an interim lecturer while negotiations went on to bring in an established scholar who would have, of course, the required PhD My replacement would be Reginald Watters who had just published a massive *Checklist of Canadian Literature and Backgrounds Materials*. I accepted the situation without regret for although I was very happy at the College I missed the more academic milieu of universities. Despite the best efforts of Colonel Sawyer the demands of military training adversely affected the cadets' performance—they complained regularly to me of always being tired and of a conflict between the compulsory nature of their military program in contrast to the total freedom of their academic work. Then too I missed the energy generated in the university classroom by the interaction of male and female students. Not that there weren't some very good students at RMC. In my fourth year class Cadet Kenneth Graham submitted a paper to me on an aspect of Joyce's *Ulysses* which was excellent. When he came to see me to say goodbye I suggested to him that should he ever leave the army he should consider taking up graduate work in English.

Within a few weeks I contacted my friend Paul Scanlon at the University of Sudbury and was offered at job as assistant professor starting in September of 1961. I spent the next three academic years at Sudbury and the summers in Europe. They were difficult years caused mainly by the fact that the university was in its earliest stages of development. There was no tenure system, library facilities were minimal, and classes were still being held all over the city in rented rooms that were unsuitable. I was a member of the Faculty Association Council and we spent a huge amount of time sparring with the Administration over our rights and obligations. On one occasion the Dean of Arts and Science announced that he had the right to visit each classroom in order to observe whether what was being taught was in line with the University's mandate! Then too we faculty felt isolated—many of us had all studied at universities throughout the world and many had traveled widely. The contrast provided between Sudbury and, say, the environs of the University of Heidelberg or Trinity College, Dublin, or Cambridge or Harvard or Toronto was shattering. Some forty square miles of the Sudbury area had been laid waste by copper and nickel operations—the area was totally barren of vegetation and there was no top soil. In summer one could escape to the lakes beyond this hellish landscape but in winter one was captive in a frozen landscape whose ghastliness could not be hidden even by the snow which was immediately polluted by the great smelters that towered above the city. The nearest city was Toronto but it was about a six-hour drive and, given the roads, much longer in winter. There were always faculty parties to while away the months but these usually degenerated into booze-fuelled affairs where people got drunk, tried to seduce each others wives or husbands, and indulged in violent quarrels over issues not remembered the next day.

It was always the same people, the same drinks, the same flirtations and seductions, the same conversations, the same feeling of an ever enduring *ennui*. But I made some strong friendships—there was always Paul Scanlon, now freed of his administrative duties to be a full-time teacher in the English Department, and his beautiful Estonian girlfriend Marit, and there was Denis Deneau and Jay Ford of the Philosophy Department. Ford was one of the handsomest men I had ever met.

The gloom of those years was accentuated by the politics of the time—the Cuban missile crisis, the building of the Berlin Wall and ever-growing threat of a nuclear clash between the USSR and the USA. From early May until early September I escaped from this world to the cities and libraries of England and Ireland and it was this escape that made me able to endure my time at Sudbury. I spent a summer at the Bodleian Museum in Oxford ("city of dreaming spires"), another in Dublin at Trinity College, others in London working out of the British Museum with one summer spent in London House, Mecklenburgh Square, an international residence for Commonwealth students pursuing post graduate studies. For holidays I traveled to Spain (Sitges and Altea), to Paris, Copenhagen, Amsterdam, Hamburg, Dusseldorf, Juan-les-Pins, St Tropez, Marseilles. In Ireland I visited my family and I usually rented a car and explored the country, very often with my father, to visit sites that he remembered vividly—the village of Lissoy, West Meath, his first posting as a police officer in the Royal Irish Constabulary (to my delight the pub owner found a very old man who remembered my father and to my further delight I discovered that Lissoy was where Oliver Goldsmith, poet, novelist, and dramatist, was raised); and to his home in Carrickbanagher, County Sligo; and to Drumcliff, not far away, to visit the tomb of the poet W.B. Yeats and read the epitaph which he himself wrote:

> Under bare Ben Bulben's head
> In Drumcliff churchyard Yeats is laid...
>
> *Cast a cold eye*
> *On life and death.*
> *Horseman, pass by!*

On one of these trips, in 1963, my father and I were in Dublin when President Kennedy visited the city. We were in a restaurant off St Stephen's

Green when suddenly all the maids ran to the windows and began waving in a chatter of excitement. I went to the door and the President's cavalcade passed by. As he stood in his car waving to the crowd the sun caught his hair turning its red and copper tones into a nimbus of gold. Like a Divinity. Eighteen months later came another tragic, final cavalcade in Dallas, Texas.

My years of isolation in Sudbury were reinforced by the fact that I had entered into a serious love relationship in the summer of 1961. She was Irish, by the name of Noeleen, very attractive I thought, a student in a teaching college in Coventry, England. I met her in London and for the next two and a half years we conducted a trans-Atlantic love affair in which we became engaged, broke it off, got engaged again, and finally ended our affair in 1963. The major stumbling block was distance. We had wonderful summers but then there were the long periods of separation. I have never regretted the relationship and remember Noeleen with love and with gratitude.

In 1964 I decided to leave Sudbury and spend a year in England finishing my PhD dissertation. There was so little time during the academic year to do serious research and the library at Sudbury was totally inadequate for my purposes. And so I traveled to London in the Spring of 1964 where I found a spacious apartment in Redcliffe Gardens, in the Earls Court area close to central London, known colloquially as Kangaroo Alley because of the number of Australian and New Zealand students living there. Very soon the British Museum Reading Room became my daily haunt from about 10 a.m. to early evening where I immersed myself in work on my dissertation now given sharper definition under its new title "James Joyce: Orthodoxy and Heterodoxy." I had already done a good deal of work in the previous two summers on the neoplatonism of Joyce's thought by relating Nicolas of Cusa, Giordano Bruno, and Giambattista Vico—important influences on Joyce—to Dun Scotus Erigena. A second chapter was concerned with the extraordinary figure of Joachim of Flora who forecast a Third Golden Age of the Holy Spirit which Joyce exploited in order to convert Molly Bloom into a Gnostic Holy Spirit. Three chapters remained to be done relating to Joyce's Trinitarianism, his use of myth, and his ironic vision. My reading in the British Museum Reading Room reflected my studies: everything written by Joyce, studies specifically about Joyce and his work, books on the philosophy of history and on comparative mythology, selected writings of Freud and Jung (Joyce in *Finnegans Wake* speaks of "being jung and easily freudened"), selected writings from Aquinas, the eight volume nineteenth-century translation of *The* Great *Commentary of Cornelius à Lapide* (Cornelius turns up in the *Portrait of the Artist as a Young Man*). Particularly interesting was *Our Examination round his Factification for Incamination of Work in Progress,* with a major essay by Samuel Beckett on *Finnegans Wake.* While Joyce was writing the *Wake* Beckett acted as a kind of unofficial secretary who would visit Joyce's Paris apartment, do a little work, and then usually fall asleep. Joyce's daughter Lucia fell in love with this strange red-haired Irishman but Beckett fled her advances.

My most interesting task was a detailed reading and study of the original manuscripts of *Finnegans Wake* which Joyce had given to his patroness Harriet Shaw Weaver for her extraordinary generosity over a number of years in supporting him. The manuscripts were kept in the British museum's Rare Books Reading Room and I was given a pair of gloves and a smooth plastic stick to turn over the leaves of each section of the work in order not to contaminate them with moisture from my fingers. A librarian sat in a gallery above and watched me as I followed Joyce's quest to write the ultimate Book of Books, *le Livre,* the Bible of modernist literature, to out-rival the most *avant garde* work of contemporary artists such as Picasso, Schoenberg, Le Corbusier, and Brancusi. The guardian librarian also watched my fellow readers below as they studied rare works by Galileo and Copernicus, the Quartos of Shakespeare, the gorgeously illuminated Lindisfarne Gospels, or the Diamond Sutra, a Chinese work printed almost six hundred years before the Gutenberg Bible.

But I preferred the great circular Reading Room with its enormous ceiling and its walls lined with books in a thousand shades of colour. One was always aware of those who had come here to read and study—a ghostly procession of writers, long dead, including Dickens, Marx, Darwin, Wilde, Shaw, and Lenin. An added benefit of the British Museum was that its wash rooms had hot running water which resulted in poor post graduate students from developing countries converting them into their favourite laundry rooms. There was also a number of eccentric readers; among them was my favourite, a middle-aged woman, who, no matter the weather, wore tropical shorts which exaggerated her sticklike legs. She took her seat, arranged her books, and very soon began writing pen poison letters which she delivered to various unsuspecting readers accusing them of various crimes. I fell within her ken one afternoon and received a letter accusing me of having robbed her. Then one day she was gone and I did not see her for about two months when she suddenly reappeared. I spoke to one of the librarians about her and he told me that she had been barred from the Reading Room because of her erratic behaviour, but when it was discovered that she had declined so catastrophically in health that her doctor feared for her life she was re-admitted to her beloved Room where, undoubtedly, she carried on writing poison pen letters for the rest of her days.

Occasionally friends or acquaintances appeared in the Reading Room. Late in the summer of 1964 I saw my old professor, A.S.P. Woodhouse, but now he no longer looked so formidable. I invited him for coffee or tea and he accepted with alacrity. I discovered he felt quite out of his depths now that he was retired and that he welcomed the chance to meet someone with whom he could talk. I made a point of meeting with him regularly and we became friends. Another face from the past was Kenneth Graham's; he had resigned his captaincy in the Canadian Army to pursue graduate studies. He was in the Library seeking a subject for an MA thesis for submission to the University of London. When he told me that his interests were in late eighteenth-century and early nineteenth-century literature I immediately recommended he read a novel for which I had the greatest admiration, William Beckford's *Vathek* of 1786. I had read it as an undergraduate and remembered it as a most extravagant combination of Gothicism and Orientalism with features that anticipated Surrealism. Beckford, one of the richest men in England, was tutored in the piano at the age of five by the nine-year old Mozart. An avid art collector he owned paintings by Mantegna, Raphael, Lorrain, and Velasquez among others. He wrote *Vathek* at the age of eighteen at one sitting, he claimed, of three days and two nights—"I never took off my clothes the whole time. This severe application made me very ill." Graham took up my suggestion and wrote his MA thesis on Beckford followed by a PhD dissertation becoming in later years an international expert in the area. Other visitors from Canada were Denis Deneau and Jay Ford who turned up in the Spring of 1965, Jay recovering from a broken engagement to a young would-be poet by the name of Margaret Atwood.

It was about this time that I also wrote two one-act plays, each at one sitting. I was at my table one evening in my Redcliffe Gardens apartment working on some notes taken that day in the British Museum when I saw a middle-aged man pass my window carrying a violin. Distracted from my work I began to wonder where he was going and before long I began to write a play which was obviously about myself in some way since the violinist had now become a writer who feared that someone was plagiarizing his material. The other character in the play, a woman, tries to point out that he may be mistaken but at the end of the play he sets off to murder the plagiarist who may or may not exist. I wrote nonstop (emulating Beckford!), without interruption, and was totally surprised, and exhausted when I finished the twenty-two-page play at around six in the morning. I called the play *Joan of Arc's Violin*. About two months later the same thing happened under similar circumstances. I was at my desk working when I remembered a visit I had made with my father to an old people's home in Ireland. When he went in to visit his friend who was a patient I sat outside in the sunshine near where two old men—in their mid seventies perhaps—were viewing the nurses passing by. I was totally surprised at their ribaldry and sexual energy which showed a capacity for life that I had not suspected. They came again to me that night in London and I began to write as before, starting about nine in the evening and finishing between six and seven in the morning. This one-act play I titled *The Gunner's Rope*. Unlike Beckford's, my "severe application" did not make me ill.

While I was certainly working very hard I was also enjoying myself for after all this was London of the 1960s, perhaps the most exciting city in the world at that time. It had taken the UK a long time to recover from the effects of the war—far longer than Germany—but by the early 1960s it had begun to shake off the drabness and the food rationing and debility of the post-war years. It was still the period of the Cold War dominated by the horror of a possible thermonuclear Armageddon which gave a kind of frenzied rhythm to daily life, *carpe diem* with an edge. The Cuban crisis of 1962 was a foretaste of what could happen. And so London played out its life with a heightened sense of hedonism and *Angst*. The theatre was unrivalled in the English-speaking world with a wealth of offerings from the Royal Shakespeare Company at the Aldwych Theatre, the Royal Court Theatre, the National Theatre, and dozens of others, featuring famous actors like Laurence Olivier, John Gielgud, Peggy Ashcroft, Ralph Richardson, and a host of new comers—Peter O'Toole, Alan Bates, and

Maggie Smith. There had been no dramatist of worth since Wilde and Shaw (both Irish) , but now the theatrical treasures of Europe, displayed in work by Ionesco, Beckett, Brecht, and Genet, among others, amazed—and confounded—London audiences. The emergence of British writers like John Osborne who introduced kitchen sink drama into early twentieth-century English pretty drawing room drama pointed to an exciting, indigenous movement. The effect of all this was only equaled by Roger Fry's 1910-1911 exhibition of post-Impressionist painters in London. My most enduring image of the plays of that period is from Peter Weiss' *The Persecution and Assassination of Jean-Paul Marat as Performed by the Inmates of the Asylum of Charenton under the Direction of the Marquis de Sade*, commonly knows as *Marat/Sade*, produced by the Royal Shakespeare Company. It is not a great play but as directed by a virtuoso like Peter Brook it became a series of *coups de théâtre*, my favourite being the scene where Glenda Jackson, playing Charlotte Corday, whips the half naked de Sade, played by Patrick Magee, with her long tresses.

London movie screens were running the work of Europe's most innovative film directors: Bergman of Sweden, Truffaut, Resnais, Godard, and Malle of France, Fellini, Antonioni, Bertolucci, and De Sicca of Italy, and the iconoclastic Buñuel of Spain (*Viridiana*). Most popular, however, were the new James Bond movies featuring an amoral British spy and his pneumatic Bond girls, as available and disposable as Barbie dolls. His battles with the USSR (thinly disguised as SPECTRE) represented the last hiccup of British colonialism in its contempt for most things not English. There was ballet at Saddler's Wells (Royal Ballet) with the forty-three-year-old Margot Fonteyn as partner to the twenty-four-year-old Nureyev who had just made a spectacular defection from the USSR.

But what most defined London in those years was the sexual freedom that had replaced the stultifying morality for so long synonymous with Britain in contrast to that of the Continent. It was propelled by one of the most revolutionary inventions of the twentieth century—the Pill—which liberated women from the curse of unwanted pregnancies. Authors like Simone de Bouvoir and later Betty Friedman popularized the idea of "Women's Liberation" which many women took to mean that they were entitled to the same promiscuity that men had always enjoyed. Pharmaceutical companies and the popular press focused on the search for the ultimate orgasm which, it was asserted, previous generations of women had not experienced. Clothes now reflected this new freedom with the introduction of the mini skirt by London's Mary Quant—the skirts were so short that, paradoxically, secretaries had to have modesty panels added to their desks to keep their male colleagues from looking up their minis. Driven by this new freedom young women from Scandinavia, Germany, France, and Italy flocked to London as would-be models, as *au pair* girls, or merely as the idle rich in search of the hedonistic lifestyle being trumpeted in the media. Discotheques sprang up all over the city. At the Rheingold Club one would meet a beautiful *au pair* girl from Denmark taking time out from her medical studies or an aspiring model from Vienna. The strobe lights flashed, the girls looked impossibly beautiful and invulnerable, and as Jacques Brel sang *"Ne me quitte pas"* the music seemed timeless.

On giant billboards across London loomed the iconic model Twiggy, a skeletonic figure who fittingly seemed to embody the (unconscious) fear of universal death in that decade. A supermodel, bereft, it appeared, of *mons veneris*, she seemed a Death-in Life invented by Carnaby Street to preside over the vast *Totentanz* that possessed the city. In the art galleries the mutilated portraits of Francis Bacon haunted the collective unconsciousness like a nightmare. *Timor mortis conturbat me.*

My favourite recreational place was the Irish Club on Eaton Square. It had a very fine restaurant, it held dances at weekends, and it sponsored a visiting programme, often with Irish speakers. Conor Cruise O'Brien, the opinionated but very talented Irish journalist and diplomat, came one night and was loudly booed when the audience disagreed with him as he tried to make the case for Ulster Unionism. There was a bar where everyone congregated between dances. I took Ross Woodman to the Irish Club one evening—on his first visit to the UK. He didn't dance but rather sat all night talking with the Irish actor Cyril Cusack who was then a member of the Royal Shakespeare Company but had just finished work on the film *The Spy Who Came in from the Cold.*

But my year in London was coming to an end when I must return to Canada. In spring of 1965 I wrote to three universities in Ontario to enquire about a teaching position. An answer came back shortly from the University of Guelph offering me a job, the telegram was signed by Murdo MacKinnon, formerly of Western, now the Dean of Arts of the newly established University of Guelph. By the time I flew back to Canada in

August I had completed my PhD dissertation which I packed in a separate bag with my two plays *The Gunner's Rope* and *Joan of Arc's Violin*. I knew very little about Guelph, but it was to be my home for the rest of my life.

Marriage, Politics, and Marshall McLuhan

It was hot on the evening of my arrival in Guelph as I walked from my hotel to the city centre which was identified by a royal crown hung over it. A large and beautiful church on a height overlooked the city—the Church of Our Lady I was told. During dinner I read through various pamphlets describing Guelph and was pleasantly surprised to discover that it had been founded at the beginning of the nineteenth century by John Galt, who was not only an astute business man but a poet and novelist and the biographer of the painter Benjamin West and Lord Byron, whom he knew well. It was also the birthplace of Colonel John McCrae, famous for his poem "In Flanders Fields."

> *Short days ago*
> *We lived, felt dawn, saw sunset glow,*
> *Loved and were loved, and now we lie*
> *In Flanders fields.*

There was also mention of the tenor Edward Johnson with whose name and career I was to become very familiar in the years ahead.

The next day I walked up Gordon Street to the hill above Guelph and past the Ontario Veterinary College—one of the oldest in North America—past Macdonald Institute, a women's college specializing in home economics, and across the campus to the Ontario Agricultural College (where McCrae had been a lecturer in the English Department). The new college devoted to the arts, social sciences, and physical sciences known as Wellington College was located in various OAC buildings pending the building of its own building. The campus hummed with activity as student numbers multiplied, as new faculty were added, as new buildings went up, all preparing for the arrival of a new and dynamic President, William Winegard, who enjoyed a special *cachet* because when he joined the Canadian Navy during the war he was its youngest officer.

The English Department faculty grew from four to twenty-five within the next few years, and a new building, Corbusier-inspired in its architecture, was built to house the new college along with a number of student residences. The university's Senate, to which I was elected in 1967, often ran beyond midnight passing rules and regulations governing the conduct and future development of the university. One of the key areas of concern was the fact that the Library's holdings were completely inadequate to handle the needs of the new departments—many of us spent hours combing catalogues to order even the most basic books to make up functional bibliographies for our various courses. In one of those early summers of the new university I was given *carte blanche* to order whatever I wanted on a visit to London and Dublin. Because there were so many splendid bargains available in Dublin I bought a large number of first editions by leading authors like Yeats, Lady Gregory, Ezra Pound, T.S. Eliot, and Sean O'Casey—the Chief Librarian who assumed I would buy books for courses at the undergraduate level was not amused.

The dramatic growth in university enrollment in these years and the creation of a number of new universities (Guelph, Brock, Laurentian, Lakehead, York, Trent) and community colleges reflected an extraordinary change in the cultural life of Ontario (and of Canada). The Canada Council, created in 1957, was given a mandate to promote "the Arts, Letters, Humanities and Social Sciences" and received initial funding of fifty million dollars. Grants from the Council subsidized ballet companies, opera companies, publishing companies (which were thus encouraged to place more Canadian materials by Canadian novelists and poets on school and university curricula), theatres, and orchestras. A string of new theatres was built across Canada (the Manitoba Theatre Centre, 1957, the Vancouver Playhouse and Neptune Theatre in Halifax, the Edmonton's Citadel in 1965, Theatre Calgary and Theatre New Brunswick in 1968, the National Arts Centre, Ottawa in 1969, for example). The Shaw Festival opened in 1962. Importantly, Canada Council grants and federal works programs helped to establish an alternate theatre that laid great emphasis on Canadian social and political issues and championed Canadian plays. The 1967 Centennial celebrations were a sign of a country come of age, a country whose de-colonization was symbolized by the adoption of a Canadian flag in 1965. It was also comically symbolized when a few years later a young Englishman named Robin Phillips, appointed Artistic Director of Canada's Stratford Festival, was challenged to a duel (with swords) on the grounds that a foreigner should not have been appointed to such a culturally sensitive post.

The most important event of these years was the entry into my life of a young woman named Renate Niklaus, from Dusseldorf, Germany, who was studying for her PhD at McGill University. She came to Guelph as a German lecturer in the summer of 1966. I thought she was absolutely striking—people often compared her to Romy Schneider, the astonishingly beautiful Austrian actress. Renate and I were married in the Church of Our Lady and our wedding cost something in the neighbourhood of three hundred dollars because she made her own wedding dress and we held the wedding reception in the house we were renting with food made by Renate and her bridesmaid, Kari, also of the German Department. And so began a marriage that endured for more than fifty years, a relationship involving fierce love and equally fierce fights to achieve an emotional and intellectual partnership, a shared love of international travel, and an enduring interest in literature that blossomed in discussing and translating German and French works into English. I had been a dilettante in my relationship with women until then, drifting aimlessly and with little emotional engagement with them, very often lonely. But now my life was changed—here was a young lovely woman who filled my days and nights. No more loneliness. Talking, dancing, laughing, making love, making plans, arguing, discovering (for me) an entirely new world of being together with someone whose variety was unending. There seemed nothing Renate could not do to perfection. In her kitchen she created wonderful dishes—slim *Wiener Schnitzel*, tasty *Rouladen* and *Sauerbraten*, *Coq au Vin*, and her speciality *Königin-Pastete* which made the Director General of the Canadian Opera Company, Herman Geiger-Torel, marvel. She bought fruits and vegetables in the local Farmers' Market, under the spires of the Church of Our Lady, and our kitchen filled with the smells of peaches, plums and apricots being bottled and of onions, gherkins, cucumbers and pumpkin being preserved in vinegar, sugar, cinnamon, and cloves. She had a sewing machine on which she made some of the children's clothing and for her beautiful doll's house she created clothes and furniture of the most exquisite character. And as she had taught her two younger sisters to sing German folk songs and operatic arias, so she taught me many of the same melodies. (When she lay dying more than fifty years later, ravaged by dementia, I sang these same songs to her as I struggled to hide my tears.) At Christmas and New Year and at parties with German friends I played the piano as we sang the songs of her youth—*Aber Heidschi bumbeidschi*, Die Leineweber, Die Gedanken sind frei:

> *Die gedanken sind frei, wer kann sie erraten,*
> *Sie fliehen vorbei wie nächtliche Schatten.*
> *Kein Mensch kann sie wissen, kein Jäger sie schiessen,*
> *Es bleibet dabei: Die Gedanken sind frei!*

And through Renate I became familiar with a great many German-language authors—Mann, Kafka, Brecht, Rilke, Dürrenmatt, Frisch, Grass, and Expressionist dramatists such as Toller and Kaiser. The Book of Proverbs speaks of the virtues of a good wife "Whose worth is far above rubies." Such was Renate.

If this description of our life together sounds too idyllic, it is. For always the shadow hung over Renate of her blighted childhood. Born in 1938 in Tilsit, East Prussia (renamed Sovetsk and incorporated in Russia in 1945), she lived with her family in Berlin (her father was a senior officer in the *Wehrmacht*). During her most impressionable years (from four to seven) she experienced the horror of Allied massive air raids, sometimes carried out by as many as one thousand bombers at their deadly business of destroying the most important city in northern Europe. Fleeing to Bavaria in February 1945, she and her family boarded the last train leaving Dresden before it was fire-bombed that night and the following day by the RAF. When we first met she would awaken me in the middle of the night with her screams; the nightmares of her childhood pursued her even as an adult. Adding to the trauma of those years was her growing knowledge as a university student and lecturer of Germany's role in the mass slaughter of millions of Jews at camps such as Dachau, Auschwitz, Majdanek, Buchenwald, Treblinka, Bergen-Belsen. The monstrous list went on and on. How does she come to terms with Germany's twentieth-century demonic history? How can she ask her students to read such authors as Goethe, Lessing, von Kleist, Schiller, Rilke, Thomas Mann when some see the very culture of which they are an integral part as being irremediably linked in some way to the brutal ideology that spawned Hitler and

Nazism? Perhaps that was why Renate turned to the writings of Erich Kästner for answers when she wrote her PhD dissertation, the same Kästner who saw his books (including the wonderful children's story *Emil und die Detektive*) burned by the Nazi in Berlin in 1933. When we were in Dusseldorf in 1970 visiting her parents she took time out to fly to Munich to chat with him about the key theme in her dissertation, the moral vision which Kästner espoused, a vision of freedom and tolerance. After a long day of discussion at his home he began to show signs of wishing to finish their work at which point his companion, a young woman, led Renate out. It was not that the master was tired, she explained, but rather that he wanted to catch his favourite TV program *I Dream of Jeannie*. A month later he sent her a letter praising her dissertation; the letter became the Preface to the dissertation when it was published in 1973 by *Bouvier Verlag* as *Erich Kästner: Studien zu Seinen Werk*. It was the last article Kästner wrote before he died a year later.

In 1966 I defended my PhD dissertation: "James Joyce: Orthodoxy and Heterodoxy." The defence, the last stage in determining whether the candidate can be admitted to those who are licensed to teach in a university, is a carefully prescribed ritual dating back to mediaeval times (and even earlier in Muslim civilization). For some two hours the candidate is faced by a panel of professors whose business it is to interrogate him or her on matters directly or indirectly related to the dissertation topic. However, an examiner may not ask the candidate about Mesopotamian Gutian-period pottery, for example, if there is no reference, direct or indirect, to such pottery in the dissertation. At the conclusion of the defence a vote is called on whether to pass or fail the candidate. There are variations on this procedure governing the defence. In Finland and Sweden candidates, who must dress in tails and white tie, are faced by officially appointed "opponents" who challenge them to mortal intellectual combat. Successful candidates must then host, at their own expense, an evening of eating and drinking for the examining board. In Spain, so highly regarded are those who are admitted to the rank of Ph.D. that they are entitled—along with Grandees and Dukes—to sit without hats in the presence of the King.

The University of Toronto at that time treated the PhD defence very seriously. The Committee which examined me consisted of nine professors, seven of them English professors from various colleges of the university, one a professor of French, and the Chair, a Professor Warder from the

Department of East Asian Studies. I was facing a formidable opponent. We met in a room at University College, civilities were exchanged, the defence began, the time went quickly. Professor Shook and Professor Lynch asked questions mainly in the area of the mediaeval figures that I had linked to Joyce's writing—Duns Scotus, Aquinas, Joachim of Flora, among others. Professor Rosenbaum focused on my analysis of Joyce's debt to Giovanni Vico and his philosophy of history. Professor Carroll was interested in Joyce's links with fellow Irish writers Yeats and Beckett, Endicott questioned me on matters bibliographical, the French professor did not question me nor did Frye. Things went very well for me as I fielded probing and far ranging questions with Warder vigilant to make sure my interests were protected and that academic protocol was observed. Last came Marshall McLuhan.

While I admired McLuhan (just months before I had sat up all night reading his *Understanding Media*), I was not intimidated by him. During my two years as a doctoral student I had run into him on a number of occasions and he was always quite friendly. On two of these occasions I attended talks that he gave to Catholic groups in the evening at church locations and there he was the most genial of lecturers, never condescending but genuinely interested in explaining, without affectation, his ideas to groups of lay people. And so at my defence, knowing that I was almost finished, I faced McLuhan without any sense of fear or foreboding. I knew that he detested linearity, that his line of questioning was likely to be unconventional, that he liked to link heterogeneous ideas in order to find a new synthesis, but I felt well prepared and ready for him. He asked his first question and my heart sank as I realized that I had absolutely no idea what he was talking about. All I remember of that question now is its random nature as if he had asked me, say, to comment on the relationship of tectonic plates to Mesopotamian pottery of the Gutian era and the relationship of both to Joyce's blindness. I sat silently, desperately seeking some linkage in McLuhan's question to my dissertation. Finding none, I told him politely that I did not understand his question. He asked me a second question and now I began to panic. Again I had absolutely no idea what he was talking about. My mind raced frantically. This can't be happening to me, I know my material, I'm well prepared, what is going on? He mentioned the Gobi Desert (I think), the invention of the machine gun and the novels of Thackeray—what has this to do with my thesis topic?

I breathed deeply, grappled with the terms that had been thrown at me, and finally confessed (again) that I did not understand the question. There was visible unease in the room. Frye's fingers thrummed ceaselessly on the table beside me, other panel members shuffled uncomfortably, and McLuhan plainly showed his irritation. Came his third question. I listened carefully, concentrating (*don't panic*), but again the question was as sibylline and unintelligible as the previous two. I knew little of the relationship of tectonic plates or the Gobi Desert to Joyce's work but there were a thousand things I did know—why he used paronomasia so frequently throughout *Finnegans Wake*; the role the Tibetan Book of the Dead played in his thinking; his opinion of Napoleon. But now I too was irritated and it showed. A mistake. Maybe he is trying your mettle, I told myself. Keep calm. *Keep calm.* A precept sometimes ignored. (As on the occasion when a female candidate under questioning by Professor Woodhouse burst into a storm of tears which, in turn, provoked Professor Kathleen Coburn, an authority on Coleridge, to rebuke Woodhouse for his callous behaviour before departing in high dungeon to give solace to the candidate still weeping with unmitigated force in the corridors of University College. While the female candidate did gain enough votes to pass she undoubtedly increased Woodhouse's misogyny. But I think I digress.) As my irritation grew as did the tension in the room. Warder cut in and terminated the questioning and the meeting. I waited outside while the votes were canvassed and was relieved when Frye came out and told me all was well, that I had passed. I could keep my hat on if I should ever find myself in the presence of the King of Spain.

When I look back on that day, now so long ago, I still cannot explain why McLuhan acted so bizarrely. If insanity can be defined as that state where one has lost touch with reality, I believe that McLuhan was insane on that day. I also believe that a partial reason for his conduct lies in the fact that he was "an intellectual thug"—his own phrase to describe himself. He purposely enraged his colleagues by hijacking a wide variety of authors—whom they knew intimately following years of study and research—to reinforce and substantiate claims in a field they did not understand, a field which of which he was a principal inventor: communications. For example, he referred constantly to the French Symbolists despite having little fluency in French, and I am convinced that he had never read *Finnegans Wake* in its entirety, that he used it mainly as academic dressing to offset his image as an intellectual *manqué*. His academic colleagues were right to resent his status as a professor of English; they were wrong not to recognize that he was really an enormously gifted and intuitive pioneer in the field of communications who was stuck in a traditional department of English. So when McLuhan was questioning me at my defence he was not interested in knowing what my thesis said about Joyce but in hijacking the traditional protocol that governed such an academic process as the PhD defence to pursue his own idiosyncratic themes. His conduct was also a deliberate defiance of Frye in his role as my supervisor—each detested the other. And his conduct that day was also a warning sign of what was to come. The following year McLuhan underwent a life-threatening operation to remove a tumour from his brain, an operation which damaged irrevocably that once splendid intellect.

In 1967 my career took a new turning. I was asked to stand as the New Democratic Party candidate in the 1967 provincial election called by the Conservative Premier John Robarts. And so began a whirlwind period of campaigning, up at six every morning seeking votes at factory gates, scrambling desperately to keep up with my lectures, department, college, and Senate meetings, and then speaking at various venues in the city and throughout Wellington County. Late at night I would read the various position papers issued by the NDP from Toronto in order to brief myself on such varied and arcane matters (to me) as housing, farm subsidies, the tax loopholes enjoyed by Big Business, *ex parte* injunctions, and what were provincial issues and what federal issues. My principal opponent was the sitting Liberal member, Harry Worton, a former baker—the federal Conservative member, Alf Hales, was a butcher. Worton was renowned, his critics said, for never having spoken in the Legislature during his thirty-year term. A local radio sports commentator, Norm Jary, represented the provincial Conservative party.

The publicity director for my campaign was a transplanted American euphonically named Homer Hogan, also a member of the Department of English, who wrote copy about me that had little relation to what I actually said or did. I often spoke at small rural meetings but when I read Hogan's account of my speeches they tackled areas (in masterful fashion) that I had not ventured into. He wrote my campaign song to an old IRA ballad tune, "Off to Dublin in the Green," which blared from my downtown Head Quarters with new words by Hogan that mocked the ruling party for not allowing women to buy the contraceptive pill:

*In Ontario no drug store
Is allowed to sell the Pill,
So we keep the population down
By sheer exercise of will.*

This was undoubtedly meant to *épater le bourgeois* but it was hardly likely to win votes in the rural and conservative areas of Wellington County.

Further aiding Hogan in publicizing my campaign was John Cripton, a student in my course on the English Romantic poets. For one of his in-class assignments he did a multi-media presentation on Coleridge's poem "The Rime of the Ancient Mariner." It was a remarkable performance in its integration of sound, illustrations, voice, and music—a skillful collage of passages from composers like Stravinsky, Prokofiev, Ginastera, and Britten—and all done with an extraordinary professionalism. The students recognized its brilliance with an ovation as I did by awarding it with a mark of 98 percent only matched later by one of my students Mary Hofstetter who went on to become President of Sheridan College, Administrative Director of the Stratford Festival, and President of the Banff Centre for the Arts.

Cripton decided that my campaign would feature what he modestly called the first psychedelic political rally in the world. It would involve strobe lighting, specially choreographed dances and sketches, beautiful girls, and conclude climactically with a speech by me, the event to take place in the venerable War Memorial Hall, University of Guelph. All took place as Cripton had decreed. The Hall filled up, dominated largely by Ontario Agricultural College students in the gallery strongly opposed to the NDP and Arts and Social Science students ("artsies") who largely supported me. As I watched from the wings, a student-faculty pick-up-orchestra played while scantily clad girls, students, and departmental secretaries danced under vision-inducing strobe lights to Cripton's politically motivated script. When my turn came, I attacked the Board of Governors for not having students, women, professors, or working-class people in its membership. I argued that university education should be free, citing common European practice. I spoke in favour of abolishing the puritanical laws governing the sale of liquor and beer in the province, I criticized the lack of housing for the poor and the government's refusal to allow the sale in pharmacies of the contraceptive, and I attacked the government for never having implemented the child daycare program it routinely promised. Every proposal I advanced was met by loud disapproval (including boos) from the gallery counter-pointed by cheers from my supporters. I departed from my text to address directly those who disagreed with me so that a wonderful dialogue developed amid the clamour and the shouting. So emotional was the evening that one professor (my supporter) hit an OAC student with her handbag and had to apologise repeatedly for such a breach of manners. It was a marvelous evening, more like a rock concert than a political rally, that bore no resemblance to today's political rallies where opponents are routinely ejected for even the politest dissent.

During the campaign I was called to Toronto for a meeting of all the candidates standing for the NDP and here I met for the first time the leader Donald MacDonald, and Walter Pitman, Stephen Lewis, and Morton Shulman, among others. The contrast between Pitman and Lewis was striking, the former engaging and full of charm, the latter cerebral and extraordinarily rhetorical. I met briefly with Shulman who asked me what riding I represented. He then told me bluntly that I didn't have a chance and cited off hand the details of Worton's last three victories in the polls. I was astonished at his memory and his frankness, but as I followed his career in the NDP (he won his riding handily) I realized that it was motivated more out of revenge (he had been fired by the Conservative government as Toronto's chief coroner) than out of a belief in NDP policy. A brilliant maverick, he became a TV personality with a program "The Shulman File," a series that featured unusually abrasive interviews. My dislike of him grew when in one interview I saw him mock Timothy Findley on the grounds that he was a homosexual and that he made little money as a writer.

But Shulman was right in forecasting that I would lose the election and that Worton would win. At the time I regretted my loss but very soon I came to recognize that I had gained valuable experience and a heightened sense of matters political. As the years went by I met many politicians—renewed acquaintance with Pitman, Stephen Lewis, and continued a deep friendship with Winegard who became a Cabinet Minister in Brian Mulroney's government. But the more I learned of politics the more I realized the truth of Lord Acton's truism, "Power corrupts, absolute power corrupts absolutely." I met ministers in Ottawa who were so insulated after a few years in office that they lost all sense of public accountability (I am thinking here particularly of Francis Fox with whom I had dealings). Rewards were handed out on a partisan basis—lawyers received the honorary title of Queen's Counsel or King's Counsel based too often on their political stripe—and the judiciary—even to the level of Supreme Court appointees—were too often chosen in the same manner. The Royal Canadian Mounted Police acted as if they were above the law, wiretapping such distinguished figures as Tommy Douglas; burning barns in Quebec in order discredit the FLQ, a Quebec separatist group; forging documents; infiltrating university student organizations; and conducting illegal break-ins. I came to recognize that political parties put party interest before the good of the nation or ethical considerations and that this had always been so. When I came to write my second novel *Power Game: The Making of a Prime Minister* these considerations were in my mind. That novel was written in the Horatian mode but it might more fittingly have been pitched in a Juvenalian key.

After the election I returned with renewed vigour to my university life with its growing numbers of students and where all around me departments were recruiting. Among these recruits were some memorable characters such as a young and personable psychology professor who used to sell *objets d'art* from his office—I bought a painting of a semi nude woman from him mainly because of its lushly wrought Victorian gilt frame. One semester when he did not return I asked Dean Murdo MacKinnon where he was and discovered that MacKinnon had fired him because his art sales were a cover for the drugs he sold to students and faculty alike. Another professor in Spanish studies, hired from the USA, was an outspoken anti-Semite who interspersed his lectures with admiring comments on Hitler. When he charged Dean MacKinnon with attempting to seduce his wife he also was dismissed. I should add that no one believed the professor's charge since his wife had one of the more unfortunate figures of the twentieth century with a face to match. At this time I organized an extension course featuring mainly lecturers from the English and Languages Departments speaking on major international writers. A young Chinese part time lecturer, married to a student doing post-graduate work in entomology at the OAC, gave me the text of her talk on a Chinese author but told me that it must be presented by her husband. Pressed as to why, she said it would not be respectful to her husband for her to speak publicly and thus claim some kind of superior status. When I pointed out that her audience might feel it was disrespectful to have her paper read by someone who did not know the subject, she finally consented to read her own paper—after discussion with her husband. An interesting end note on this matter was that when I met her husband I discovered that though he spent his time working with insects he risked his life in doing so because of an extreme allergy to many varieties of these insects.

This was also the time of the flower child and the hippie who dreamed of a new Golden Age leavened by love and pot. *Hair* and Elvis Presley and the Beatles and The Doors were all the rage and students waved their Little Red Book of Mao, unaware that his touted Chinese Cultural Revolution was, in reality, the most brutal assault on China's cultural heritage and institutions in its history. Harvard professor Timothy Leary promoted psychedelic drugs with the mantra, "Turn on, tune in, drop out." In my class on Blake in one of these years there was a young man who listened so intently to my lectures and with such appreciation that I looked forward to meeting him when he turned in his first paper. Instead, he made an appointment to see me about six weeks into the term and when he appeared it was to announce that Blake (and I) had persuaded him of the truth of the Blakean aphorism that "The tigers of wrath are wiser than the horses of instruction." He was dressed for a journey to a cottage somewhere up north, he told me, taking only one suitcase, a volume of Blake's poetry, and a knapsack of marijuana. He had found what he wanted and now the university could offer him no more. I wished him well and we parted and I never saw him again. But I think that in some strange way he was a true disciple of Blake who understood the aphorism, "The road of excess leads to the palace of wisdom." Of course, Leary may have been his guru, not Blake.

In the English Department I soon became friends with John Harney who had run as a federal candidate for the NDP. He was a brilliant young academic who had published various poems in the Chicago magazine *Poetry* (joining fellow contributors T.S. Eliot, Robert Frost, Wallace Stevens, and Robert Bly). Dinner parties at his house were always a delight featuring good food and political talk, the *pièce de résistance* being a post-prandial concert performed at full volume by Harney on his Scottish bagpipes. John soon left the Department to take up the post of Secretary of the Ontario NDP, later winning a seat in the federal parliament. He lost that seat after two years when he went sailing off the coast of Greece broadcasting messages to the mainland demanding the resignation of the Greek colonels who had seized power there—his constituents felt that he should really be at home looking after their pensions and passports and other such interests. Fluently bi-lingual, he later re-incarnated himself as Jean-Paul Harney in the hope of revitalizing the Quebec wing of the NDP.

It was hard not be political at this time when students in North America and Europe were rioting against what they perceived as repressive and criminal governments. In the USA they conducted sit-ins on campuses and marched on the Pentagon to protest the butchery in Vietnam, French students protested colonial rule and their Government's atrocities in Algeria, and in Germany the visit of the Shah of Persia to Berlin in 1967 triggered student unrest. In 1969 when I was acting Chair of the English Department I had dozens of applications from American professors at established universities seeking a position with our Department because of fear that their sons might be drafted into the armed forces. It has often been argued that television coverage from the battlefields of Vietnam brought about its end. But the influence of the draft was also of great importance for now that affluent students could be sent off to fight and die in an unpopular war their parents—very often associated with universities, the media, and large corporations—exercised great pressure to safeguard their sons. The war in Afghanistan has been largely fought in the twenty-first century by an American volunteer army, made up mostly of the disadvantaged and people of colour, and there have been no comparable marches on the Pentagon or sit-ins on college campuses. It is always comforting to be able to combine political idealism with self-interest.

Canada and Canadian universities also shared this sense of *Sturm und Drang* featuring sit-ins and anti-war marches. In Quebec, in 1970, the *Front de Libération du Québec* (FLQ) kidnapped Pierre Laporte, a Cabinet minister, and murdered him—they may have been encouraged by General de Gaulle who came to Quebec in 1967 to infamously declaim, *Vivre le Québec libre*. Given the fact that De Gaulle's Chief of Police for Paris had killed hundred of protestors against the Algerian War in the early 1960s (in addition to collaborating with the Nazis in the deportation of French Jews to their deaths), de Gaulle's words rang somewhat hollow and justified the Canadian government declaring him *persona non grata*. But in general, the 1960s was a good period in Canada with Conservative and Liberal governments led by Diefenbaker, Lester Pearson, and Trudeau capped by Expo'67 at Montreal. It is a mark of Canadian moderation that the strongest protests at the University of Guelph were marked by a short and civilized sit-in at President Winegard's office and the hiring by the student body—without consultation with the University—of an anti-establishment poet.

And so it was that the poet Irving Layton came to the campus in 1969. Short, stubby, with an leonine mane and a swagger born of a *machismo* that he flaunted like a matador, he installed himself for a term in one of the student residences where he announced scandalously that he was open to meet the student body, pen ready and his pants unbuttoned. I had long admired Layton's poetry and thought his 1959 *A Red Carpet for the Sun* a volume of international stature. In his poetry he harnessed the irrational and the sexual in a way that was new to Canadian poetry and his flaunting of his own *persona* and his attacks on what was conventional in politics, art, and literature made him as public a figure in Canada as Dylan Thomas had been a decade earlier in the UK and the USA. Shortly after he arrived on campus, I invited Layton to lecture to my third-year class. He read poetry in a powerful guttural voice where he seemed to crush each word before spitting it out. After hearing a recording of, say, T.S. Eliot reading in his arid, deacon-like voice, a Layton reading was a pleasure, full of passion and denunciation, combining preaching with a prophet's power and incantatory rhetoric. He was also a teacher of unusual reach who generated controversy wherever he went. During his time as poet in residence on the Guelph campus it took the form of students who worshipped him and others who attacked his poetry for its demagoguery and disdain of women and its hatred of the WASP culture of which they were a part. Renate and I invited Layton often to our house and in the course of many evenings we discovered that the *persona* he cultivated so assiduously did not truly correspond with the reality. This was clearly evident in the deep attachment he had to his wife Aviva when she came to Guelph occasionally to visit him. But that deep attachment threatened his sense of himself as a Don Juan and so he sacrificed it for an illusion of himself as a great lover, poet, and voluptuary. But, as he ruefully admitted to us, the female undergraduates were suspicious of him and while they were drawn to his growing celebrity they were not willing to trade their dreams of marriage for someone who so obviously despised that institution.

Irving came to us many evenings when we had good dinners with lots of wine and light classical music—at that time a favourite of ours was

Gluck's "Dance of the Blessed Spirits" and Rodrigues' *Concierto de Aranjuez*. After dinner there was more wine and Layton would ask for the music which he loved—Theodorakis' score for the film *Zorba the Greek*. Arm in arm, Renate, Irving, and I danced the evenings away to the music of the *bouzouki*. On those evenings Irving saw himself as another Zorba destined to teach WASPish Canadians from Newfoundland to British Columbia to dance to the orgiastic music of his poetry. After Layton left the campus I seldom saw him but I continued to read his poetry with interest. He published a number of poems equalled in quality by only a few of his peers, but few of his peers would have allowed themselves to publish so many poems that were careless and a reproach to the artistry that had once so adorned his work. W.B. Yeats was a poet that Layton admired and he might have learned from his example for Yeats is pre-eminently the poet of middle age and old age. When he was almost fifty he wrote "The Coming of Wisdom with Age" where he declared:

> *Through all the lying days of my youth*
> *I swayed my leaves and flowers in the sun;*
> *Now I may wither into truth.*

Yeats went on to publish some of the finest poetry of the twentieth century; Layton, drawn into political controversy and rootless in his personal life, lost his way and his vision of the nobility of the craft of writing. My last meeting with him was at a Canada PEN dinner-dance in Montreal in 1990. With some maliciousness I suspect, his Quebec hosts had placed him at a table with the feminist Betty Friedman whom he despised. I saw him watch, with a kind of sad lust, as young women writers from countries around the world danced by him and all the time Friedan, between mouthfuls of chicken, held him captive with statistics about the enslavement of women in North America. Dear, driven Irving, you were truly a force of nature. Rest well and blessings on your weary poet's head.

About this time I wrote a short play *The Ram* which arose out of my preoccupation with the tragedy of the Holocaust. In the play a German officer accused of complicity in the killings is interrogated by a Jewish American officer who is appalled when the German argues with seeming sincerity that the Holocaust was a part of God's plan and merely another facet of the mystery of the origin of Evil in the world. It was broadcast in 1967 by

Radio McGill, Montreal. When I was asked by some students in the University of Guelph Drama Society to direct a one-act play which would be entered in the Inter-university drama competition of Ontario I suggested we present the premiere of *The Gunner's Rope* which I had written in London, England. The students were agreeable and so I and my co-director, a young woman studying at the Veterinary College, worked hard to prepare the two students playing the roles of two old men who must decide which one will die so that the other may live on two pensions. The first round of the competition was held at McMaster University in Hamilton with plays by Sartre, Ionesco, and Anouilh entered by other university drama groups. To my surprise the adjudicator awarded us first place. I invited him for a drink afterwards and so I met Ely Yost, then a high school teacher, who was beginning to become known as a host on the CBC. Bald headed, with an infectious laugh and enthusiasm, he talked of his long interest in drama but very soon veered to his favourite subject which was movies and here he spoke with what seemed like encyclopedic knowledge. I was not surprised when a few years later he became host of the long-running CBC program "Saturday Night at the Movies" when he interviewed celebrities connected with the films he loved. *The Gunner's Rope* had a further life. In 1969 I sent it to the CBC with my other London play *Joan of Arc's Violin* where they eventually landed on the desk of Robert Weaver, the *éminence grise* behind such writers as Mordechai Richler, Alice Munro, Timothy Findley, and many others. Weaver liked my plays and had both of them broadcast by the CBC. He followed that by commissioning a further radio play from me *The Doctors' Wife* that involved multiple murders; in our correspondence he addressed me as Hitchcock, after the famous film director.

A measure of my involvement with university life is that at one point I discovered that I was on twenty-one committees covering everything from departmental committees on tenure and promotion to College committees like the B.A. Board of Review to Senate committees such as that on Academic Administrative Organization which over a two-year period from 1968 to 1970 examined the relationship between the four colleges of the University and devised a new administrative structure; Wellington College became two colleges—the College of Arts and the College of Social Sciences- and Macdonald Institute received new focus as the College of Family and Consumer Studies. The Department of English developed an MA program and that entailed reading and directing MA theses. I also sat for two years on the Committee of Ontario Universities (the President and one professor for each university) which provided me with an over view of the educational scene at a time when the student population was exploding. I published a number of articles in the *Canadian Association Universities Bulletin* exposing the consequent lowering of academic standards. Until the middle 1960s, for example, all students entering language courses at university level had at least five years high school education in that language. Now that requirement was dropped and highly trained professors were forced to teach their students the A B Cs of French and German and other languages. Even in professional courses such as engineering, students had to be given remedial training in mathematics and physics in contrast to the early 1960s when they had entered university well prepared. Perhaps nothing could have been done to prevent such dilution of standards—the students were still as intelligent and eager to learn. It was the system that was failing them. I myself, lacking modern languages, took a course for one semester in Italian and another semester course in German but I never had time to achieve fluency in either language.

While sitting on the Committee of Ontario Universities between 1970 and 1972, I finally met the Premier of Ontario, John Robarts, who granted the Committee an interview, or perhaps I should call it an audience. He was a patrician figure, in his middle fifties, handsome, remote. He talked to us for ten minutes, speaking from a prepared speech, and then, surrounded protectively by aides, he left the room without answering questions. The next time I met him was in September 1982 at the Gala Concert celebrating the opening of Toronto's Roy Thompson Hall. It was a very high-profile occasion with dinner served in the Hall before the concert—vintage wines in crystal glasses, food catered by Winston's, formal wear, medals and decorations to be worn. At one point I sat down on a large bench by myself to eat dessert when I was joined by a man I recognized immediately—John Robarts. We said good evening, but he seemed not to want to become engaged in conversation and so we sat side by side in silence as we ate. I was surprised that no one approached him to congratulate him on his services as a politician or merely to offer good wishes. Perhaps the inaccessibility he had so cultivated throughout his political life kept well-wishers at a distance. I was very shocked when a month later I read that he had committed suicide by use of a shotgun, exactly as his son had done at the age of twenty-one.

    We worked hard and we played hard. We had many friends including Renate's colleague in the Department of German, Manfred Kremer and his wife whose company Renate especially enjoyed because of shared German interests. In summers Renate and I traveled widely. To Dusseldorf, Germany, and its charming and sophisticated *alt Stadt;* a tour of Ireland, a country Renate only knew from the travel account *Irische Tagebuch* by Heinrich Böll; and our first trip to Dubrovnik, Yugoslavia. Winston Churchill in a famous speech had spoken of an "iron curtain" that had isolated Eastern and Central Europe and its great cities. I wanted to travel behind that curtain and to see something of Communism and so in the summer of 1968 Renate and I drove into Yugoslavia via the Ljubljana Gap and south east to Belgrade. We drove though mountain passes and towering mountains with roads lacking guard rails of any kind while racing rivers thundered below and through villages with names undecipherable to us, villages that had little changed in a thousand years. In the inns there were roaring fires because high in the mountains it was cold. And there were huge hams hanging in the bars and beers unknown to me and wines and liqueurs with no labels that tasted wonderful after a hard day's driving. In the course of a month we visited Sofia in Bulgaria, then on to Varna on the Black Sea, to Bucharest, Rumania, and finally Budapest, Hungary, preparatory to visiting Prague. My memories are of fields of sun flowers in sun drenched fields, truculent border guards (entering Hungary, one confiscated my copy of William Manchester's biography of J.F. Kennedy), restaurants offering a wide variety of dishes that usually turned out to feature only *Jamón* or *Schinken* (surprisingly, German was the language of tourism in the Eastern Europe we visited). Accommodation varied from huge hotel rooms to boarding house rooms filled with the stale smell of potatoes and cabbage, and a censorship of most Western newspapers so severe that in Varna I was reduced to "reading" a daily Dutch newspaper that, inexplicably, was in the local library. We stayed for two weeks in Varna where on the beach we met many people—mainly East Germans, Romanians, and Russians—who were eager to learn from us something of the West. When we talked of politics they immediately fell silent or used code words among themselves. When they said that they liked jazz very much this was as far as they would go in admitting an admiration for things Western and when they blamed food shortages on the bureaucrats this was their way of condemning the *apparatchik* for their dachas and mistresses and access to shops that sold Western foods and luxury items which they were denied. We had intended to finish our trip by driving from Budapest to Prague for we had heard a great deal about the "Prague spring"—the relaxation of censorship in Czechoslovakia and the flourishing of such writers as Milan Kundera, Václav Havel, and Josef Škvorecký, and the stage designer Josef Svoboda whose multimedia show *Laterna Magika* had astonished audiences at Montreal's Expo'67. On the morning of 21 August as we were having breakfast in our hotel in Budapest we noticed great excitement, alarm even, at the adjoining tables and discovered that Russian armed forces had invaded Czechoslovakia and that Russian tanks were on the streets of Prague. We changed our plans and drove instead to Vienna and then for the last two weeks of our European holiday to Murnau, in Bavaria (in Guelph the local newspaper ran an article under the title "Bensons may be trapped in Prague"). Years later when I invited Škvorecký (now living in Toronto) to lecture at the university we spoke of that tumultuous summer.

During this summer vacation Renate continued work on her PhD dissertation. Her subject, Erich Kästner, seemed a fitting one given the totalitarianism that we saw all around us in Communist Europe. But what surprised us in Europe was a virulent anti-Americanism especially evident in France and England which dismissed the USA as a frontier country, with inferior educational institutes and little culture. (Canada was usually dismissed with variations on Voltaire's quip characterising the country as *Quelques arpents de pèige*). But the more I traveled in Europe (which I loved) I was struck and dismayed by its bloody history and I was forced to examine the role of the intellectual in European society and how, especially in the twentieth century, the intellectual class had too often been complicit in the crimes born of such monstrous ideologies as Hitler's National Socialism, Leninism, Stalinism, and Fascism—and colonialism. Throughout the 1950s and 1960s reports of the gulags operating in the USSR were widely documented in the West (Solzhenitsyn's *A Day in the Life of Ivan Denisovitch*, a chilling account of the horrors of the gulags, was published in 1962) yet French intellectuals such as Camus, Merleau-Ponty, Sartre, and de Bouvoir shut their eyes to these mass imprisonments and torture. The invasion of Czechoslovakia unfolding not a hundred kilometers from where I was staying in Murnau did shock the world into a truer understanding of what the stakes were in the Cold War and a truer understanding of the sophistries of so many European intellectuals who espoused Communism, sometimes out of a misreading of history, but too often out of an anti-Americanism rooted in ignorance, envy, and elitism. But every Revolution has its benefits and the West benefited from the many Czech artists who fled abroad like those Hungarian artists who fled in the wake of the abortive Hungarian Uprising of 1956. Škvorecký, for example, settled in Toronto and established *68 Publishing*, which promoted those central European writers whose voices totalitarianism could not tolerate.

More concrete values occupied me in the next few years following the birth of our first son Ormonde in 1970. I think his birth was especially significant for me because I was then forty-two years old and highly attuned to the rhythms of life and mortality. The sonnets of Shakespeare which I taught each year were full of this theme suggesting that only art and children could compensate one for the penalty of our individual birth and death. And it was also at this time when Renate defended her PhD dissertation at McGill University that we bought the house in which we still live almost fifty years later. It is a large, red brick house with stone lintels and decorative cornices, designed by an English architect Cornelius J. Soule, whose houses and public buildings can be found from Port Hope, Ontario, to Victoria, British Columbia. Built in the year 1887 for the Mayor of Guelph, Colonel A.H. MacDonald, for the sum of 2,500 pounds, it is a large, airy red brick house, 43 feet by 34 feet, on a lot that measures some 270 feet by 210 feet. Situated at the corner of Palmer St and Queen St., it is one of five large houses built on the hill fronting Queen St. thus giving a view of the city centre below. The ceilings on the ground floor of our house are eleven feet high with massive windows in the dining room and the living room. The design of the house allows for the morning sun to light the breakfast room and in the evening the western sun floods the living room. The Chinese-inspired staircase leading from the first floor to the second floor presents a fine sweep from the top of its twenty-two steps; when we gave parties this crimson-carpeted staircase provided a dramatic backdrop for the women in their evening gowns. At the top of the stairs is a large bookcase holding hundreds of books. Adjacent to it we have our study with two desks, and more books, for Renate and for me. My desk overlooks the lawns of the garden and the swimming pool.

From our bedroom we have a view over the city of Guelph and from it we can see the spires of St George's Church and the Church of our Lady. Our property abuts on probably the most impressive house in Guelph, Tyrcathlen, the stone Rectory built for Archdeacon Palmer from Dublin, Ireland (later Bishop of Toronto) who supervised the construction of St George's Church. It was renamed Ker Cavan in the 1920s by its new owner Harry Higinbotham, who besides being a very wealthy insurance executive was the patron of his fellow Guelphite Edward Johnson, the internationally acclaimed opera tenor.

In 1971 my father died at the age of eighty-four. Peacefully, in his bed. I did not feel the same sense of pain and trauma that I had experienced when my mother died, but I did feel an immense regret at the passing of a man I had always loved deeply, a man whom I also admired for his strength and good looks and charm. And how he could tell a story! There was no hesitation, no seeking to remember. Always the exact detail, "It was in 1911 in Tipperary on a Saturday morning, when I was on duty at the fair that it happened . . ." In memory I hear his voice and I rejoice that we shared so much during his life.

So it was that in 1971 we settled in our home that I grew to love with the passing years and where I sit now in my study in 2018, looking from time to time at the garden below, at the rock garden and the flower garden we started and at the bushes and trees we planted, grown from saplings to twenty feet high. I have grown to love this city where I finally settled, this city with its limestone buildings and its hills traversed by rivers and always the sounds of church bells and the music of the carillons. But if we were now finally settled in a beautiful house there was new work to be done. From the mediaeval world of wandering scholars and Gothic glory, there came again into my life those two doomed characters I had come to know so well—the philosopher Abelard and his lover, the nun Heloise.

Of Canadian Opera and Irish Poets

In those years—the 1960s and 1970s—music continued to play a very important in my life. Dean MacKinnon, himself a lover of music, wisely decided that Wellington College should have a Department of Music. His inspired choice to head the department was Nicholas Goldschmidt, an unlikely candidate because he lacked the kind of credentials one associates with an academic position. But he also lacked the pedantry that too often comes with entry into the hermetic world of academia. A product of Vienna's State Academy of Music where he was a student for six years, on graduation Goldschmidt became a conductor working in the many provincial opera houses and concert halls of Austria and Czechoslovakia (where he was born), in the process obtaining a practical knowledge of the vast repertoire of European opera and *Leider*. In one of these provincial opera houses (in Troppau, Czechoslovakia) he met the young conductor and stage director Herman Geiger-Torel who would join him and fellow Czech Arnold Walter in founding the Canadian Opera Company after the Second World War. Fleeing Europe to escape the Nazis, Goldschmidt eventually arrived in Toronto, becoming such an established figure by the 1960s that he was responsible for advising on all aspects of the performing arts relating to the celebration of Canada's Centennial in 1967. Such a man was unlikely to be satisfied with running a small university department and very soon he decided that Guelph should become the home of a great music festival. He would transform this small city of some 35,000 people into a venue rivaling Salzburg or Edinburgh. If Benjamin Britten could create a world-class music festival in the tiny village of Aldeburgh, England, and Tom Patterson an acclaimed theatre company in the village of Stratford, Canada, he, Goldschmidt, could do the same in Guelph. *Fiat festival musica!* And so it came about as he ordained.

There were other factors at work, of course. One does not merely order a universe into existence unless one is God, and Niki (as he became known to us) never did reach the status of Divinity, although he may have sought it. Successful festivals have characteristics that are born of association with special places (like Salzburg and, yes, Woodstock) and personalities (Mozart, Wagner, Britten). But Guelph did have a certain *cachet*—it could lay claim to such nationally known figures as Colonel John McCrae and Edward Johnson. The last name was especially potent in launching the Guelph Spring Festival—Johnson had been internationally known as an opera singer, he had sung under the baton of the great Toscanini, and had not Puccini himself created the tenor roles in his operas *Gianni Schicchi* and *Il Tabarro* for Edoardo di Giovanni as Johnson was known in Italy. But there was a further outreach—Johnson's daughter Fiorenza married Colonel George Drew, a prominent Conservative politician who later became Premier of Ontario and finally the Canadian High Commissioner in London. (Billy Bishop, the famed flying ace, was to be best man at their wedding but had to beg off at the last minute.) A Guelph Spring Festival could benefit from such an interface of politics, fame, and culture.

Niki was determined from the start that the Festival would feature an opera and his choice of Britten's *The Prodigal Son* as the Festival's first offering was an inspired one. It is a magnificent work blending the biblical simplicity of a New Testament parable and the theatricality of Japanese Noh theatre. The all-male cast is small—four principals with chorus, and an eight-piece orchestra. It was first performed in the church at Orford, Suffolk, England, as part of Britten's Aldeburgh Festival which led Niki—lacking an opera house—to tour Guelph's many churches. And there to hand was the perfect venue—The Church of Our Lady, majestically sited on a hill where all could see it! Designed by Joseph Connolly, a pupil of Pugin, the famous English architect, it is a smaller replica of the Cathedral of Cologne, Germany, with a magnificent exterior and a spacious interior with seating capacity (and good sight lines) for some eleven hundred people. Niki would be the musical director of the opera and for his stage director he imported Lode Verstraete, well known for his work in Belgium—one of Niki's uncles had been a diplomat in Belgium which explains the choice. Bill Lord, who had worked with Niki at the Canadian Opera Company, was the designer and his most imaginative stroke was to call for a stage-platform to hold the set which would be within the altar area. This presented daunting logistical problems since the opera's production had to be accommodated to the demands of the church where Mass, baptism, funeral services, and other ecclesiastical functions were conducted daily. The platform, reaching fifteen feet in height, was on such a steep rake that the singers had great difficulty in walking on it. John Cripton, a student in one of my classes, built it on a farm outside Guelph and arranged for its transportation and set up. Niki (and Murdo MacKinnon) drew me (willingly) into this web and so I became the Festival's unpaid Administrative Director and production manager for the North American premiere of *The Prodigal Son*. I, in turn, called on the resources of the University's Department of Drama—some of its staff were as expert as those at the Stratford Festival or the Royal Alex in Toronto. I also called on the resources of a local lawyer Peter Gifford to help me with budgetary matters--he and his wife Marilyn soon became close friends. By the time Verstraete arrived from Belgium three weeks before opening night, much had been done—Niki's work with the singers was well advanced, the set had been constructed, the costumes were being made by Malabar of Toronto to Lord's design; and a detailed timetable governing every aspect of production had been developed. Verstraete pronounced himself pleased.

Opening night, 3 May 1969, was splendid, pleasantly warm. When *The Prodigal Son* began at eight thirty the Church of Our Lady was still glowing with the light of the evening sun, and as the opera progressed and the sun's light diminished, artificial lighting was gradually introduced. At the opera's close a single pool of light bathed the centre stage as the prodigal son was reconciled with his father and his brother. It was at once a magnificent spectacle and a moving ritual and audience and critics alike sang the company's praise. Especially moving in the role of the prodigal son was a young Canadian tenor Garnet Brooks who would later play the leading role in my opera *Everyman* and in the Chorus was Gary Relyea who would play the role of Dr Shadow in another of my works *Psycho Red*. My opinion about the fallibility of critics was confirmed by Nathan Cohen of the *Toronto Star* who praised the performance lavishly but damned Britten's music for its "sameness" which, he pontificated, "leads to monotony."

So began my twenty-year association with Niki and the Guelph Spring Festival which was one of the most enjoyable learning periods of my life involving as it did working with some of the most gifted people in the fields of opera and dance, puppetry, drama, set design and costume. As a child growing up in Ireland I had learned of the violin prodigy who was Yehudi Menuhin—what a pleasure it was then to meet him on a number of occasions in Guelph and especially on the occasion when, with his sister Hepzibah in attendance, he rehearsed "Music for Solo Violin" by Harry Somers which was to receive its world premiere the following day. Perhaps the most memorable concert I heard was given by Marilyn Horne who was then at the peak of her career. It took place in 1971 in the university's 800-seat War Memorial Hall which is intimate and enjoys fine acoustics. The packed audience roared its approval as Horne demonstrated the truth of the claim that she was arguably the finest mezzo soprano in the world. When she sang the aria "O Mon Fernand" from Donizetti's *La Favorite* she tossed off the challenging coloratura passages with absolute assurance. After the concert she came to our house with her accompanist Martin Katz for dinner and to chat with a small group of friends closely involved in the festival. Ravi Shankar came that year too, his contract specifying in detail the height of the platform that would have to be erected on the stage, the kind of carpets to be used, and even the brands of tea to be available to him. Because of such detailed commands we expected a martinet but on meeting him after his concert in the home of an Indian physician resident in Guelph he proved the most delightful of guests.

A genial adjunct to festival going is the attendant hospitality—dinners and cocktail parties. It was at one of these that I met Charles Wilson, a composer who had taken his doctorate in composition at the University of Toronto. He was an organist in one of Guelph's local churches, a music teacher in a high school, and the conductor of various choirs. He disliked social gatherings being a rather aloof man with a penetrating glance and with little time for idle chat. We discovered a mutual interest in the fact that he had set to music a poem by D.G. Jones, a former professor in the OAC English Department. He told me that though he had written music for most genres, including oratorio, he wanted to write an opera but had not yet found a suitable libretto. I told him that maybe I had a story, a radio play, *Heloise and Abelard*, that he might like to read. He read it, liked it ("perfect," he said), and so began a collaboration that was longer and more arduous than I expected. During the summers of 1969 to 1972 Renate and I, with our son Ormonde, would join the Wilsons at their summer property on Lake Paudash, near Bancroft, northern Ontario. It was a beautiful property on a large lot which Wilson had brought from the poet Jones whose own summer home was just around the bay from us.

And so at Lake Paudash the summers fled. During the day Charles worked on his score and I on my libretto, but there was plenty of time for family swimming, and reading, and boating. In the evening Charles would often play to us on a spinet the music he had written that day and I shall always associate *Heloise and Abelard* with the sound of that spinet and the haunting cry of the loons on the lake. Not that our collaboration was all loons and spinet music. There was the seemingly endless task of revision, discussion of the line the story should take, analysis of character and situation and motive, the necessity to seek a new approach when we could not agree. Wilson had said my radio play was "perfect"; since it took me four years to rewrite it to his satisfaction I was reinforced in my opinion that composers are more given to hyperbole than writers. I remember only one interruption to our routine when in the summer of 1969 we rowed across the lake to a rented room in a motel that had television to see two American astronauts walk on the moon.

The art of the librettist is a very difficult one and there are no schools where one can learn it and there are no books on the subject. One reason perhaps is that the work of the librettist is much underrated; when we speak of an opera the librettist is rarely mentioned. It is Bizet's *Carmen*, Strauss' *Die Fledermaus*, Puccini's *Madama Butterfly*. And yet, to take an example, one could make a very good argument that the libretto for *Carmen* by Henri Meilhac and Ludovic Halévy is as much a work of art as Bizet's music. It is a marvel of swift characterization and narrative with a love-hate story at its core which the libretto's other elements complement. When Carmen dances the *habanera* in her opening scene and speaks of love, she also speaks of its danger—*Si tou ne m'aimes pas, je t'aime;/Si je t'aime, prends garde à toi*—and the librettists have done their work so well that we know that Carmen and her lover will die as surely as Shakespeare's ill-fated Desdemona and Othello. Meilhac and Halévy (a member of the *Académie française*) were men of the theatre who enjoyed great and well-deserved popularity in their time—both Bizet and Offenbach owe a great deal to their extraordinary ability to write libretti that positively cry out for operatic treatment. There are, of course, many cases where a weak libretto is redeemed by the music. Schikaneder's libretto for *The Magic Flute* is a case in point which, despite its faults, provoked some of Mozart's most ravishing music. I yield to no one in my admiration for Oscar

Wilde's best work, but I consider his play *Salomé* to be a second-rate piece whose flashy appeal is grounded in a fake exoticism that is indulgent and gross. And yet in its German translation by Hedwig Lachmann it was the catalyst of the magnificent score by Strauss. The librettist must live with the knowledge that ultimately an opera will be succeed or fall by the quality of the music; that and that alone will decide its fate in the opera houses of the world.

Each libretto presents it own difficulties. The major problem when writing about historical characters (as in *Heloise and Abelard*) is to make sure that they are not overwhelmed by the history of which they are a part. In *Antony and Cleopatra* and *Romeo and Juliet,* for example, Shakespeare exploits the historical background to complement and heighten the tragic love stories. We may remember little of where the events of *Antony and Cleopatra* take place ("in several parts of the Roman Empire") or why, but we can never forget the doomed Egyptian Queen and her Roman general. They dominate the play's action at all times. In my opera I had to wrestle with keeping Heloise and Abelard centre stage while at the same time I had to provide the history of a time little known to contemporary audiences—the ecclesiastical world of the twelfth century. I think the libretto is daring in that it did not compromise in trying to convey this world—it demanded large scenes incorporating Heloise's Convent with its Chorus of nuns, a large tavern scene, a wedding in a church, and Abelard's trial scene with its Archbishops, Bishops, Priests, and Onlookers. It was daring also, I think, in its use of Latin for many of the choruses; even in the scene where Abelard and Heloise declare their love,. I had Heloise sing in Latin counterpointed by Abelard's English.

> *Sicut vitta coccinea labia tua*
> *Et eloquium tuum dulce.*
>
> *Thy lips are as a scarlet lace*
> *And thy speech sweet.*

When I now compare my original radio play with the completed libretto I am struck by the differences. Entire scenes were dropped and new ones written. I rewrote the castration scene twenty-one times finally reducing my original four hundred words or so to fourteen. A new and important character, Bernard of Clairvaux, was added. Long speeches and soliloquies were written out, and the language of the radio play (it was a poetic drama) was drastically revised because it was too musical; if the libretto needed music, Wilson said, he would supply it. I came to accept that music takes precedence over words; the librettist may write a scene which he considers very good only to have the composer reject it because at that point in the opera he needs an ensemble in order not to destroy the opera's architectonics which he has been carefully building. A composer thinks in terms of formal relationships—how to balance choruses with solo and ensemble work and how to complement that with orchestral writing. The librettist thinks primarily in terms of plot and character and symbol. Ultimately what a good librettist must learn is the paradoxical truth that he is at his best when he "writes out" as much as possible so that the music may usurp and perform the traditional elements of dramatic writing. Ultimately, the best libretti, like the purest style, are distinguished by their discretion.

Perhaps the key difficulty facing the contemporary librettist is that very often, unless he is a trained musician, he cannot read what the composer is writing. In that sense I was writing blind since while I could read the piano score I was not sufficiently trained to read the orchestral score. Although the theme of *Heloise and Abelard* is a very old one, Wilson was determined not to write "mediaeval" music, a kind of operatic *Carmina Burana*. Having studied under Lukas Foss (himself a student of Hindemith) Wilson often writes in a non-diatonic style with wide jumps in the intervals for the singers. But if I cannot read what my collaborator is writing serious difficulties may arise. I may write a scene intended to end on a note of defiance, but the composer, favouring another interpretation, can retain the librettist's words but subvert them by means of orchestral texturing or any of the musical modalities available to him. A piano score provides only a suggestion as to what an orchestral score, written for full orchestra, offers. It is only when the librettist hears his work performed in full operatic form that he can make a judgement as to whether the composer has been true to his intentions and at that point there is little he can do about it. The correspondence between Richard Strauss and von Hofmannsthal is the *locus classicus* documenting the difficulties that can arise when two men of genius collaborate and Strauss' opera *Capriccio* (written after von Hofmannsthal's death) is an explicit exploration of the question as to the relative importance of words and music in an opera. I should add that Charles Wilson and I continued work on a new opera as late as 2012.

To return to the writing of *Heloise and Abelard*. Until the summer of 1970, when we had completed two acts of the opera, Wilson and I had been indulging in an act of pleasant folly. No one had commissioned us to write an opera, few in the world of music even knew we were writing one, yet here we were watching the moonlight and listening to the loons and writing a grand opera for a very large number of soloists, for a chorus that would ultimately be fifty in number, and for a large classical-sized orchestra. But as so often happens in fairy tales where love and lunacy coincide, a Fairy Godmother appeared on the scene. Ruby Mercer, editor of *Opera Canada*, and herself a soprano who had made her debut at New York's Metropolitan Opera in 1936 after being auditioned by Edward Johnson, heard about what we were doing from Wilson's wife while at a Guelph Spring Festival cocktail party. She asked to read the libretto, and was so impressed by it that she praised it to Dr Herman Geiger-Torel, Director General of the Canadian Opera Company, and insisted he read it and hear what was written of the score. That was the essential contact. Wilson played the music for Geiger-Torel, he too was impressed, he took it to his Board, and in 1970 the COC announced that it had commissioned a new grand opera *Heloise and Abelard* to celebrate its Silver Anniversary. Scheduled for production in September 1973, it joined the only other two operas commissioned by the COC—Healey Willan's *Deirdre*, to a libretto by John Coulter, and Harry Somers' *Louis Riel*, to a bilingual libretto by Mavor Moore and Jacques Languirand. Geiger-Torel also announced the names of the other operas to be performed in the 1973 season: Wagner's *Die Götterdämmerung*, Rossini's *The Barber of Seville*, Lehar's *The Merry Widow*, Verdi's *Rigoletto*, and Bethoven's *Fidelio*.

In 1970 my student John Cripton graduated and left Guelph to take up an appointment as Coordinator of Cultural Activities at Dalhousie University. He was no sooner there than he began to display those gifts that would soon make him an impresario on an international scale that would dwarf Goldschmidt, bringing to Canada major artistic groups from Russia and China and organizing festivals and Expositions worldwide. Within a year he commissioned Wilson and myself to write an opera which he would stage in 1972 at the University's Rebecca Cohn Auditorium. Choice of subject was left to us. My thoughts immediately turned to *The Summoning* of *Everyman*, a masterpiece of mediaeval drama which I had long admired. I may have been drawn to the theme by having worked so closely on Britten's three church operas—*The Prodigal Son* (1968), *The Burning Fiery Furnace* (1971), and *Noye's Fludde* (1972). And I had also been involved with the Festival's mediaeval play *The Life and Death of Herod* in 1969 (featuring the wonderful actress Kate Nelligan as the Virgin Mary) which also influenced me in my choice of subject matter.

The plot of *The Summoning of Everyman*, written about 1500, is starkly simple. God sends Death to tell Everyman that the hour of his death is at hand. Because I knew the play well, having taught it my university classes and because I remembered vividly a production at University College, Cork, in 1949, I wrote the libretto very quickly. While I admired the play greatly I made a number of alterations the major one being to cut those sections at the end of the play which are in the nature of a sermon inculcating Christian virtues. In order to provide more dramatic tension and also to add colour to the original cast—Good Deeds, Cousin, Kinship, and so on—I introduced two new characters. I gave Everyman a Paramour in order to add a new dimension to his humanity and I added a Devil because all good drama needs an antagonist. In my version the Devil is not the villain of the piece; rather, he is a servant of God whose bidding he carries out faithfully. As I read further into the background of the play I was delighted to discover that there is an Ur-Everyman in Sanskrit literature which also features a devil. It was only after I had finished my work that Renate told me that Hofmannsthal had also introduced the Devil into his play *Jedermann*. But I tried always not to interfere with the noble simplicity of the original and to relate the rhythm of my work to its intensity and inevitability which is achieved through a striking unity of time, action, and place. I felt very strongly that in writing this libretto I was like a sculptor whose work is to unfold the form that is hidden in its material body of stone. As soon as I had given my text to Charles Wilson the inevitable task of collaboration began, but now with an increased sense of urgency. The premiere of *Everyman* would take place in Halifax, Nova Scotia, in April 1973, to be followed by the premiere of *Heloise and Abelard* five months later in Toronto.

In 1970 I met Professor Alexander Norman Jeffares, MA, PhD (Dublin), MA, DPhil (Oxon), F.R.S.A., F.R.S.L., Honorary Fellow, Australian Academy of the Humanities—better known to his friends and colleagues as "Derry." He was a grand swashbuckler of an academic, as formidable in his drinking, conversation, and witticisms as in his multitudinous writings and literary undertakings. Born in Dublin, he first lectured in Classics at Trinity College, Dublin, before taking his DPhil. at Oxford on the work of W.B. Yeats. This led him to Mrs Yeats, widow of the poet, who entrusted to him a treasure trove of unpublished work by Yeats which formed the basis of Derry's outstanding critical biography on Yeats written when he was twenty-nine years old. A Chair in English Literature at the University of Adelaide, Australia, soon followed and a few years later, in 1957, Derry returned to Leeds University to build probably the finest university in the UK in the fields of American, Anglo-Irish, and Commonwealth literary studies. At that time Professor Woodhouse of Toronto wielded enormous power in placing his PhD students all across Canada, but his power was dwarfed by Derry's influence in placing his Leeds students in English Departments all over the world from the India subcontinent to Africa, to the Middle East, and the Orient.

In 1970 Jeffares had come to Canada on one of his travels and stopped off in Guelph at the invitation of Dean MacKinnon. He gave a lecture on the life and writings of Yeats in the university theatre that was eventually to be named the Nicholas Goldschmidt Music Room. It was as entertaining a lecture as I had heard to that time, so entertaining that afterwards many of the academics who heard him dismissed it as mere pablum. Without knowing in any detail the extent of his publications and, I suspect, without having read his authoritative biography of Yeats, they mistook Derry's witticisms for shallowness, his wide ranging allusions to the literatures of a number of Commonwealth countries as grandstanding, and the *bravura* of his sixty-minute lecture without notes as a reproach to their own tightly scripted lectures which changed little over the years.

The following day I had coffee with Derry when he asked if he might attend one of my classes. About a week later, after he had left to go on to universities in Western Canada, I received a hand written note from him inviting me to lecture at the International Yeats Summer School in Sligo, Ireland, that summer. I was delighted to accept for, to paraphrase Chaucer, once the academic year is over and the innumerable essays graded and the wearying departmental meetings adjourned, scholars then long to go on travels. It pleased me also to think that I was returning to a place only a few miles from where my father and my ancestors had been born and lived and died and that my students would be drawn from all over the world.

In the two summers that I taught in Sligo I came to feel that Derry Jeffares had taken on the job of Director in order to surround himself with the kind of people that he liked—men and women who formed a fascinating band of intellectual adventurers like himself who loved high talk, good whiskies and wines, and who were very far from the dry as dust stereotypes of the professor. There was Kevin Nowland, Professor of History from University College, Dublin. About five foot, four inches, he looked like a leprechaun and was everyone's favourite because of the comic way he sang Irish songs in the evenings when lecturers and students gathered in the lounge of the Sligo Hotel overlooking the river where the swans swam—the swans that so poignantly symbolized mortality and immortality for Yeats:

> *Among what rushes will they build,*
> *By what lake's edge, or pool*
> *Delight men's eyes when I awake some day*
> *To find they have flown away?*

John Montague the poet was there too, very conscious of the fact that many called him the worthy successor to Yeats. He was a great source of gossip, regaling us with tales of shared debauchery in Paris with Samuel Beckett and the French poet Claude Esteban, and of his adventures in America with poetry-besotted university girls. He and I were on a panel when I, perhaps incautiously, remarked that the age of the epic was long gone only to be reposted by him that he was even then in the process of writing the great Irish epic. *Touché*! When his next volume of poetry *The Rough Field* came out a year later I read it carefully, admired it, but concluded that it was anything but an epic.

It was a mark of Derry Jeffares' generosity that the American scholar Richard Ellmann was among us for he had published his very fine book on Yeats in 1948, the same year that Derry brought out his biography of the poet. Since then Ellmann's monumental and critical biography of James Joyce had established his reputation as possibly the finest English language biographer of the twentieth century and earned him a place—certainly in Sligo—as an honorary Irishman. There were Canadians too on the teaching staff including Anne Saddlemyer, an authority on the Irish dramatist J.M. Synge, who was later to succeed Robertson Davies as Master of Massey College, the University of Toronto. At our Sligo school she was more celebrated for her tap dancing which was her favourite recreational sport. From Cork in the south of Ireland came Sean Lucy, a professor there, to lecture on metre and rhythm in Anglo-Irish verse. To our delight Lucy's talk turned into a concert in which he sang song after song in Gaelic and English to illustrate his theme. Years later in Toronto I heard him give the same lecture invested with even greater *brio*.

Two other poets on our faculty were Geoffrey Hill from Leeds University and Seamus Heaney from Queen's University, Belfast. Hill was an extraordinarily intense person seemingly quite different from his very relaxed Sligo colleagues, but he surprised me one evening when after the hotel bar had shut he told myself and an American professor Lester Connor that he felt inspired to write a poem but that he needed the ambiance of a graveyard to help summon his Muse. Not a whit abashed we set off to discover a graveyard but found the entrance locked. Again, not a whit abashed we climbed over the railing and there Lester and I walked together among the graves while Geoffrey Hill communed with his poetic *daemon* beneath a Yeatsian moon that sailed overhead. I have now before me on my desk a hand written poem by Hill which may indeed be the sepulchral poem that came to him that far away night in a Sligo graveyard.

Seamus Heaney, then a handsome thirty-something years of age, had already established a name for himself with two volumes of poetry that hinted at possible greatness, promise fulfilled when, many years later, he won the Nobel Prize for Literature. His enduring theme, like Montague's and so many Irish writers, was the trauma inflicted on the psyche of Ireland by the imposition of an alien culture and the amputation of the province of Ulster. Heaney was the most accessible of men, down to earth, open, democratic in all his instincts in total contrast to his eminent predecessor, the enigmatic, aloof Yeats with his aura of the occult and the hieratic.

There were also Brendan Kennelly (who had just published his translation of the Gaelic epic *Táin Bó Cúailnge*), Thomas Kinsella the poet, Conor Cruise O'Brien (who thrived on controversy, baiting Orangeman and Catholic nationalist alike), Senator Michael Yeats, who had something of his famous father's aura of ethereal remoteness, and Balachandra Rajan, a savant from India, relocated to the University of Western Ontario. And then there was Mary Lavin reading from her short stories.

I had first come across Lavin's work in the late 1940s when I read her novel *The House in Clewe Street*. I was immediately captivated by its elegance of style and uniqueness of voice. Now, so many years later, hoping to meet her I went to lunch in the hotel where most of the faculty stayed and by good luck she was sitting alone in the dining room. I joined her and in the course of our conversation there was mention of her husband. I must have touched a sympathetic chord in her nature for she told me that when she first attended University College, Dublin, in the late 1930s she had fallen in love with a handsome fellow student who seemed to reciprocate her feeling, only to discover that he was in training to become a Jesuit priest. They parted and some years Mary married a lawyer, and had a happy marriage and three daughters. When her husband died in 1954, she received a letter of condolences from Australia, from the Jesuit student she had loved so much who did indeed become a priest. Correspondence followed, her priest returned to Dublin, and they fell in love again. With permission from Rome, he left the Jesuit Order and they married. As Mary finished her story, she said, "Here is Michael Scott, my husband," and, as if on cue, a very handsome, slim man about her age entered the dining room and joined us. Years later when I met the Irish classical pianist Veronica McSweeney she said that Lavin's second marriage had caused a great scandal among certain people in Dublin, always fond of malicious gossip, who felt that a woman should be content with one husband and not run after a second, especially not a Jesuit priest.

And so during the summers of 1970 and 1971 I flew to Ireland and joined the faculty of the International Yeats School. It was the most satisfactory and productive educational experience I have ever had. The distinguished Yeats scholar, Professor Henn of Cambridge University, had been one of those who most influenced the beginnings of the School and he had wisely insisted that it should be totally independent of any university or institute of higher learning, that there should be no academic entrance requirements, that there should be the utmost freedom in the interchange between teacher and pupil, and that there be no institutional recognition of completed work such as a diploma or degree or any sort. And so it was. Teachers and students took meals together, went on trips together, drank in the pubs and danced together. And the result was the most committed of students, many with university degrees, others with none, but all driven by the desire to know more about Yeats and his contemporaries. They came from Europe—mainly France, Italy, Germany, and Scandinavia, the USA (the largest contingent), and Japan. The latter is hard to explain but one possible explanation may relate to Yeats's interest in the Japanese Noh drama. Henn's wise advice was violated in only one respect: many American nuns, the most assiduous of students, attended the School and because their Mothers Superior needed some assurance they were not spending their time frivolously, Derry had designed a small diploma especially for them which stated that they had earned the highest distinction in their studies.

While the main emphasis of the curriculum was on the work of Yeats, that emphasis was conducted within the historical, economic, political, and literary context of nineteenth and twentieth-century Ireland and included such contemporaries of Yeats as Oscar Wilde, Bernard Shaw, Lady Gregory, J.M. Synge, Sean O'Casey, George Moore, Oliver St John Gogarty, and James Joyce. There were two lectures in the morning, seminars in the late afternoon, performances of plays, mainly by Yeats, in the evenings, and lots of dancing where these students from Europe and Japan learned Irish steps to the accompaniment of fiddle, banjo, and *bodhran*. There were also excursions to places like Coole, Ballylee, Innisfree, Yeats's Tower in Galway, and to Lissadell House where Yeats had known Eva Gore-Booth, poet and suffragette, and her sister Constance, the Countess Markiewicz, condemned to death by the British for her role in the 1916 Easter Rising:

> *The light of evening, Lissadell,*
> *Great windows open to the south,*
> *Two girls in silk kimonos, both*
> *Beautiful, one a gazelle . . . .*
> *The innocent and the beautiful*
> *Have no enemy but time.*

But as we went about our peaceful ways in Sligo we, the faculty, were intensely aware of the gravity of the political situation in the North of Ireland, and especially in the area of the city of Derry, an hour's drive from Sligo. Here the ancient animosity between the Protestant North and the Catholic South (symbolized by the rabid Reverend Ian Paisley and the twenty-one-year-old nationalist Bernadette Devlin) had flared dangerously. Full scale rioting had broken out in Derry and Belfast in 1969 and so dangerous was the situation that the government of Eire directed the Irish Army to establish field hospitals along the border to provide medical help in case war broke out. The danger of a war pitting the armed forces of the North and South against each other with horrendous consequences seemed very real. When Seamus Heaney, himself from Derry, published his 1975 volume of poetry *North* it showed a new engagement with the nightmare of Irish history and its attendant violence echoing the themes Yeats had sounded fifty years earlier in his *Tower* volume. When I visited my family in Belfast those two summers the city was like a war zone—houses blown up, traffic lights down, burned buses by the roadside, soldiers with armored cars, and paramilitary police everywhere as helicopters clattered overhead night and day. One evening I went with a friend from highschool days, Kieran, a medical doctor, to a club for a drink. We were stopped at three points and questioned by security guards before gaining entrance. The waitress, a good-looking young woman, chatted with us. She likes you, Kieran said, if you want, I'm sure she will sleep with you. But not for money. The waitress was, in fact, a medical student. With the breakdown in civil order and the ever present danger from bombings and assassinations, there had also followed a breakdown in morals. The club we were in was probably targeted. Who knew when it would be bombed? Men from the IRA had entered Kieran's medical office on two occasions and demanded the keys to his car at gun point. "Eat, drink, and be merry, for tomorrow . . . " He would emigrate, Kieran said, but he felt he was too old. He wasn't too old, but he did die a relatively young man, a victim, I was sure, of the dangers and the stress of those days.

When I look back on those summers in Sligo, there is one lecture that stands out in my mind. Given by Professor Henn, it was titled "The Property of the Dead" and while ostensibly about Yeats's life-long attendance at séances in order to communicate with the dead, the lecture turned into a confession that Henn had himself in later years attended séances where he said that he had spoken with Yeats and with many of his dead friends. I remember vividly the shadows of evening fall on us as we listened in astonishment to Henn, now an old man, as he moved from the safety of the professional lecture to the dangerous level of personal revelation. He died not long after. Henn's was the last lecture of the 1971 International Yeats Summer School and two days later we said our goodbyes and departed,

I to Canada, glad to leave behind me the images of a gutted Belfast and the ghosts of so many Irish who had died and suffered for a freedom that always seemed so close and yet remained a cruel dream.

> *We have fed the heart on fantasies,*
> *The heart's grown brutal from the fare;*
> *More substance in our enmities*
> *Than in our love; O honey-bees,*
> *Come build in the empty house of the stare.*

The Bulls of Ronda

Christians link the word "Sabbatical" to Sunday, their day of rest, Muslims to Friday, and Jews to Saturday. The concept of a sabbatical derives from passages in the Book of Leviticus where it is ordered that the soil of Israel lie fallow every seventh year when Jews must refrain from buying and selling and when both land and humans enter a year-long period of spiritual healing and recuperation. It also derives from that passage in the Book of Genesis where God too enjoys a sabbatical: "And He rested on the seventh day from all His work which He had made." Happily the idea was taken up by universities where every seventh year professors may apply for a leave of absence, usually with pay, for travel, research, and for rest. Leave is not granted automatically. The professor must submit an application setting out why he or she wants leave, and what he hopes to do during that time. It might seem that universities would be flooded with requests from faculty seeking to travel abroad to further their research activities, but in fact only a small number apply. This is because most cannot afford the costs associated with re-locating to another city or country to conduct research. It is also a fact that many professors simply run out of ideas after a few years of teaching and prefer not to leave the comforts of their university and home town. But I ardently wanted a break in order to write and to travel. And so it was that in 1972 I began thinking about what I would do were I granted sabbatical leave.

I commenced researching a story I had come across about a German soldier who had been executed by Nazi officers in a Canadian prison camp in the Netherlands because he had deserted in the final days of the war. What I found so striking about the incident was that the execution by firing squad had been carried out with the approval of the Canadian military authorities acting in strict accordance with international military law. I made voluminous notes, I flew to Ottawa to consult the pertinent files in the National Archives, and I made a rough plan to order them with a view to using them for a play. Simultaneously I also began making notes for a documentary play about the Conscription Crisis of 1944 when Canada came close to breaking up over Quebec's determination to resist conscription and when Canadian generals considered staging a revolt against the Government of Canada in order to get the additional manpower they claimed to need. It was on the strength of the latter idea that I was given a leave of absence for the year 1972–73. But where to spend this precious year? I thought about spending it in Ireland or Germany but soon decided against that. Renate and I wanted some place new to both of us, a country where everything was different in terms of language and customs, a space where we might see life with a new vision, a place that would excite the imagination Very soon we settled on Spain.

In the meantime, I had a lot of work to do because early in 1972 the publishing firm Methuen commissioned me to compile an anthology of Canadian plays. When I began work there existed only four anthologies of Canadian plays, all devoted to stage plays. But remembering my year in Saskatchewan when I used to listen so eagerly to drama broadcast by the CBC, I decided that my anthology should be a multi-media collection offering stage, radio, television, and film plays. Very soon I contacted Stephen Mezei, the editor of *Performing Arts in Canada*. Stephen was the very image of the *émigré* intellectual. A Hungarian who had fled his country in 1956 after the Russian invasion to settle in Toronto, he was as interested in Canadian writing as in the various new French, German, and Hungarian plays and novels he spoke about so vividly. Conducting most of his business in cafés, he showered me with advice and scripts. Robert Weaver of the CBC, who had broadcast my own plays, helped me with my choices of radio plays, and George Jonas, another Hungarian *émigré,* gave me access to a number of CBC television plays. The published anthology *Encounter: Canadian Drama in Four Media* contained three one-act stage plays including *Overlaid* by Robertson Davies and *Still Stands the House* by Gwen Pharis Ringwood; two radio plays by Michael Cook and Mavor Moore; two television plays, one by Sinclair Ross better known for his novel *As for Me and My House*; and Joan Finnigan's magnificent film play *The Best Damn Fiddler from Calabogie to*

Kaladar, produced by the National Film Board of Canada, and featuring a young woman, Margot Kidder, who would go on to play the role of Lois Lane in the *Superman* movies. I finished work on this anthology the day I left Canada for Spain, but I knew from my research that I would return one day to the long-neglected subject of Canadian drama and theatre.

Freed now of teaching and university duties and with my anthology at the publisher, it was time to go to Spain. We flew to Dusseldorf, Germany, in late August to visit Renate's family. We picked up a car and drove via Munich, where the Summer Olympic Games were in progress, to Leoben in Austria. Renate's sister Marianne was living here with her husband Werner, a professor and Head of the Engineering Department at the university. A brilliant young man in his thirties he had worked at the Max Planck Institute for Iron Research in Dusseldorf, and later for Siemens. His dream, he told me, was to build his own yacht. The evening before we left Leoben for Spain reports came in via radio and television of the massacre at the Olympic Games of eleven Israeli athletes by the Palestinian Black September group.

I have always loved travel, and especially by car. If one flies, say, from Paris to Rome or to Vienna, one misses so much—the changes in scenery, the foods and wines that in Europe may differ completely within a fifty-kilometre drive, the hidden villages off the major routes criss-crossing a continent that offered a way of life little changed in some ways from a century before. And so I laid out the map and plotted a course from Vienna to the south of Spain. We had a good car, enough money to live relatively well, and we had our two-year old son Ormonde through whose eyes we would receive fresh impressions of the exciting new world ahead us. The journey took us east through Villach, Austria, and then southwest as we climbed to the mountainous country around Udine, Italy, before descending into Venice where we stayed. It was my second visit to what I have always regarded as the most theatrical city in Europe, theatrical in its famous St Mark's Square and in the gold and black gondolas that seem so exactly right for the canals that snake through the city, theatrical in the ever unfolding vistas of piazzas and bridges and churches that spoke to me of Giorgione, Titian, Tintoretto, Byron and his menagerie of mistresses and animals, and Thomas Mann's beautiful Tadzio. After Venice across northern Italy, past Sirmione (where the poet

Catullus lived and where he wrote his finest love songs), Milan, Turin, and southwest again to Perpignan on the French-Spanish border. In Barcelona we must switch from speaking French to Spanish. *"Esta señora se llama Renate Benson." "Quisiera una habitación doble tranquilla."*

In Barcelona we did indeed find a *hotel tranquilla* a block away from Gaudi's astonishing architectural anachronism, the *Sagrada Familia*. The next day we drove south following the coastal highway past Benidorm (soon to become a German outpost catering to Germans seeking S*auerkraut* and German beers so as not to feel homesick), Alicante, Murcia, and on to Granada in Andalucia and a leisurely visit to the Alhambra. Just before Málaga we stopped at Nerja, a small village in a spectacular setting overlooking the Mediterranean, and I remember what a wonderful feeling of sheer freedom I felt as I realized that I had a whole year ahead of me to discover this new country and perhaps to discover things about myself. We finally arrived in Torremolinos, not far from Málaga, where we stayed in the *parador* and rested—it had been a long trip, with the driving sometimes risky, especially in the mountains and on the east coast *cornice*.

We were now on the Costa del Sol, that classic curve of the Mediterranean that ends at the Straits of Gibraltar, known in classical times as the Pillars of Hercules, one resting in Europe , the other in Africa. Because Torremolinos was a tourist centre with all that that implies we drove back and forth, as far west as Estepona and Marbella until at last we found the perfect place—Rio del Sol. It was an enclave of eight villas on a small hill in Torre Blanca, a little way from the town of Fuengirola; each villa had two stories with spacious balconies which gave on wonderful views of the Mediterranean, villas which were clustered around a pool. The entire enclave was smothered in flowers and trees—bougainvillea, oleanders, fig, almond, and olive trees. There was even a grove of trees at the bottom of the hill where nightingales sang by day and night. By the sea, several minutes walk from our villa, was a village, Los Boliches, made up of a few streets with cantinas and shops and restaurants. The tourist hotels which had just begun to encroach on the area were empty; the sun seekers from northern Europe had now flown, reluctantly, to their jobs in Manchester and Paris and Berlin and Helsinki. The life of the Spanish people around us had resumed its regular and ancient rhythms, undisturbed by the temporary onslaught of a foreign ethos. Europe stopped at the Iberian mountains separating Spain and France, separating Spain from the democracies of western Europe, and from their languages and their cultures. Spain in 1972 was still in many ways an eighteenth-century state, temporarily given over to fascism; it was ruled by *El Caudillo*, General Franco, and his Falangist Party—the omnipresent Civil Guardia represented the iron fist of the dictator. But even the Guardia could not contain the undercurrents of rebellion; in Catalonia the people yearned for independence from Madrid and in the north the Spanish Basque movement *Euzkadi Ta Azkata* fought for regional autonomy with bombings and assassinations. In the coming months I learned a great deal about Spain from the Spanish writers and painters whom we met in the *cafés* of Los Boliches and Fuengirola.

Life now took on a pattern. In the morning there was shopping where we learned new words—*pan*, *pescado*, *carne*, *legumbre*, *fruta*, *vino*, *mantequilla*. Important words, as old as civilization. Words necessary if one is to live. We learned that there was a club, the British Club, not too far away, in Benalmádena, where we could get Spanish lessons. The club was very British, a retreat for all the retired doctors and dentists and lawyers and businessmen who had come to Spain for the cheap living and the *frisson* of living in a foreign country and who, like Germans on the Costa Brava, wanted all the familiar comforts of home—proper English tea, bridge parties, English beers and Scotch whiskies, and people like themselves. Not foreigners. Our teacher turned out to be a Swede who has lived on the coast for many years; he was a jazz player and much of the class was spent as he expanded (in English) on his love of Louis Armstrong and Dizzy Gillespie and other of his heroes. But week by week we began to acquire a working vocabulary and greater fluency in Spanish.

Afternoons were spent writing, I on my play about the Conscription Crisis of 1944 and Renate correcting proofs of her Erich Kästner book. Although we had a large villa with lots of space, we did not have an office; we wrote on the kitchen table or on the dining room table, sometimes by the pool when it was hot enough to sunbathe and swim. But after three weeks in Rio del Sol I had not been able to write a single scene of my proposed play. Ottawa and its politics seemed so remote, even antithetical, to all that the Costa del Sol represented. In some of the *cafés* there was flamenco where the vividness of the scene evoked the present, not the past. When we left the *cafés* late at night we saw the two members of the Guardia Civil, distinctive in their tricorn hats, standing under the bridge just below our house, a reminder of the ever watchful presence of Franco, the old man in Madrid now in the last years of his life. A history was being played out here which began to exercise a stronger hold on me than the political machinations surrounding the 1944 Conscription Crisis.

One day posters went up everywhere, it seemed. The bullfight! A *corrida* to be held in Fuengirola. Positively the last of the season! Famous matadors, noble bulls. Spain's unique contribution to the world of culture and of sport. Franco himself approved of bull fighting as he approved the cult of the Virgin Mary; they represented the vigour of the Spanish male and the purity of Spanish women. The bullring of Fuengirola was small but the *corrida* retained, somewhat shabbily, its centuries-old pageantry. A small band played, a lone steward on horseback led the *paseo*. First the matadors, followed by the *banderilleros* and the *picadores*. The matadors spread their ceremonial capes on the *barrera*, the trumpet blew, the red gate opened, and the first bull came charging into the ring. Then followed two hours of slaughter. The *picadores* bored their steel lances deep into the muscles of the bulls pushing and goring the animals so that the spectators booed the cowardice of the matadors who dared not face the animals unless they were viciously wounded and thus rendered less dangerous. The matadors were third rate, totally unknown on the national scene, and when they came to the actual killing of the bulls they stabbed them to death unable or afraid to come in over the shoulder where a bravely directed thrust between the collar bones and into the heart's aorta would take down a bull in seconds. I was sickened and angered by the venality of what I saw and within a few days I began to write a short story about what I had seen, attempting to present a very different picture than that associated with Hemingway's portrayal of the world of bull fighting. He was certainly aware of the shoddy practices of the matadors—the shaved horns, the beatings about the kidneys of the bull sometimes before they released it into the arena, the savagery of the *picadores*—but he opted most often to glamorize what is essentially a brutal blood sport.

When I had written my short story, I read it to Renate who without hesitation told me that while I thought I was writing a short story she was convinced I was writing something else—perhaps a novel. As usual, she was right. And so began the mysterious business of finding out what it was that I so urgently wanted to say. As I thought more deeply about the nature of bull fighting and its relationship to Spanish culture, I decided that I must visit the home of bullfighting, the place where it all began—Ronda, a city over the mountains to the north of where I was living. In November we took the mountain road to Coín where the countryside leveled south of Casarabonela before the mountains that encircled Ronda. The road reeled precariously through the Sierra de Ronda and the landscape, with the earth blood red, reminded me of the desolate drought-ridden area south from Murcia to Almería. We drove higher and higher where the metalled road gave way to hard red clay and where the valleys far below allowed for no mistake in driving. It was a relief to come in over the mountains to the city of Ronda along the Avenue Dr Fleming and past the *plaza de toros* to the Hotel Victoria Reina. It was also a surprise to discover that the poet Rilke had lived in the hotel where he wrote parts of his *Duino Elegies*, a volume comparable in importance, I have always felt, to T.S. Eliot's *The Wasteland*. In one of those gestures so characteristic of a nation whose archetypal literary figure is the knight Quixote, the hotel had retained Rilke's room exactly as it had been almost forty years ago—a bed, a table and chair, a collection of his work on the shelves, a framed yellowing bill of 1913 that showed his monthly expenses. I did not write down any of these details at the time—they remained firmly in my mind.

The next day I visited the town. A bridge over a deep gorge links both sections of the city; the various Guidebooks draw attention to the dramatic quality of the gorge and bridge but say nothing of the killing of hundreds of people here in 1936 during the Civil War, many of whom were thrown into the gorge. The same way the dead horses were thrown there after they had been killed in the bullfight. I also visited the *plaza de toros*, walking through the faded neo-classical entrance into the arena. This was the birthplace of modern bull fighting in the late eighteenth century. To the right of the President's Box I entered the dispensary, a bleak, sterile room where cabinets on one wall displayed surgical instruments carefully laid out: scalpels, needles, fine saws, bandages. At the centre of the room was an ugly metal table which was bolted to the floor under a bank of powerful lights. A Christ on a crucifix presided over this room of pain and of occasional death.

My novel gradually began to take on its shape. My protagonist is a young Canadian (possibly my *Doppelgänger*), he comes to Spain to find poems written by a Spanish poet who has been murdered. I think at that point I had Rilke in mind, but a more important association was with Garcia Lorca, the Spanish poet, murdered in 1936 by the Falangists, and whose plays *Bodas de Sangre* (*Blood Wedding*) and *Amor de Don Perlimplín con Belisa en su jardín* I had long admired. These two poets gave me artistic co-ordinates in plotting my novel and they gave me a political sub text that steered me clear, I hoped, of the clichés that too often defined Spain to foreign observers—guitars and castanets, mantillas, the bull fight, and all the cultural paraphernalia associated with that most popular of operas, Bizet's *Carmen*. Spain was all these things, but it was much much more. In the 1970s it was a patient emerging painfully from the national trauma of the 1930s when a Spanish general baited the philosopher Unamuno with the cry, *Muerta la intelligencia! Viva la Muerte!* and was cheered by the Nationalists. It was also the time when La Pasionaria rallied the Republican forces with the slogan *No Pasarán!* even as her hero Stalin was conducting mass purges of intellectuals, Ukrainians, and senior Soviet Army officers.

The pawns were the young men who knew little of the ideologies of the warring parties—Communism, Nazism, and Fascism—and died for slogans whose meanings they never understood. Picasso's searing painting of the bombed out Basque village Guernica became a prophetic image of what was to come—the immolation of Coventry, Hamburg, Dresden, Hiroshima, and Nagasaki and so many cities in the Soviet Union.

In September theatre director Gino Marrocco wrote to me from Toronto saying how much he admired my plays *The Gunner's Rope* and *Joan of Arc's Violin* (recently published) which he wished to stage at his Backdoor Theatre. Following their production, he wrote again to tell me how well they had been received (which pleased me) and that he had discreetly added dialogue in various places to strengthen my work (which did not please me). In *The Gunner's Rope* there is a scene where one of the characters "hangs" himself. The actor playing the part had a morbid dislike of playing this scene and refused to do so in rehearsal, despite Marrocco's insistence that nothing could go wrong. But the actor did agree to play the hanging when the play was actually performed. On opening night he kept his word but, despite all precautions, the rope burned his neck so badly that he had to be taken to the hospital for treatment.

Charles Wilson and I corresponded constantly on changes and additions to *Heloise and Abelard,* a correspondence that would continue until I returned to Canada in September. In October Wilson wrote that some of the key singers had been selected—Don McManus to play Heloise's uncle, Fulbert; Allan Monk to play Abelard; Emile Belcourt as Bernard of Clairvaux. They were seasoned singers—Monk would go on to a distinguished career at the Met in a couple of years and Belcourt was a regular with London's Sadler's Wells Opera Company and other European companies. It seems that the part of Heloise had been the most difficult to cast with Wilson rejecting the various proposals put forward by Geiger-Torel. Then Wilson attended the COC's production of *Eugene Onegin* where he was stunned by the leading lady, Heather Thompson, in the role of Tatiana. She too had extensive experience with Sadler's Wells and the COC but somehow Geiger-Torel had not thought of her for the role. He, Wilson, and Victor Feldbrill, who was to conduct the opera, auditioned Heather and they agreed unanimously that she was ideal for the part—even Canadian soprano Ricky Turofsky who had passionately wanted the role conceded that she was the perfect choice. The other key members of the team have also been chosen, Leon Major as director, Suzanne Mess as costume designer, and Murray Laufer who will design the set. They are all well known in the world of Canadian music and theatre and were the team responsible for mounting the 1967 COC opera *Louis Riel*. Major, it seems, is busy reading up on mediaeval philosophy and theology and is of the opinion that the most powerful force in the opera is the Church which will dominate the action. I was disturbed by this because I have intended the focus to be at all times on the lovers and their relationship. Shakespeare's *Romeo and Juliet* is not about the quarrels of the Montagues and the Capulets—that is necessary but incidental background. I had chosen to put the name "Heloise" before that of Abelard in order to focus the tragedy on that remarkable woman who far outshone Abelard in the depths of her love. Wilson went on to say that the vocal scores have been printed and are in the hands of the singers. He has been very busy completing scores for *Everyman* and for his children's opera *The Selfish Giant* (based on the short story by Oscar Wilde) which will be premiered in December 1973.

My novel had now progressed to the point where I had identified some of my key characters and themes. I began with my protagonist Mark Gibson being interrogated in Ronda by Colonel Cortés, a police officer who warns him to steer clear of political matters. Gibson meets the woman, Elena, who will possibly be able to help him locate the missing poems (which he has translated) of the murdered poet Lorenzo Gayarre. He goes to a hotel at Mijas where he meets a brother and sister, Rafael and Leonora, who have also known Gayarre but he gains no useful information. At this point he receives a note from Elena arranging a meeting in Morocco.

At this point I had no conscious idea as to why my characters would visit Morocco but I knew that I must go there if I was to write about this new location of which I knew nothing. And so Renate and I, with Ormonde, set off in our car. First along the coast past Marbella to Algeciras, and then by ferry across the straits to Ceuta, Morocco. Our journey led us through Fez and Casablanca and through sand storms when everything was sheathed in a fine red dust so that the sun itself turned a bloody red until we reached our destination Marrakesh, cradled by the snow-capped Atlas mountains. Our hotel, La Mamounia, was on the Avenue Mohammed V. We did the usual things, went shopping in the *souks* with their fine carpets and kaftans—Renate bought a beautiful kaftan in a rich black material with silver trimmings which she may wear for the premiere of *Heloise and Abelard*—we visited ruins like the El Badi Palace which spoke of the past glories of Muslim architecture, and we visited the Place Djemaa El Fna. It was a large square surrounded on four sides by shabby run-down shops and buildings, alive with thousands of people. Most appalling was the sight of a long line of beggars standing arm in arm, left hands holding out wooden bowls for alms. The beggars were blind and festered with sores. In another place human bodies were laid out for view, men and women, some without arms or legs, some with hideous wounds and deformities. Across from them, as if in contempt of their rotting bodies, acrobats danced on ropes, jugglers spun bright objects in the air, ballad singers chanted songs in ceaseless repetitive cadence. Flute music in another place showed snake charmers at work, the cobras rising from dirty burlap bags, menacing and darkly bright, throats swelling and cresting with controlled venom. A few *dirham* lay on a copper plate before them, the reward for a morning's work.

That night we went to a restaurant, the Gharnatta. It was evening and dark and it was in a part of the *medina* where taxis could not travel so it was a relief to come in from alleys that seemed threatening to find such a beautiful place that was more like a mosque than a place of eating and drinking. The walls soared to galleries thirty feet above, the centre of the building held a fountain around which were grouped enormous copper cooking utensils, the walls were stuccoed and mosaiced in elaborate designs, the wood work painted in the *zouak* style. There were only four other customers, Moroccans we guessed, who sat on cushions as they ate. We followed suit and began a very good dinner. But as we ate I had the feeling we were being watched. And then a man in a *bournous* with a *tarboosh* appeared and introduced himself as the proprietor and asked if he might join us. He spoke excellent English and was very interested in learning who we were and what we were doing in Marrakesh. When we had finished our main course he clapped his hands and a tray of drinks, alcoholic and sweet, came. After dinner he invited us to see his house which was actually attached to the restaurant. It was a large building, decorated in the most extraordinary manner for a private home. The proprietor told us that he was replicating various aspects of the Alhambra in Granada which explained the ornate geometrical patterns wrought into arabesques and the painted tiles and the profusion of filigreed arches.

Marrakesh was the highlight of our visit to Morocco. Back in Rio del Sol we resumed our life—going to the market, walking by the sea or driving to the tiny village of Mijas for lunch, swimming in the pool, Spanish lessons at the British Club. Ormonde, now almost three years old, is learning to speak Spanish from our maid Rosa and speaks German with his mother and English with me. We wrote mainly in the afternoons, Renate on her Kästner book and I on my novel now given a title—*The Bulls of Ronda*. The visit to Morocco gave me a new character, a former SS officer once accused of war crimes who like so many other Nazi officers fled Europe. My SS officer may or may not be guilty of murdering the poet Gayarre. I do not know yet. I have decided that Leonora and Raphael will be from the Basque country and I already noted correspondences between the Basque independence movement and the Irish Republican Army that may be worth developing. I have now got my five major characters whom I am destined, it seems, to follow—at this point I do not know where.

Visitors arrived from Canada from time to time. In January of 1973 Charles Wilson and his wife Jennifer flew to Spain for a final face-to-face conference on *Heloise and Abelard* and we combined sightseeing with detailed analysis of what we have done so far and what remains to be done. The text of the libretto on which the music hangs must be finalized very soon for use by the principals. The conductor will need lead time to study the piano score because this is a new work and the sooner he gets the full orchestral score the happier he will be. The director will also need a "final" libretto and score in order to determine how he is going to present the work and gear that vision to more mundane matters such as blocking, lighting, movement, and so on. When we saw Charles and Jennifer off at Málaga Airport, I am struck by the fact that when I next see him it will be in Toronto at rehearsals of our opera.

In April Barbara Wolfond, opera singer and friend, comes to visit us just before the world premiere of my opera *Everyman* and one evening she sings to us from the vocal score. I visualize the last-minute preparations at Dalhousie University in Nova Scotia, Canada, and telegraph my good wishes to Wilson and the company. The premiere comes and goes and finally Charles Wilson writes to me. He is ecstatic. *Everyman* was so relentless in its emotional intensity, he wrote, that audiences were too stunned to applaud after the last light faded. The *Globe and Mail* music critic John Kraglund has praised the premiere in an article headed, "*Everyman*: Skilled Elegance." The CBC will broadcast the opera in May; it should prove the perfect *entré* to the premiere of *Heloise and Abelard* in September.

Easter in Spain is dominated by the religious spectacles that play out during Holy Week in all its major cities and towns. We drove to Málaga on Good Friday where we spent most of the day watching the huge procession that made its way through the city—bishops, priests, monks, soldiers, lay men ominous in their Klu Klux Klan-like costumes, men sweating under the floats they carry to the directions of a barbarous gong. The floats hold life-size statues of the Virgin and of the crucified Christ. There are no women in the procession but occasionally a woman will break away from the crowd to reach ecstatically to the Christ figure. These Easter Week processions are religious in character but they also seem atavistic and of a piece with the blood sacrifice of the bull ring. The statues of Christ are gruesome in their realism—blood streaming from the five wounds like the blood on the flanks of a wounded bull. One remembers Goya whose *Saturn devouring his Son* is so realistic, so offensive, in its cannibalistic detail that he intended that it never be seen by eyes other than his.

My novel took on its final direction in May and June when to my surprise elements from earlier writings clamoured to be heard. My 1952 play

The Crowing of the Cock (which I had submitted to Dublin's Abbey Theatre years before) had featured the kidnapping of a British officer by the IRA and I had developed that in my Mexican novel. My protagonist Mark Gibson will find himself involved in a Basque plot that will spell disaster for all involved. But as I began to work on this development I was also forced to work on an article for Ruby Mercer's magazine *Opera in Canada* on the genesis and development of *Heloise and Abelard* and on writing a synopsis of the opera that the Canadian Opera Company will offer in its program. By the time I had finished the last two tasks the plot line of my novel indicated that the location of the novel's catastrophe would take place in the Basque country of Spain and so we made preparations to leave the Costa del Sol at the end of June and go there. We traveled by way of Seville where we visited the Cathedral with its astonishing *retable* before which boys dance at Easter, Seville with its echoes of Mérimée who found his Carmen at the Tobacco Factory, the city of Don Juan, murderer and seducer, softened by the sound of lute and operatic gallantry. After Cordoba to Linares where Manolete died in the ring and over the *Paso de Despeñaperros* ("The Pass of the Killing of the Dogs"), which separates Andalucia from the heartland of Spain. When we stopped for an evening in Aranjuez, just outside Madrid, a film crew was at work on another remake of *The Three Musketeers* with Faye Dunaway, Charlton Heston, and Michael York. The next day we visited the Prado. I was anxious to see its unrivalled collection of Spanish masterpieces but there was another reason: I needed to walk through its rooms because I had already visualized my protagonist having a crucial meeting there with my fictional Leonora Duran.

After a few days we traveled north again through Burgos, finally leaving the high tableland behind as we crossed the Ebro to Victoria and finally entered the Basque country. *País Vasco.* Within two days we found an apartment in a rather nondescript building on Calle Biarritz, San Sebastián. Once regarded as among Europe's finest resorts, the city is situated splendidly on a bay overlooking the Concha and Onderatta beaches with the Isla de Santa Clara on the horizon. But after the Civil War international tourists stayed away preferring the beaches and nightclubs of Biarritz, just over the French border. At first we found it difficult to adapt to life in San Sebastian—we missed the bright colours of Andalucia, the light, the flowers, the days of never ending sunshine. The Basque country was so dark, it seemed, so geared to work. And it rained a great deal. But gradually we began to appreciate its virtues—the people who were friendly and yet reserved, who were deeply religious but far removed from the histrionic Catholicism of Andalucia, a people who yearned for freedom from a central regime which forbade the use of their Basque language, a people who spoke guardedly to me of these things after a time. It was a good place in which to plot and write my final chapters.

One day in late June Renate and Ormonde and I drove out of San Sebastián to Irún close to the French border and then to the tiny village of Endarlaza under the mountains of La Rhune. Just beyond that there is a river, the Rio Bidasoa, which forms a natural border between Spain and France. It was a rainy day, rather cold. I got out of the car and walked down the bank of the river where I broke off a long branch so that I could test the speed of the river and its depths. Renate watched in some amusement as I made my rough measurements. But I had found what I wanted. The clues I had planted throughout the novel led to this place—the conclusion to my novel would take place here at this river where Mark Gibson would finally learn the message suggested to him by the killing of the bulls in the arena at Ronda.

We left Spain at the end of June and drove through France to Dusseldorf, taking time out to stop in Soissons, northern France, where in 1121 a Church Council condemned the writings of Abelard as heretical and ordered his books burned. This climactic scene in Abelard's life is also the climactic scene in my opera.

> *Burns now in the flame his book,*
> *Symbol of the man.*
> *Now he's at his Golgotha,*
> *And his noon-day cry.*

Soissons and Berlin. Erich Kástner and Peter Abelard. *Plus ça change, plus c'est la même chose.* In Dusseldorf there was mail waiting. A letter from a young man named John Steffler, asking me if I will supervise his MA thesis on the poet William Blake. I agreed. It was a reminder that very soon I must return to a life of teaching Chaucer and Milton and Shelley and Yeats and to department and college meetings and to the never-ending business of marking papers and all the work associated with the life of a professor. A letter from Vida Peene, in charge of the Canadian Opera

Guild, requested me and Renate to be in the Receiving Line at 5.30 pm before the premiere of the opera. I agreed. Geiger-Torel wrote to thanks me for my synopsis of the opera and Bruce Chalmers, Administrative Director of the COC, wrote to ask whether I can get a final script to him so that COC may print the libretto for sale. I agreed. (Over the years the libretto became a very rare item fetching many times the original price of three dollars.) Ruby Mercer wrote on behalf of herself, Joanne Mazzoleni, Mabel Krug, and Barbara Wolfond inviting Renate and me to a reception following the opera at her apartment. I agreed.

At the end of July I received a long letter from Charles Wilson. He told me that *Everyman* had been broadcast by the CBC on July 10 and 12; that he has been rehearsing the Chorus for *Heloise and Abelard* (twenty women and thirty men); the orchestral score is complete except for Act 1—the copyist is a slow worker; the electronic music for the wedding scene is now set up for four channel playbacks—two speakers in the gallery and two by the stage; he has selected three timbres on the synthesizer to match the four principal singers in order to achieve a kind of timelessness during the dream wedding sequence. In the second week of August he will begin coaching Heather Thompson (Heloise) and Allan Monk (Abelard). Charles also wrote at length of the new formal wear he has ordered to be tailored (by Morris Gay) for the premiere: a deep blue-black material with bits of silk on the lapels, pants with the cummerbund built into them, a straight Edwardian-cut jacket with white shirt, and a blue silk bow tie. I replied that since I could not hope to match his sartorial splendour I would attend the premiere in jeans, a sweater, and a sombrero.

By mid August my desk was clear. I had only one other obligation—to attend the week-long Commonwealth Universities Congress in Edinburgh, Scotland; President William Winegard and I were to be our university's representatives. My only memories of that Congress are of talking with the President of an Indian university who told me he had an enrollment of 112, 000 students, and of sitting in a lecture hall besides the Duke of Edinburgh who attended faithfully for two afternoons and spoke with his usual conviction and scorn for received opinion. After that we flew home to Canada in the last week of August. We had been away for a year and a day. I had completed the first draft of my novel, *The Bulls of Ronda* and Renate had also got her book on Kästner ready for publication. But I had other thoughts on my mind—on September 8 I had a rendezvous with a story written twenty years before in Belfast, Ireland.

LANDSCAPES OF THE MIND

The O'Keefe Centre, Toronto, financed by multi-millionaire E.P. Taylor of the O'Keefe Breweries interests, opened in 1960 with the premiere of Lerner and Lowe's *Camelot* starring Richard Burton, Julie Andrews, and Robert Goulet. This set the pattern for the Centre which has always been a roadhouse for international theatre attractions featuring such performers as Marlene Dietrich, Maurice Chevalier, and Judy Garland, and companies such as New York's Metropolitan Opera and the Kirov Ballet. Perhaps the most dramatic incident to occur there took place in 1974 when the Russian ballet dancer Baryshnikov, starring in *Don Quixote*, raced off the O'Keefe stage into a waiting car to seek refuge in Canada.

The O'Keefe Centre (later renamed The Sony Centre) is a vast performing area seating over three thousand in two tiers; the stage measures 125 feet by 60 feet, the proscenium 60 feet by 30 feet. In contrast, London's Royal Opera House seats just over two thousand in four tiers, while its proscenium measures 48 feet by 40 feet. Although the Centre was further hampered by poor sight lines and acoustics, in 1961 the Canadian Opera Company moved from the Royal Alexandra Theatre to the O'Keefe Centre seeking larger audiences. When I walked out on the vast stage of the Centre on September 4 shortly before the first full dress rehearsal of *Heloise and Abelard* I felt overwhelmed. All around me carpenters were still at work making final adjustments, technicians were adjusting lights, in the dressing rooms the singers were finishing their make-up and donning their costumes, and members of the Toronto Symphony were tuning their instruments, impatient to begin. I went backstage to wish Heather Thompson and the other principal singers good luck (*"merde,"* "break a leg," "*toi toi toi*"). The voice came over the sound system, "Heloise. Five minutes" and I felt not only overwhelmed but apprehensive. When I had begun writing my libretto in Belfast almost twenty years before I had never envisaged all this—the millions of dollars invested, the arrival of music critics from across Canada and from the USA and England, the possibility of failure.

The final days leading up to the premiere were packed. I had classes to teach and lots of university business to attend to. Family members were arriving in Toronto from overseas and from parts of Canada and the USA. Hotel rooms had to be booked, dinners arranged, and press interviews given. Perhaps these distractions were a good thing allowing less time for worry or nervousness. The evening of the premiere (8 September) arrived, the audience filled the great theatre, the lights lowered, the conductor Victor Feldbrill entered to applause, his baton led the orchestra into the Overture, and the curtain rose on Heloise, severe and beautiful in her Abbess's habit, as she dictated a letter to her amanuensis:

> *O, my François,*
> *To you the dearest of his friends,*
> *And mine. I write to ease the sorrow of heart*
> *That has overtaken me*
> *Since I heard of Abelard's death.*

And so the evening fled quickly as the tragic passion of Heloise and her priest lover was played out.

My most striking memory of that evening was the difference between listening to the piano score which Wilson often played to me as the composition of the opera progressed and hearing the opera with orchestral. I realized how powerfully an orchestral accompaniment can strengthen mood and character development and especially how it can amplify emotion. In later years I grew more and more impressed at the phenomenon that was the development of the European orchestra, a development comparable, I have always thought, to that of the Gothic cathedral. At first glance the composer has, seemingly, a very limited palette based (in Western music) on a scale of only seven main notes. But when one listens to a Bethoven symphony or, to take an extreme example, to Mahler's Symphony No. 8, with its scoring for an orchestra of some 170 players and a chorus of 850, this seemingly limited palette can achieve an enormous variety of sound. No wonder the Greek philosopher Pythagoras held that music was a branch of the divine science of mathematics and that its harmonies echoed the mathematical proportions of the universe. The truly pure of heart were blessed, he believed, with the ability to hear the music of the spheres as Adam and Eve did in their prelapsarian Eden. The reality is that the orchestral composer has many other tools at his command beyond the notes with which he works. For example, the five components of the orchestra—strings, percussion, brass, woodwind, and keyboard—allow for multiple shadings associated with their various instruments. No two violins sound alike, no two oboes. The wind section of the orchestra offers the flute, oboe, clarinet, bass clarinet, bassoon, French horn, and English horn. Further, the flute family includes the piccolo, the concert flute, the alto flute, and the bass flute and, for special effects, one can employ the recorder and the tin whistle. Although the flute and the cello may play the same note it will sound different because of harmonics and the same is true of all the other instruments. And composers who want a very special sound may also commission the building of instruments as Wagner did when he had a tuba, the Wagner tuba, built for his "Ring" cycle. Composers are also intensely aware of the importance of selecting the appropriate key for a work; a symphony transposed note by note from the key of G to the key of E flat will sound quite different. I had never been more aware of the extraordinarily varied timbral palette that a great orchestra can offer than when I first heard the entire grand opera that was *Heloise and Abelard*.

The following morning the critics of the *Globe and Mail*, the *Telegram*, and the *Toronto Star* were respectful but not as enthusiastic as Wilson and I might have wished. The nub of their criticism echoed my fears regarding the staging of the opera. They saw the opera as having a dual focus—the story of the lovers and that of the struggle between Abelard and the Church. Leon Major the director, taking this duality to an extreme, allowed the representatives of the Church sitting on bleachers to dominate the action. The *Toronto Star* critic William Littler noted this pointing out that the protagonists of the opera "shrink particularly in the presence of the church." Interestingly, foreign critics were much kinder that those from Canada. Alan Blyth of *The Times* of London praised the opera enthusiastically, noting that it was "among the best new operas of the past decade, certainly surpassing anything heard in Britain, Tippet and Britten excluded."

It is unfortunate that in the twentieth century new operas rarely get a chance to be heard again. In the nineteenth century operas that failed on first performance were often given a new life as in the case of Puccini's *Madama Butterfly* whose La Scala premiere was a total fiasco but whose second revised presentation some months later at Brescia's Opera House opened the doors of opera houses throughout the world. The Paris premiere of Wagner's *Tannhäuser* was a spectacular failure but he was allowed to revise it for another production. It too was a failure and was withdrawn after only three performances before going on many years later to become a standard work in the operatic repertoire. Most composers and librettists argue wryly that there should be a foundation of some sort devoted primarily to the second presentation of new operas to allow for modification if necessary (as was the case with Wagner and Puccini) and to allow audiences and critics to re-evaluate these works which may have productions differing totally in direction, staging, lighting, and in the quality of the leading singers.

The case of *The Summoning of Everyman* offers an interesting perspective on these remarks. The premiere at Dalhousie University, Nova Scotia, was essentially a university production; only the starring and difficult role of Everyman was played by a professional singer from outside the community—Garnett Brooks, who had sung in various opera houses in Europe. This university production was received with such critical acclaim (especially when it was broadcast by the CBC) that the Stratford Festival of Canada offered it in its 1974 season along with Menotti's *The Medium*, starring Maureen Forrester. *Everyman* was directed by Michael Bawtree who had to hand all the resources of the Stratford Festival, with Garnett Brooks reprising the title role. And yet the *Globe and Mail* critic John Kraglund who had praised the Dalhousie University production so highly wrote that the Stratford production "was an arena staging ... which had the effect of making it a wholly different opera" because it diffused the intensity of the action. Many years later the opera was again produced by Guillermo Silva-Marin's Opera in Concert where the starkness of the setting allowed for full appreciation of the libretto and the music. So it is that a change of directors, production values, singers, or venue can affect the way in which a work of art is received. I have always cherished the wish that one day the Salzburg Festival would mount my *Everyman* in tandem with its annual presentation of the same play *Jedermann,* by Hugo von Hofmannsthal.

University matters continued to be the main business of my life—teaching, supervision of MA theses, committee work, book reviewing, search committees (for Chairs, Deans, a President—Donald F. Foster), and senate committee work. I was very lucky in that I loved my work, especially my contact with students. People occasionally remarked to me that I must find it boring teaching the same courses year after year. But I did not. I never spoke from a written text and so I could vary my material in line with what I might call the dynamics of the lecture room. The students varied in their response to the material asking different questions and seizing on different points of interest. And sometimes I came across an exceptionally gifted student whose work and insight and intelligence recharged my own academic batteries. Such was that student John Steffler who had written to me from Spain wanting to write his MA thesis on the poetry of Blake. We met in my office and I was so impressed by him that I told him I did not want to get in his way and that he should go off and write the thesis which I would read when it was finished. He did, I read it, it was excellent—probably the finest thesis I have ever been associated with—he took his degree and went off to Newfoundland and Labrador as a university lecturer where he wrote a number of volumes of poetry and a novel, *The Afterlife of George Cartwright*, which I consider a Canadian classic.

And then there was Florence, an undergraduate student from Nigeria, whose husband was taking a doctoral degree at the Ontario Agricultural College. Florence was plump with an ever-present smile and the kind of presence that radiated contentment and goodness. And she was very pregnant which seemed to please her mightily. One day during class early in the Fall semester we were working on Wordsworth's "Intimations of Immortality" ode when we came to the lines:

> *Hence in a season of calm weather*
> *Though inland far we be,*
> *Our Souls have sight of that immortal sea*
> *Which brought us hither,*

> *Can in a moment travel thither,*
> *And see the Children sport upon the shore,*
> *And hear the mighty waters rolling evermore.*

When I invited comments on the passage Florence said she thought the lines referred to the fact that we somehow retained memories of being in the waters of the womb and that these memories never leave us. As she spoke she put her hands on her stomach and said that when her baby was born she was going to read these lines to it. The days and weeks went by and Florence grew bigger and bigger and she became the centre of attention in our classroom. The women students consulted with her on their problems and their fears and hopes and the men students showed a surprising degree of solicitude, opening doors and carrying her bags and books as she drew nearer to the week when her baby would be born. But soon, too soon, Florence did not appear and one day a woman student stood up and tearfully announced to the class that Florence's baby had died. I never saw Florence again. In the years that followed I always thought sadly of Florence when I lectured on Wordsworth's great ode, taking comfort in a later passage:

> *We will grieve not, rather find*
> *Strength in what remains behind;*
> *In the primal sympathy*
> *Which having been must ever be;*
> *In the soothing thoughts that spring*
> *Out of human suffering;*
> *In the faith that looks through death,*
> *In years that bring the philosophic mind.*

Richard, a graduate student in my seminar on the poetry of Yeats, was a very unusual young man. My students were required to make an oral presentation on a topic before their fellow graduate students who would then question them or seek additional information. Students would later present me with this oral work in written form so that I could grade it. Richard's presentation was excellent but a week passed, then two, without my receiving his paper. I sent for him and he said he was extensively revising it, that I would receive it soon. Two further weeks went by and no paper. One day a young woman, Richard's wife, appeared in my office to tell me that he was sitting up night after night working on his paper but was unable to finish it and that she feared he was endangering his health. At the undergraduate level the same thing had often happened. Unable to get any written work from Richard, for the first and only time in my professional career I referred him to the university's Psychological Services for help. He dropped out of my class and it was over a year before I met him when I discovered that he had become a real estate salesman and was very successful. He told me that Psychological Services had sent him to a medical doctor who specialized in treating people with serious heart and lung problems who needed help in overcoming their addition to smoking. In his first session with Richard the doctor discovered a severe traumatic event in his background that caused him, under hypnosis, to clench his right hand as if in *rigor mortis*. Six further sessions were necessary to enable the doctor to get Richard to clench and unclench his hand with ease. No sooner was the cure complete than Richard gave up any academic ambitions and settled contentedly into a lifestyle which he claimed to be thoroughly enjoying. I was so impressed by Richard's story that I made an appointment with his doctor and underwent hypnosis to cure my own addition to cigarettes—I had been smoking two packs a day for twenty-four years. One session of fifteen minutes was successful and in the years since then I have never smoked although I remember nostalgically my enjoyment of a cigarette or a cigar with a good coffee and a fine cognac.

The year 1975 was a very good year because in January our second son Shaun was born. Renate and I loved him from the moment of his birth but his brother Ormonde did not. It was as classic a case of sibling rivalry as I had ever seen. Ormonde had been very close to us—for the first years of his life he called me Eugene and his mother Renate. From his birth we took him everywhere we went—late night parties, flamenco shows in Seville that only began at ten o'clock in the evening, family gatherings in Ireland and Germany. We did not have any modern or doctrinaire concept of parenthood that stressed letting children grow up freely or allowing them to live in unconventional ways—it was merely that in many situations it was impossible to get baby sitters or, more frankly, because we enjoyed having him with us wherever we went. But then came Shaun—a baby who demanded enormous attention which shunted Ormonde, firstborn, off to an emotionally-depleted siding. I was fascinated by the irrationality of his reaction to his sibling—an irrationality predetermined by his genetic code which drove him to defend his emotional territory that included his parents, his toys, his friends, his space. It took some eight years for Shaun to win over his brother and then the capitulation was complete. They became best friends, bound by blood and countless psychological campaigns by a younger brother whose multiple roles in entertaining his brother may have led him to a professional career as an actor and to Hollywood.

Only one event marred the very good year that was 1975—the death of my sister and my twin, Bernadette, who died of a painful cancer leaving behind a husband and children. She had begun training to be a nurse but never finished. Life can be very unfair and I have often thought how blessed I have been in contrast to Bernadette, the human being who shared the same womb as I.

Following my return from Spain I had spent a great deal of time working on my manuscript of *The Bulls of Ronda* until it was finally ready to be sent to the publishing firm of Methuen where is was immediately accepted for publication. It was released in 1976 with editions in Canada, the USA, the UK, and Australia in both hardback and paperback. I was surprised to discover that in general the foreign reviews were more favourable than the Canadian reviews and once again I was struck by the discrepancy of critical reaction. But, paradoxically, writers are generally not disturbed by such discrepancies cheering themselves by citing the case of so many writers who have been rejected only to later achieve international fame. Wordsworth thought the poetry of Blake clearly demonstrated that he was mad, Byron damned Wordsworth as one who shows that "prose is verse, verse merely prose, / Convincing all, by demonstration plain," and the learned critic Lockhart dismissed Keats' poetry as "driveling idiocy." In our own time Joseph Heller's *Catch-22* was rejected by twenty-two publishers, Robert Persig's *Zen and the Art of Motorcycle Maintenance* by more than one hundred.

Following the success of *Heloise and Abelard* and *The Summoning of Everyman*, the Guelph Spring Festival commissioned Charles Wilson and me to write a new opera that, given budgetary limitations, was to have a small cast, a small orchestra, and a unit set. It would be premiered in 1977.

I spent at least two years researching different subjects and especially that of Undine, the underwater sprite, as told in the novella by Friedrich de la Motte Fouqué. I had already sketched a scenario for the latter subject until I finally decided that I would not rely on an historical or mythological story line but would seek to write in a contemporary mode that drew upon the genre of the detective story and modern psychiatry. I was also influenced in this regard by the fact that Wilson was eager to write an opera in which he would avoid such traditional operatic conventions as arias, avoid establishing definite keys, avoid tonality in favour of atonality, and instead use similar patterns of orchestral sounds instead of the Wagnerian (and Verdian) *leitmotif* to advance the opera's action. It was an audacious plan, but we were both interested in dramatizing states of mind and psychological landscapes rather than in following the tyranny of conventional plot. Stockhausen, Berg, and the interior monologue of James Joyce were our avatars, not Bellini and Dickens.

Still involved with the Spring Festival throughout the 1970s I saw many artists of international stature wing their way to Guelph—Jon Vickers, Yehudi Menuhin, Colin Graham, Judith Forst, Krzysztof Penderecki, Betty Comden and Adolph Green (who wrote the screenplays for *On the Town*, with Frank Sinatra and Gene Kelly, and *Singin' in the Rain* with Kelly), Peter Pears, Ernst Krenek, Siobhan McKenna, and many others. The Canadian tenor Jon Vickers came often to perform at the festival because while he wintered in Bermuda he loved his farm north of Toronto. Additionally, he was delighted to sing at a festival presided over by Niki Goldschmidt who had given him voice lessons as a young aspiring tenor. Barrel-chested, with beetling eyebrows, he was the most intense artist I ever met. To see him in the role of Florestan in Bethoven's *Fidelio* was to witness a degree of artistic and moral commitment unparalleled by any other singer. In 1974 Vickers performed the role of the Male Chorus (sung by Peter Pears in the opera's premiere) in Benjamin Britten's *The Rape of Lucretia*, with Colin Graham (a close friend of Britten) directing. It says something for Niki's powers of persuasion that one of the most famous tenors in the world and a director who was accustomed to work in the most prestigious theatres in the world came to Guelph to perform in a High School auditorium. As a man, Vickers was conservative in his likes and dislikes; for example, he condemned with his usual intensity those who worked behind the scenes in the opera houses of the world, claiming that they spent their time featherbedding and that they made too much money. This from the highest paid tenor in the world! When he received a well-deserved honorary degree from the University of Guelph in 1983 we chatted as we donned our academic robes prior to walking across the campus for Convocation. My fellow professors probably thought we were speaking of musical matters but in fact Vickers was telling me jokes of which he had a never-ending stream. His convocation address was in character—he took as his theme the French Revolution which, he argued, was the source of most modern ills. But it is the work of a great artist which redeems him and the imperfections of a man like Vickers pale before the magnitude of his talent.

Unlike Vickers, Menuhin was the most unassuming of men. I had known of him since I was a child and still remember my mother reading newspaper accounts of the child prodigy who played his violin in the world's capitals from the age of seven and consolidated that early fame in a life time devoted to music. When he came to Guelph with his sister Hephzibah as accompanist on the piano, he also played a work he had commissioned from the Canadian composer Harry Somers—a twenty-minute long monophonic "Music for Solo Violin." I was there when Menuhin rehearsed the piece in War Memorial Hall as was Hephzibah. At the conclusion Menuhin turned to his sister and asked, "what do you think?" She pondered the question for a long time and finally replied, "challenging." I had no idea whether she approved or not. On another occasion I accompanied Menuhin, now Sir Yehudi Menuhin, Order of Merit, when he visited Guelph's Farmers' Market which operates on Saturdays under the shadow of the beautiful Church of Our Lady. When he heard a local fiddler play, he stopped to talk to him and then proceeded to play a tune on his very inferior fiddle. It was certainly a change for Menuhin who at the age of twelve practiced on the famous 1733 Prince Khevenhüller Stradivari violin.

In 1976 the Guelph Spring Festival presented one of its most daring evenings simply titled "Penderecki: A Tribute to Krzysztof Penderecki." In his early forties, the Polish composer already enjoyed an international reputation. When Niki Goldschmidt decided to stage this concert he invited Penderecki to come to Guelph to conduct the concert and to choose his own music. The result was a feast fit for connoisseurs of avant garde music: "Strophes"; *Ecloga*; String Quartet, No 2; the *Miserere* and "*Stabat Mater*" from his "St Luke's Passion, for Mixed Chorus, *A Capella*"; "*Capriccio* for Solo Cello"; and "From the Psalms of David"—for Mixed Chorus and Instrumental Ensemble. To perform this music to the standard of the *maestro*, Niki drew on some of Canada's finest musical talent—soprano Mary Morrison, flautist Robert Aiken, cellist Gisela Depkat, The Festival Singers of Canada, The Orford Quartet, The Nexus Percussion Ensemble, and narrator John Horton. The concert was to be held in War Memorial Hall and Niki and I accompanied Penderecki there when he first went to check the hall's acoustics. He pronounced them to be very fine but there had to be one change—there was a very large curtain behind the stage . It would have to go. A stagehand pulled it back to reveal a wall that that not been painted in years and which was covered in graffiti. What would our audience think! But Penderecki was not to be moved and down the curtain came to give him the kind of acoustic finesse he wanted. The concert was a stunning success, the *maestro* was delighted, and Niki arranged a little post-concert part at a local hotel for our guest. Present were Sheila Goldschmidt, Murdo MacKinnon and Elizabeth MacKinnon, and Renate and me. I remember it was a very hot evening and when we arrived at the hotel room our hostess Sheila said she was sure I would like a drink. I asked her for a cold beer but she apologized profusely and said she only had French champagne! During the evening we had plenty of time to chat with Penderecki. He was a smallish bearded and mustached man, very like the image most people have of a cloistered professor. He chatted in English, and in French and German (with Niki and Renate). At one point in the evening when he learned that I was working on a libretto for a new opera he told me that he also was at work on a large scale opera based on Milton's *Paradise Lost*, with libretto by the gifted British playwright Christopher Fry. He was very interested to learn that such English Romantic poets as Blake and Shelley held that Satan was in fact the true hero of *Paradise Lost* and that Blake believed that Milton "was of the Devil's party without knowing it." When his opera was premiered one prominent critic in Chicago praised it highly while Harold Schoenberg of *The New York Times* (who had reviewed favorably the Ottawa performance of *Heloise and Abelard*) damned it.

In 1976 an exciting manuscript came across my desk—it was a play, *Memoir* by John Murrell, a young playwright just entering his stride. *Memoir* is a two-hander featuring the actress Sarah Bernhardt as she dictates her reminiscences to her servant and secretary Pitou. I was immediately struck by the elegance of Murrell's language, the way he was able to capture so well the atmosphere of the *Belle Époque,* and by the vivid vignettes he offered of many of her contemporaries such as Oscar Wilde. Although the Guelph Spring Festival's mandate related almost entirely to music, I managed to convince Niki to present the world premiere. The director, Erik Salmon, wanted Wendy Hiller (Bernard Shaw's favourite actress for many years) for the role of Bernhardt but when he was unable to get her up he signed up the Irish actress Siobhan McKenna. Because I had long admired McKenna's work, I asked her to dinner. Born in Belfast, and raised in Galway in the west of Ireland, she was a tall woman, big boned, with beautiful eyes and a voice of great distinction. She drank whisky and wine, she smoked incessantly which gave her voice a husky timbre, and she loved salmon, eating it at every opportunity. Well aware of her fame as an actress, she was very much the *diva*, but in private she was most companionable with lots of tales about her work in the theatre. Fluent in Gaelic, she had translated Bernard Shaw's *Saint Joan* into that language—her 1954 London appearance in the role of Joan (in English) was a triumph which she followed up four years later by playing that most special of roles—Hamlet. She fell in love with *Memoir* when she first read it—indeed the part of Sarah Bernhardt fitted her like a glove. But she hated her Guelph accommodation—a rather grim suite of rooms on the university campus. Because Renate and I were going off to the Bahamas for a holiday, and because she had often said how beautiful she thought our house was, we offered Siobhan the use of it for two weeks. I like to remember her walking about our home rehearsing her role or consulting Joanna Richardson's *Sarah Bernhardt and Her World*—she left us her signed copy with a note of thanks.

The play's premiere was applauded by most of the press and *Memoir* went on to play Dublin, London, Paris, and the major cities of Europe and was translated into some twenty languages. The sole dissenting critic was Gina Mallet of the *Toronto Star* who was often very aggressive in her criticism, so aggressive that a number of Toronto theatre groups tried—unsuccessfully—to have her fired because she was not sufficiently enthusiastic about Canadian plays. Her defence was that she disliked the barns in which they were staged and the fact that she had to walk over dirty straw and horse and cow manure to take her seat.

The creation by Charles Wilson and me of a new opera proved much more difficult than did the creation of our previous two operas. At one point, in the Spring of 1976, Wilson and I were at such cross purposes as to how the story line should develop that I suggested we abandon our collaboration. I had begun by writing a draft with the title "A Detective Story," later finalized as *Psycho Red*, where I would have the audience solve the crime from clues that I would supply throughout the work. Gradually a number of themes began to coalesce. My novel *The Bulls of Ronda* was also a detective story in which a man caught between two women, Elena and Leonora, is destroyed. The women, meant to be Janus images of each other, suggest that it is difficult to define what is good and what evil and to suggest that perhaps they are twins (my twin Bernadette was on my mind). I noticed also that in my various drafts I had already named the two women of my opera Elena and Leonora. Then too memories of the doctor who hypnotized me into stop smoking began to interest me and he gradually became my fictional Dr. Shadow, a psychiatrist. But instead of making him the kind of all-powerful scientist too often presented in the media, I became interested in the man rather than the doctor-scientist. At this point I made Elena and Leonora one and introduced them to Dr Shadow in order that this person with a dual personality might be cured by his psychiatric and hypnotic–based techniques. Consequently, the murder would not be a crude physical one but rather a spiritual or psychic killing. I was not drawing on the movies "The Three Faces of Eve" or "Sybil" for this business of multiple personalities but on Joyce's *Finnegans Wake* where I first came across reference to Dr Morton Prince's classic study of dissociation of personality. *Psycho Red* is about psychiatric practice but it also suggests that that in a sense we are only healthy if we cherish creatively our neuroses.

When I mentioned the composer Berg earlier I had in mind his opera *Wozzeck*, which is based on Büchner's early nineteenth-century play. Few people who attend this opera for the first time are bothered by the modernity of the music precisely because the music—orchestral and vocal—is only one element of the opera and is complemented by another element—the modernity and starkness of the dramatic and psychological action. In a sense *Wozzeck* is theatre rather than opera. I tried for the same kind of thing in writing the libretto for *Psycho Red.* I wanted it to be called something other than "opera" to indicate I was trying to find a new form which is why I called it a "mindscape in music." I also borrowed from the other arts which explains why I chose to incorporate a ballet in this mindscape. I had always intended to have a chorus but I did not want it interrupting or slowing down the action of the work. It soon became evident that the chorus represented states of mind rather than real characters and since I had not given the chorus words to sing Wilson and I decided that it should be an extension of the orchestra. Accordingly we tucked them away in the pit with the orchestra. Wilson's music echoed the unconventionality of this mindscape. He devised his own notation system to enable the performers and orchestra to follow his multiple tempi and asymmetrical rhythmic groupings. Further, he laid out the entire score in a time-grid of seconds and insisted that while the conductor would conduct in the conventional patterns the conductor's beat was not meant to indicate the accentual beat for the individual performers—their accents were to be executed independently of both the conductor and the other performers. Because of the complexity of the score Wilson decided there should be a second conductor who would cue the singers and so a young musician Robert Cooper was hired.

When *Psycho Red* was completed Goldschmidt set about getting a director (Wilson would conduct). But he met with refusal after refusal—would-be directors found great difficulty reading the score. Michael Bawtree who had conducted our *Everyman* at the Stratford Festival turned it down telling me he thought the music "monstrous." Finally, Goldschmidt, remembering that the opera contained a ballet, sent the score (by diplomatic pouch) to Canada's foremost choreographer Brian Macdonald who was then at work with Stockholm's Royal Ballet. A rehearsal pianist at the Royal Opera House led him through the score and he agreed to direct. To play the three main roles Gary Relyea, a young baritone with a beautiful voice, was contracted for the part of Dr Shadow, while seasoned veterans Alexandra Browning would play his wife and Jean MacPhail the dual role of Leonora-Elena. It would seem all was set for a smooth rehearsal period and premiere. Renate and I invited Brian Macdonald to stay in our home, but we saw very little of him because while he was preparing *Psycho Red* he was also commuting between Guelph and Stratford where he was choreographing Bernstein's *Candide* and preparing two new works for Montreal's *Les Grands Ballets Canadiens* also being presented by the Guelph Spring Festival.

Rehearsals began in the middle of April and all went well at first. But it soon became evident that Relyea was having difficulties in Act 2 and seemed overwhelmed by his role. On April 27, nine days before the premiere which was scheduled for Saturday 6 May, he did not turn up for rehearsals and could not be located. When Niki finally established contact with Relyea's wife she told him that her husband would not be returning to the cast. He was intimidated by the difficulty of the music and he seemed also to be haunted by the character of Dr Shadow who suffers a mental breakdown in the opera. Ever resourceful, Niki phoned the baritone Alexander Gray who had just finished an engagement in Calgary, he was free, a score was flown out to him, he accepted, and arrived in Guelph two days later. To help him with the difficult role, dates for the opera were altered. The premiere would take place on Wednesday 10 May and there would be only one other performance on the following day. Here was the making of one of those legendary breaks that singers dream about—replacing an ailing singer at the last moment and scoring a great artistic triumph as when Pavarotti gained international attention replacing di Stefano in 1963 in *La Bohème* at Covent Garden or Martina Arroyo replacing Birgit Nilsson in *Aida* at four hours' notice. But it was not to be. Charles Wilson began working with Gray for up to twelve hours a day but after five days, on 4 May, Gray told Brian Macdonald he found the part of Dr Shadow too difficult and fled back to Calgary.

At this point it looked as though the opera would have to be cancelled. I was shocked by this turn of events because I felt that it would be almost impossible to get the opera produced by another company and because I believed it deserved a hearing. Niki called a meeting of Macdonald, Murdo MacKinnon, and myself and various options—including cancellation—were considered. Finally, someone suggested that Relyea was secure enough in Act One and if he could be persuaded to return perhaps he could remain seated at his desk throughout Act Two reading his patients' files which would be, in fact, the score. Relyea was contacted and after much hesitation he accepted. Macdonald then redesigned Act Two to allow for its leading actor, to be deskbound, and the opera opened to an audience eager to hear a work that had already caused so much controversy.

It would be an understatement to say that the audience was taken aback. Not only did it find the music difficult but it found the story of the opera almost incomprehensible because it was now so overlaid by a ballet played by two men and two women. When Macdonald had first begun rehearsing the opera, the ballet took place midway in the piece; in his new blocking of the opera caused by Relyea's dropout the ballet dancers were introduced at various point to suggest those movements that Relyea was unable to carry out. I had a great deal of sympathy for the audience since even the critics who had been briefed before the premiere professed puzzlement. John Kraglund, writing in the *Globe and Mail*, said, "If I had discovered what the piece was all about, I would offer a brief synopsis," but he did go on to write, "once one has a firm grip on the story, I suspect the score with its strongly percussive rhythms will bring the work quite effectively out of the musical theatre mold into the operatic one." Critic Gerald Manning wrote, "There is no question that *Psycho Red* is an achievement of major importance in contemporary opera." Wilson the composer has always felt that *Psycho Red* is his best work and I echo that opinion while hoping that when the work is staged again under less dramatic conditions its merits will be more clearly recognized. A final note. The case of Gary Relyea provides a cautionary note to all artists—do not allow your manager to book you into a role before you have made sure that you can prepare it thoroughly while fulfilling your other engagements. Browning and MacPhail had to play roles as difficult as that facing Relyea—they were prepared, he was not.

In the middle of these activities I was also at work on a new novel, this one based on a Canadian subject. My years working for the NDP following the 1967 provincial election had made me familiar with many of the figures on the provincial political scene and with some on the national scene in Ottawa. In addition, I had been reading a number of books on past Canadian Prime Ministers including John A. Macdonald, Mackenzie King, John Diefenbaker, and Pierre Trudeau. And a merry band they were. Macdonald, when not recovering from bouts of prolonged drunkenness, accepted huge bribes from a railway mogul who was rewarded with the contract to build the Canadian Pacific Railroad. William Lyon Mackenzie King, Canada's tenth Prime Minister, abhorred alcohol, admired Hitler, and cultivated séances where he communicated with his dead mother, his dead Irish setter dogs, and Leonardo da Vinci, and confirmed the wisdom of his political decisions by use of a crystal ball and a Ouija board. Such reading was fertile soil for a political satire and so between 1976 and 1980 (with a winter of preparation in Longboat Key, Florida), I worked very hard on my tale of a young Member of Parliament (Julius B. Kaiser) who is vaulted into prominence as a prospective Prime Minister of Canada and who acts as a gauge of the moral values of the federal scene in Ottawa. In my *roman à clef* I took aim at a large number of sacred cows—Cabinet ministers with their foibles and sexual appetites, civil servants and their expense accounts, Canadian relations with the USA, bilingualism, the RCMP, Russian diplomats, pollsters, television "personalities," among others. I had no expectation that my novel would improve matters in Ottawa for I was aware that satire is a mirror in which we see only the faces of others. The novel was published in 1980 under the title *Power Game: The Making of a Prime Minister*. Critical reviews were favourable, the major qualification being that my view of the Canadian political scene and its politicians was too improbable and much too harsh.

But, in fact, Julius Kaiser, the protagonist of my *roman à clef*, was a shrinking violet compared to the figure on whom he was based—Pierre Trudeau, the fifteenth Prime Minister of Canada and its most improbable. A casual Montreal *bon vivant*, he had endorsed the politics and ideology of the New Democratic Party of Canada until, in 1968, he became a Liberal when offered a safe seat. In order to satisfy Quebec representation in the Cabinet he was appointed Minister of Justice and later became Prime Minister based largely on popular perception (fostered by the media ever alert to promote someone who guaranteed headlines) that he was "cool" because he was a bachelor, because he sported a cape and a rose in his lapel, because he wore sandals to Parliament, and because he didn't really care deeply about politics or anything else. In an age of the flower child, the Beatles, and drugs, he was a perfect icon of the *Zeitgeist*. Perceived in the halls of Academe as a liberal intellectual, he invoked the War Emergency Act (Martial Law) which suspended essential civil rights across

Canada because a Minister of the Crown had been murdered by *Le Front de libération du Québec* (FLQ); only twice before had the Act been invoked—at the outbreak of the First and Second World Wars. A year later Trudeau confirmed the eccentricity of his judgment by marrying Margaret Sinclair, thirty years his junior. Read today *Power Game: The Making of a Prime Minister* may be seen to reaffirm the wisdom of the saying *Plus ça change, plus c'est la même chose* and the savage truths of the aphorisms from Machiavelli that introduce each section of the novel.

CAN LIT AND THE COLONIAL CRINGE

The year 1980 ushered in the busiest decade of my life. It began when I took over the editorship of a small journal, *Canadian Drama/L'Art dramatique canadienne*. Dedicated to the promotion of Canadian drama, it had been founded five years before by Rota Herzberg, born in Austria, at a time when there was no journal devoted exclusively to the study of Canadian drama and theatre. Although the print run was small—three hundred copies—the journal was on the subscription list of most of the major libraries in the English-speaking world and thus its influence was out of all proportion to its print run. Very soon I had the journal format redesigned, I obtained a federal grant to help with publication costs, and I developed a strong editorial board. For the next ten years I published two issues annually and complemented the journal's scholarly articles with the publication of original play scripts and translations of French-Canadian plays.

The first issue of the journal under my editorial control was devoted to Commonwealth drama because I wanted to get a perspective on what was happening in drama in other countries with a colonial past like Canada's and a common language—English. Were there any characteristics that linked us? In what ways did we differ? A number of critics have made the case that a distinguishing mark of the Canadian identity is a sense of space, space as represented by the garrison, the wilderness, the North (whether geographical or mythic). Did Australian novels and plays use such markers? How did the representation of the Australian Aboriginal differ from that found in Canadian literature? Was the Outback the equivalent of the North in Canada and did both have symbolic values? South Africa had a colonial past but what effect did the policy of apartheid have on its literature? These were questions which exercised me at the time and contributors from Australia, New Zealand, South Africa, the Caribbean, and Nigeria attempted to answer some of these questions in my first issue of *Canadian Drama/L'Art dramatique canadienne* . An additional benefit was that I struck up an epistolary friendship with a number of experts in various parts of the Commonwealth who would be very helpful when later I began work on a very large Commonwealth literary project.

What was remarkable about the theatrical scene in English Canada at that time is that while it had grown in importance it had been virtually ignored by the academic community and by publishers. There were a number of practising playwrights—John Herbert, James Reaney, George Ryga, David Fennario, George Walker, David French, Sharon Pollock, Judith Thompson—and the scene in Quebec was even more vital with a host of new dramatists of whom the most outstanding was Michel Tremblay. But the work of these playwrights was not being introduced into university curricula—the many professors who now taught Canadian literature knew nothing about either the history of Canadian drama and its plays or about the theatrical milieu in which these plays were produced. Additionally, there were no anthologies of full-length Canadian plays that could be used in university courses. In taking on the editorship of *Canadian Drama* I hoped to remedy in some degree this situation. I placed great emphasis on the publication of original Canadian stage, radio, and television plays and on historical plays that reflected Canadian interests. I included plays by Marc Lescarbot, Timothy Findley, Gwen Pharis Ringwood, Herman Voaden, Robertson Davies, W.H. Fréchette, Léon Petitjean and Henri Rollin, Pierre Petitclair, Elzéar Paquin, Marcel Dubé, and Anne Hébert. The journal published essays on their work while drawing attention to Canadian dramatists of previous centuries writing in both English Canada and French Canada. Because there were few translations into English of French Canadian plays, Renate and I spent long hours translating Lescarbot's 1606 masque *Le Théâtre de Neptune en la Nouvelle-France*, the first play to be performed in North America, Fréchette's *Papineau* (1880), Paquin's *Riel* (1886), and three plays by Anne Hébert: *Le temps sauvage*, *La Merciére assassinée*, and *Les Invités au procès.*

I had always admired the work of Robertson Davies who was internationally acclaimed for his novels, especially his Deptford trilogy. Almost unknown, however, was his dramatic *oeuvre* that included such plays as *Overlaid*, and the full length *Fortune, My Foe*, *A Jig for the Gipsy*, *Gen-*

eral Confession, and *Question Time*. I designed an issue of the journal as a *Festschrift* featuring an annotated checklist of his plays, a number of scholarly essays relating them to his other miscellaneous writings, and I published for the first time Davies' own stage adaptation of his novel *The Leaven of Malice*. Davies wrote me of his pleasure at this belated *homage*.

I also published a number of theatre Calendars—lists of plays with dates of production, casts, directors, set designers, and so on. Two of these Calendars (fully illustrated) documented the history of the Charlottetown Festival from 1965 to 1985 and Festival Lennoxville which ran from 1972 to 1982. I also published important materials that no commercial publisher would touch, given their limited and specialized appeal. A good example of this was Patrick B. O'Neill's checklist of Canadian dramatic materials from the seventeenth century to 1967 which comprised more than five thousand entries. I published this enormous list in two separate issues so as not to impose too heavily on the journal's readers but I was determined to redeem these plays so long buried in neglect. *Esse est percipi*. Bishop Berkeley's famous dictum affirms that a thing does not exist if it is not perceived. I too believed that Canadian dramatic literature would not exist until it was perceived as existing. And it did not matter if there were no masterpieces in O'Neill's checklist. In order for a great literature to exist it must be preceded by a host of minor writers who provide a sense of tradition that will nurture the individual talent of the great writers that will follow. Only specialists study the work of Irish writers Griffin, Banim, Maturin, Carleton, Mangan, and Boucicault, minor writers mostly, but they fed the imagination of a generation of later writers like Wilde, Shaw, Yeats, Joyce, and O'Casey. When I published Petitjean and Rollin's *Aurore l'enfant martyre* I was aware that it was a very inferior melodrama, but I was also aware that although it ran in Quebec for thirty years no translation into English existed. I commissioned a translation because I was convinced that the play said something significant about French Canadian aesthetic taste and sensibility that might usefully be compared to English Canadian sensibilities. It was for this reason also that I published a special issue of *Canadian Drama/L'Art dramatique canadienne* on Louis Riel, that transformative and divisive figure, where the views of French-Canadians academics were often in sharp contrast to those of English-speaking academics. I also included in that issue two original plays whose subject was Riel.

I edited the journal for ten years and because I had no staff it was a very heavy task that involved editing all materials, finding reviewers for books, communicating with authors about their essays (which sometimes involved suggesting changes or modifications), and proofreading. But the reward was great for I had, so to speak, a ring side seat at the emergence of a modern native drama where I met nearly all those who had a special interest in Canadian drama. Again, this was to prove essential some years later when I undertook an even larger collaborative project directly related to firmly establishing Canadian drama and theatre as an essential element of Canadian literature as a whole.

In 1981 Macmillan of London commissioned me to write a critical study of the writings of John Millington Synge, Irish playwright. I had always been fascinated by the man and I admired greatly the plays I had read or seen on stage, especially *Riders to the Sea* and *The Playboy of the Western World*. At this time I offered a graduate course under the title "Modern Irish Writers," a title elastic enough to accommodate whatever author I wanted to examine, whether it was Yeats or Shaw or Joyce. I had never offered Synge but I now proceeded to do so. For thirteen weeks I led my MA students through his work and in our seminars my students presented papers on many aspects of the plays and prose writings. All this helped me greatly in preparing my book. I could not help noticing how germane Synge's life and work was to my own work in promoting the study of Canadian drama and theatre. A highly educated man who knew six languages, Synge was living in Paris when Yeats urged him to find his artistic materials in Ireland. As Paul Gauguin, abandoning Paris, found his métier in Tahiti, so Synge found his on the desolate Aran Islands where the people spoke only Gaelic. Here he heard the archetypal story of a son who killed his father which became the basis for his explosive *Playboy of the Western World*—explosive because it was met by riots when it first played at Dublin's Abbey Theatre. The most useful scholarly texts that I continually consulted when researching my Synge book were those by the Canadian scholar Ann Saddlemyer and by the poet Robin Skelton. When the book was published it earned very good reviews—one critic spoke of its "luminous treatment." I was most pleased by a letter from Skelton praising it and by the fact that Derry Jeffares wrote to me not long after publication to invite me to write an essay on Synge for a book on Irish writers and the theatre to be edited by his Japanese son-in-law.

Another aspect of my busy life at this period was my involvement with The Writers Union of Canada. It was remarkable that up to 1973 when the Union was founded that writers in Canada lacked even a model trade book contract and a minimum royalty. Canadian writers were virtually invisible and writing, it was generally agreed, was the business of publishers. The founders of the Union, including Margaret Atwood, Graeme Gibson, and June Callwood, were determined to change this state of affairs. Margaret Laurence was named titular head of the Union until novelist Marian Engel was elected as its first Chair. In 1978 I joined the Union and attended my first Annual General Meeting at Lake Couchiching. I shared a cabin with the writer Matt Cohen but saw little of him. He was remarkably dour, speaking only when spoken to, and displaying a chameleon-like behaviour that I learned was caused by the fact that he was a regular pot smoker. The person whom I remember most vividly from that weekend was June Callwood. Tall, immaculately turned out, and very striking in a way that reminded me of the actor Katharine Hepburn. A past Chair of the Union, she was a brilliant journalist, an inveterate proponent of civil rights, and a ghostwriter—she ghosted film director Otto Preminger's autobiography, for example. I also met Alice Munro who told me she was terrified at meeting so many strangers. We chatted about mutual friends from the University of Western Ontario where she had been a student, I took her to the bar, got her a drink, we danced, and soon she began to enjoy the evening. But throughout her life, even when she had achieved international celebrity, Munro never felt at ease in large gatherings.

In 1979 I became Chair of the Union's Grievance Committee which dealt mainly with disputes between publishers and writers when I first became friends with Mary Kainer, the Union's Executive Director, a remarkable woman who later became a remarkable artist. In 1982 I was elected first Vice Chair (Robin Skelton was Chair) which meant that I automatically became Chair of the Union for the year 1983–1984. Working with Skelton proved a good introduction to the job. He was a fascinating character, powerfully built with a luxuriant beard and hands that glittered with rings on all fingers. A lover of Irish whisky, he could out drink anyone I ever met. When he and I discussed Union business it was always in a pub of his choosing or in the bar of the Victoria Hotel at the south end of Yonge Street, Toronto. It was a cheap cheerful kind of hotel with thirty-watt bulbs in its small spartan rooms, but it had a fine Victorian bar with no television or radio to interfere with good talk. And if Skelton drank a lot it did not seem to stilt his creative output. A professor at the University of Victoria, he had published literally dozens of books (including work on Synge), he founded a journal of international calibre, *The Malahat Review*, which he edited for many years. Most intriguing to me was the fact that he was a practicing druid who had once gone to Ottawa to exorcise the evil spirits that threatened the creative energies of the Canadian Parliament. And he loved intellectual horseplay. He sent me a limerick which he said "may cause you to groan":

> *W.B. Yeats*
> *when asked about the rates*
> *for Thoor Ballylee*
> *said "This inn is free."*

Not to be outdone, I replied with a limerick that may have made him groan:

> *Erwin Piscator*
> *Was not piscatorial*
> *But he* was
> *Directorial.*

Skelton and the Chairs who had gone before him—Margaret Laurence, Marian Engel, Graeme Gibson, David Lewis Stein, Andreas Schroeder, Timothy Findley, Charles Taylor, June Callwood, Harold Horwood, Margaret Atwood—constituted an eminent set of predecessors and a fascinating cross section of Canadian literary personalities.

Margaret Laurence was Chancellor of Trent University when I first met her at a meeting of the Canadian Association of Irish Studies where she was the guest speaker at the Association's dinner. When she learned that I was to introduce her she phoned me at my home to tell me how apprehensive she was about the occasion and to find out what I intended to say in my introduction. I assured her that it would be purely *pro forma* and complimentary but that did not still her anxiety. She phoned me on two further occasions with the same concern. When we did meet prior to the dinner she was beautifully dressed, clutching an empty glass, and very nervous.

I offered her a drink and she asked for a double whisky and later another. We sat together at dinner where she drank wine with such abandon that I became nervous about her ability to deliver her speech. My introduction was brief and complimentary and I watched in surprise when I saw Margaret go to the podium and deliver a speech rich in wisdom and humour that showed an exact sense of the occasion. And never a slip. But the psychological strain must have been severe. When she committed suicide not many years after this meeting I mourned a woman who had achieved such distinction and acclaim in the world of letters and who yet lived a life dominated in later years by alcoholism, loneliness, and fear.

I met Marian Engel in the early 1980s when she had already achieved some prominence for her novel *Bear* whose rather improbable plot concerned the erotic relationship of a librarian and a bear. She seemed to me a person whose patina of cheerfulness disguised an inner loneliness rooted in a sense that her life had been a waste. When word came to us at a 1984 Council meeting of The Writers Union, which I was chairing, that Marian was in the hospital and lacked a radio, the assembled members quickly raised a couple of hundred dollars and had a radio sent to her. In that same year she died. Her successor as Chair, Schroeder, was very different in temperament. He was a man of enormous energy whose best known book then was an account of his time in prison on a narcotics conviction. He was a Mennonite as was Rudy Wiebe, later a Chair of the Union; at one meeting the two had a strong difference of opinion expressed in language that ranged from "fuck you" to "screw you." I had always thought of Mennonites as the gentlest of people but I now revised that opinion.

I first met, or rather encountered, Timothy Findley at an Annual General Meeting of the Union; he was sitting face down on a table, when I approached him to introduce myself. But he was totally drunk and was quietly and very publicly sleeping it off. I never saw him in his role as Chair of the Union but was told that at one meeting when a motion became encrusted with multiple amendments he ran outside the room, close to tears, and had to be coached back. After that a sympathetic membership spared him difficult amendments at future meetings. I got to know him very well in later years and found him to be the kindest of men (especially to younger writers) and an enduring champion of all liberal causes. Charles Taylor was the most unlikely of the Chairs I met. The son of one of the wealthiest men in Canada, he had made a distinguished career as a journalist. He dressed like a businessman, he ran the Union as if it were a business, and when his term was over he disappeared to write his books and race his horses. Harold Horwood, a former liberal member of the Newfoundland legislature and a fierce opponent of Premier Smallwood, ran Union meetings with an iron hand. He was a devotee of Robert's Rules of Order which ensured that few dared challenge him on how to run a meeting; it also helped that he and the poet F.R. Scott (also a lawyer) had drafted the Writers Union's Constitution.

Atwood was the most brilliant of these people who chaired the Union in its early years. She was rarely challenged on a ruling because she was so obviously right and the speed with which she conducted a meeting was remarkable—Graeme Gibson said that any meeting was too long for her. When members rambled on Atwood would summarize what they wished to say and have it framed as a motion, debated, and done with in a way that won my admiration. I saw that same brilliance in other ways. When the University of Guelph granted her an honorary doctorate in 1985 she stayed at our house. We had dinner followed by drinks and delightful chat until it got quite late. As we were breaking up Atwood asked Renate for the use of a typewriter as she wished to write up the speech she was to deliver the next morning at Convocation. I was surprised because it had been my experience that most people receiving an honorary doctorate were nervous about the occasion and took great pains with their speech, writing it and rewriting well in advance of Convocation day. The next morning I discovered that Atwood had not used our typewriter because she felt it might interfere with our sleep. Her hand written Convocation speech was a triumph in its wit and humour and erudition. There were some at that time who resented this brilliance and also resented her refusal to suffer fools easily. I remember one CBC television interview in which the interviewer showed clearly that he had not read Atwood's new book and so incurred her extreme displeasure. The camera was slow in going to break and showed the interviewer's face, shock written all over it. *This can't be happening to me*, it said. In later years Atwood grew more tolerant but there was always an edginess to situations in which questions were put to her or when she had to defend the causes she espoused.

When I became Chair in 1983 my Council and I inherited a motion which stated that writers in the Union would boycott readings arranged for them by the Canada Council (for which they were paid) unless the Council undertook to allow non-fiction writers access to the Reading program and pay them a reading fee as it paid writers of fiction (novelists, short story writers, poets, dramatists). For example, Margaret Laurence was paid when she gave a Canada Council reading; Pierre Berton, a non-fiction writer, did not qualify. The boycott would go into effect in October—I had five months to resolve this very difficult issue.

Another matter which was to occupy me for my term was that of obtaining payment for writers for the use of their work. If I go to the theatre I pay a fee to see the play, at the movie house I pay to see a film. This arrangement was standard practice and universally accepted. But if I borrowed a book by Leonard Cohen from the library I did not pay a fee for the use of his intellectual property. The Union made this one of its priorities and I made it my primary objective. Accordingly, I met with Ministers and MPs in Ottawa and with executive members of the Library Association of Canada who were opposed to paying authors a fee, what the Union called Payment for Public Use (PPU, a rather unfortunate acronym). Their opposition drew the wrath of Robertson Davies, who in a stinging rebuke in the Union's Newsletter characterized public librarians as "a class of civil servants . . . who are tireless in their efforts to enlarge their own salaries" at the expense of writers. The most telling argument for implementing PPU—later known as Public Lending Right (PLR)—was that most European countries, including Iceland, had adopted it in some form. In soliciting help for our campaign the only writer who refused to support us was Barbara Amiel, a former communist sympathizer but now a right-wing journalist, who wrote to me condescendingly that any writer worth her salt (specifying herself) did not need a handout from government. I replied, in non-diplomatic terms, pointing out that she was at odds with writers throughout the world who were far more distinguished than she. Many years later Amiel wrote of herself, "I have been a bitch all my life." I have no wish to dispute that assessment. In contrast to Amiel, Bob Rae, soon to be Premier of Ontario, supported the Union's position privately and publicly and generously.

In trying to secure Canada Council funding for non-fiction writers I met on a number of occasions with Timothy Porteous, Director of the Canada

Council and a close friend of Prime Minister Trudeau, and with Naim Kattan who was responsible for the literature section of the Council. A writer himself, deeply read in Jewish, Arabic, French, and English literatures, Kattan listened sympathetically when I argued my case but his problem (and Porteus's) was that the Council simply did not have enough money. I managed to win a concession—an important one—that *if* the Council were to receive increased funding from the Government a program for non-fiction writers would be the first to be funded. With that concession, and after consultation with my Council who included members representing the Atlantic provinces, Quebec, Ontario, the Prairies, and British Columbia and the Yukon, I called off the boycott. Because no funding had yet been provided, it was a controversial decision (there was even vague talk of impeaching me). But only one member resigned in protest. In 1984 the Canada Council did indeed receive additional funding and in that year the sum of $400,000 was finally allocated to finance readings by non-fiction writers. I had gambled and won and so escaped impeachment.

Negotiations to obtain Public Lending Right dragged on but when I received a letter from Brian Mulroney, the Leader of the Conservative Party, on 23 January 1984, promising that his party would "continue to press for speedy adoption" of PLR, I knew that it was only a matter of time before we would get it. In order to pressure the Government further I arranged for our Annual General Meeting to be held in Ottawa in May and instructed the staff to make arrangements to have our members march through the streets of the city to Parliament Hill. When I informed the membership of the march, some were disturbed, feeling that we would be perceived as troublemakers, if not as anarchists. Their fears were dispelled when, some time later, I informed the membership that the Governor General of Canada had invited Union members to Rideau Hall following the march.

The march took place on a very rainy Saturday, under escort by three police cruisers. Soaked but unbowed we assembled in front of Parliament where I spoke to our members. The rain pelted down, the upraised faces under the umbrellas hopeful that we could persuade Government to help us, one face especially poignant, that of the writer Jean Little, with her eye-seeing dog at her side. Janet Lunn, Audrey Thomas, and I then proceeded to a meeting with the Minister of Communications, the Right Honorable Francis Fox, who, in Guelph two years earlier, had promised to implement Public Lending Right. Gaining access to the Minister was like trying to run a blockade—we were passed from ante room to ante room by young aides until finally we gained the *sanctum sanctorum*—the Minister's office. Janet Lunn (my vice-Chair) and I had made detailed preparations as to how we would conduct the meeting—rationally, persuasively, coolly, friendly—but Audrey Thomas had her own idea. Immediately on meeting Fox she pinned a label on his jacket reading, "He's pretty, but can he type?" The meeting went on for about twenty minutes—all rationality spent—and we left. Mr Fox made no promises. We had failed. But some eighteen months later we got what the Union wanted—Brian Mulroney kept his word. But Audrey Thomas never did find out whether Fox could type.

It was a relief in 1984 to be freed of Union work because it had occupied so much of my time. Every Monday for a year I had travelled by bus to Toronto (I was able to work on the bus) and spent until late evening doing business with our Executive Director, attending to the multitude of detail relating to various Union committees, meeting with writers and publishers, preparing for meetings with the provincial and federal governments, reading briefs. At the same time my university load was, as always, heavy. In addition to my teaching duties and academic writing there were many duties of the kind associated with a busy professor—assessing academic projects for the Canada Council, acting as External Examiner for PhD candidates, reading materials relating to those seeking promotion from the rank of associate professor to that of full professor, reviewing books, writing letters of reference for students proceeding to graduate school, chairing panels.

Such work was usually routine but one panel which I chaired at the Harbourfront International Festival of Authors in 1985 proved difficult. The topic was "Writers in the Nuclear Age" with panelists Ursula LeGuin, USA, Gert Hoffman from East Germany, Margaret Atwood, and Kenzaburo Oe of Japan. When Mr Oe began to speak I sensed an obvious disquiet in the audience. I leaned forward to hear what he was saying when it struck me that he was speaking Japanese. I approached him to ask him not to do so when I realized that he was in fact speaking in English. When question time came Mr Oe was spared even a single question. Not so Atwood. Despite the fact that Atwood had spoken with her usual brilliance and incisiveness, a number of women in the audience displayed open hostility to her. At that time Atwood had not achieved the iconic status she acquired years later and many, especially women, resented her independence and feminism because that seemed a reproach to the roles they were playing as housewives or women who were unable to understand or accept the demandingly free lifestyle and audacious choices taken by Atwood's female characters. When an Atwood speaker in a poem says that she fits her lover as a fish hook fits an open eye, it was an assault on Madison Avenue's packaging of happiness as having a husband who drives a GM or Ford car, having white teeth (by Pepsodent), and having well behaved children who eat cereal (Kelloggs) for breakfast. But how do you catch a fish if not with a hook!

Travel to other universities was also a demanding and rewarding feature of my life at this time. I lectured at a number of Canadian universities including Memorial University, Newfoundland; the University of Toronto (to Hans Eichner's graduate students in German—Eichner admired Shelley's *Prometheus Unbound* but professing not to understand it he called on me); the University of British Columbia, replacing Mavor Moore at the last minute with a speech on Canadian drama to a plenary session of the Learned Societies of Canada. On the international scene I lectured at universities in the USA, New Zealand, and Australia. In 1986 I was named Visitor by the Vice-Chancellors of New Zealand's universities and invited for a five-week tour giving lectures at the universities of Victoria, Canterbury, Otago, Massey, and Auckland. Because I was called on to give only two lectures per week, I had a great deal of free time to read New Zealand authors and to come to know and admire their work. Among these were Janet Frame, Maurice Gee (I thought his Plumb trilogy to be among the finest novels I had ever read), Kerry Hume, and Albert Wendt. In Otago I attended Greg McGee's *Foreskin's Lament,* a play comparable in its influence on New Zealand theatre to that of Ray Lawlor's play *Summer of the Seventeenth Doll* on Australian theatre.

The pleasure of such travels is the making of new friends and contact with academics with specialized knowledge. Two very useful future contacts were with Terry Sturm of the University of Auckland and Howard McNaughton of the University of Canterbury, who were deeply involved in promoting the literature of New Zealand which, like Canada's, had long been neglected. On a lighter note, I was invited to dinner by one professor, locally famous for having once represented New Zealand at the Olympic Games as a long-distance runner. He had a favour to ask of me. His current girlfriend lived in New York and in order to spend time with her he had secured a temporary position in a university there, the appointment to start in three weeks. The problem was that the course he was to teach included a segment on Canadian authors. He knew nothing of the subject, could I brief him as we ate our lamb and drank an excellent New Zealand wine, tell him who the key authors were, and what books he should read. I obliged and I must have been of some service for though I scanned the newspapers assiduously for some time after there were no reports of a New Zealand professor in the New York area who had been dismissed for academic incompetence.

My most vivid impression of New Zealand was how its aboriginal people, the Maori, were treated. Every museum and art gallery that I visited had rich representations of Maori art and historical artifacts celebrating their culture, and at various public lectures and events that I attended there was always a Maori person either presiding over the proceedings or acting as co-chair. I wondered at the greater sensitivity shown the Maori by governmental agencies than that shown Canada's native peoples by their government and came to the tentative conclusion that the wounds of dislocation and dispossession inflicted on the Maori were too recent to be easily ignored. White colonizers (the *Pakeha*) had come late to New Zealand in the person of Captain Cook and the wars on the native people that inevitably followed were only settled by the Treaty of 1840. It is a tribute to the courage and resilience of the Maori that they never gave up their national identity which had its roots in Polynesian culture.

In the 1980s Renate and I also enjoyed travel unrelated to our academic careers. Werner, my brother-in-law in Austria, had finally built his dream sailing boat and so began years of flying into Vienna, motoring through Yugoslavia to the port of Rijeka on the Adriatic where we boarded the "Marianne," and explored that magical sea coast as far south as Dubrovnik until the Balkan wars broke out in 1991. My memories are of summer weather, hot during the day under a cloudless sky, when we swam in the nude off the boat, and of cool nights. One evening as we lay at anchor near land watching the sun go down, monks in a monastery on the hill above began singing their evening service. As the sea turned a deep red from the setting sun their evening prayer died away and left me marveling at how blessed such moments are. Another summer when the boat was being repaired in Rijeka, we lived in an apartment in the hills overlooking the city of Dubrovnik. Our host was a German professor married to a Yugoslavian who insisted that she was a citizen of the ancient city of Dubrovnik, a heritage nobler than that associated with the Yugoslavia that had been cobbled together by Marshall Tito. One evening our hosts gave a party to coincide with the official opening of the festival of Dubrovnik. The guests were mainly Yugoslavian writers, artists, scientists, and musicians, many of them part of the diaspora that had led them to the USA, Canada, and Australia. We talked mostly of the arts and of travel but the threat of imminent war was ever in our minds as news came in daily of the approaching dissolution of the nation. As darkness fell that evening, fireworks on platforms out at sea exploded signaling the opening of the festival.

In 1981 Leonard Conolly joined the University of Guelph as Chair of its drama department and we soon became good friends because of our mutual interest in Canadian drama and theatre. His wife Barbara became closely involved in work on L.M. Montgomery before moving on to play an important role at Broadview Press. With Renate we made a formidable working quartet! Hardly had Conolly arrived on campus than he began contacting Canadian dramatists and theatres and all those associated with Canadian theatre—actors, directors, designers—in order to convince them to leave their scripts, prompt books, letters, posters, contracts, set and costume designs, and their unpublished memoirs to the University of Guelph. Over the years the collection grew until it is now was the finest in its field, widely available and easily accessible. And hardly had Len arrived on campus than we decided that we would collaborate on a comprehensive reference work on Canadian theatre and drama. In 1984 we approached Oxford University Press Canada, in the person of William Toye, its Editorial Director. Toye was not only a man well versed in literature but someone who had a wide knowledge of Canadian art and promoted it in his company's publishing programme. In 1983 he edited *The Oxford Companion to Canadian Literature*, the first work to treat comprehensively and without condescension its subject. By a quirk of fate, I had reviewed Toye's *Companion* and while I wrote favourably of it I registered one serious objection—it contained very little about Canadian drama and neglected almost completely Canadian theatre.

We met Toye in his immaculate bachelor's home situated just off the junction of University Avenue and Bloor Street in downtown Toronto. A slim, well preserved man, beautifully dressed, he had the endearing habit of exploding into laughter at the most unexpected moments. He asked us to tell him why he should publish our proposed book and listened carefully as we described briefly the kind of book we had in mind. When we had finished our presentation Toye told us to begin work right away; Oxford University Press Canada would publish it. He also commissioned us both to collaborate on a smaller book *English-Canadian Theatre* which we wrote as work on the *Companion* progressed.

Although Conolly and I knew a good deal about our subject there was a vast amount that we did not know. In order to provide the comprehensiveness and accuracy we aimed for we recruited experts from across Canada beginning with an Editorial Board, drawn from across the country, that would advise us on what entries to include and, importantly, identify scholars with the expertise to write these entries. We carried out a carefully rehearsed plan—we secured a grant to fund the first meeting of our Board; we made an application to the Social Sciences and Humanities Research Council of Canada and secured a substantial grant enabling us to hire a secretary and a research assistant and to provide funds to bring Board members to Guelph for a number of editorial meetings. These ran at weekends and lasted some eight hours on Saturday and three hours on the Sunday morning when we determined what and who should be in the *Companion* and, a delicate matter, how many words would be allowed to each entry. Pride of place went to the entries "Drama in English" and "Drama in French" which, combined, ran to some 26,000 words. Major authors like Robertson Davies and Gratien Gélinas were allocated up to 2500 words each; lesser known writers (often beginning their career) were awarded not less than three hundred words. Entries on drama and theatre in each of the provinces were awarded up to 5000 words in order to provide an overview of the historical context in which playwrights wrote and theatres flourished. Considerable attention was paid to Canada's theatrical past through dozens of entries on theatres (location, size, facilities, repertoires)—some of which no longer existed—and to many writers, actors, producers, directors, and managers. When Conolly and I received these entries we checked them for accuracy (essential in a reference book). Sometimes articles had to be ruthlessly pruned in order to meet the allocated word count or to clean up sloppy writing. Interestingly, we did not have one complaint from our contributors about changes made to their entries—the editorial "we" which sent these contributors their corrected entries loomed too large to be challenged. Because we felt that an Index would be invaluable, we asked the Computing Centre at the University of Guelph to design a computer-generated index but the result was so ridden with errors that Conolly and I spent many evenings in the summer of 1989 fixing it. By the time we had finished our three-year task we had identified 158 contributors who wrote 703 entries; the Index (the first *Companion* to have one) ran to 63 pages with more than 40,000 references. The *Companion* was liberally illustrated with photographs, posters, and sketches. When the *Toronto Star* offered Kenneth Tynan the post of drama critic in 1971, he is reputed to have asked, "Is there a Canadian theatre?" Our book was intended tas a reposte to that condescending quip.

Our *Companion* turned up lots of fascinating materials such as the entry on Ambrose Small who at one point in his career controlled thirty-four theatres in Canada and the USA. Following the sale of his theatre interests he deposited a cheque for one million dollars in a Toronto bank on 2 December 1919 and promptly disappeared that day never to be seen again. It was alleged, but not proven, that his wife and her lover had murdered him and burned his body in the furnace of the Grand Opera House, London, Ontario—a theatre he had owned—which has given rise to the belief, still held, that his ghost haunts the building. On a less weighty note, the entry on the Palace Grand Opera House, Dawson City, the Yukon, records that while the theatre did offer legitimate theatre such as Goethe's *Faust* it also catered to less refined tastes; "Arizona Charlie" Meadows, who built the theatre, showed off his shooting skills in an act where he shot glass balls from between the fingers of his wife until one evening he shot off one of her fingers. With some justification, she refused to perform further in that act. The entry on Toronto's Theatre Passe Muraille relates that the theatre was going into bankruptcy when management decided to present a documentary—the pornographic *I love You, Baby Blue*—which made so much money that management was able to buy the building.

Published in 1989 *The Oxford Companion to Canadian Theatre* was officially launched at a reception in the Royal Alexandra Theatre, Toronto. In the weeks following the critics had their say and it was overwhelmingly laudatory. Mavor Moore who had been associated with Canadian theatre since the 1930s wrote in a *Globe and Mail* review, "Atoning for the sins of imperial snobbery": "it will be an instant and essential national and international resource for scholars, critics, and theatre-goers." Take that, Kenneth Tynan. Len and I were pleased. But already we had both signaled that this *Companion* was only the beginning of our collaboration for in the Introduction we wrote, "we are now eyeing the rich literatures of the British Commonwealth, and expect to sally forth soon on an even longer voyage of editorial exploration than the one we have just concluded."

During this period I maintained my close association with the Guelph Spring Festival as a Board member and Budget officer as the Festival continued to offer outstanding fare. In 1980 "A Tribute to Ernst Krenek" brought the composer to Guelph to hear selections from his work that included his notable String Quartet No.6, written in 1936. Niki Goldschmidt fought hard to have him at the Festival in the face of a Board of Directors that knew little of Krenek and doubted his drawing power at the box office. The Board was right. Attendance at the Krenek concert was probably the worst in the Festival's history—some fifty people in a hall that could accommodate more than eight hundred. I enjoyed the concert but I was saddened by the decline in the eighty-year old composer's fortunes. As a young man in the 1920s he had quickly gained a place in Viennese musical circles, he had married the daughter of Alma and Gustav Mahler, and he had gained international fame with his 1926 jazz opera *Jonny Spielt auf*. But when the Nazis declared his music to be "degenerate" (thinking Krenek a Jew), he emigrated to North America teaching music in various universities, including a period in the 1950s at Toronto's Royal Conservatory of Music. Krenek was one of a great number of European intellectuals and artists who fled abroad; a few flourished but too many failed—lonely, homesick for their way of life now lost, deracinated—while some, despairing like Ernst Toller and Stefan Zweig, committed suicide.

In the early 1980s I occasionally taught a class in creative writing when I often invited published writers into my classroom to talk about the craft of writing. I heard of a young lecturer at the University of Guelph called

Robert Munsch who had just published a children's story *The Paper Bag Princess* which was selling very well. He came to my class and spent the first twenty minutes talking about the business of writing—it was boring. But then he said he would show my students how he actually wrote stories whereupon he began to improvise, using mime and jokes and anything at hand to stimulate his imagination. It was absolutely wonderful and completely entertaining. That evening I drafted a letter to Niki Goldschmidt about Munsch suggesting strongly that the Festival should feature him. Unlike Krenek, he played to a full house of over eight hundred in the 1984 Festival, which marked the beginning of his very successful career.

One of the joys of the Guelph Spring Festival was seeing the emergence of a new Canadian talent. When in 1986 we offered the North American premiere of Peter Maxwell Davies' *The Lighthouse*, I first heard the tenor Ben Heppner and knew immediately that this young man was destined for greatness in the opera houses of the world. Two years later the Festival presented the world premiere of the opera *Saint Carmen of the Main*, based on the play of the same title by Michel Tremblay, music by Sydney Hodkinson. Tremblay flew to Guelph from Montreal for the opening. He was a large man in physical stature who reminded me of the Oscar Wilde I had seen in photographs, but he was gentle in conversation and not given to Wilde's conversational virtuosity which was less a conversation that a display of his own verbal brilliance. Over dinner Tremblay told me how favourably impressed he was by the way the Festival treated its artists. I was puzzled by his evident enthusiasm until I discovered later that a newly established Guelph limousine company had chauffeured him from the airport at no cost to the Festival in a stretch limousine of enormous length in order to promote its image in the city.

And so family life, teaching and publishing, travel, the business of The Writers Union of Canada, and music occupied me in this decade. In 1984 I received a phone call from Margaret Atwood which led me into the world of international letters.

PEN AND THE SWORD

My relief at being freed from my role as Chair of the Writers Union of Canada was short lived because Atwood (then a visiting professor at the University of Alabama) told me on the telephone that the English Montreal branch of PEN International was contemplating dissolving the centre, she thought we in Toronto should take over from Montreal, she was too busy, she was out of the country, so would I take on the job of recalibrating a PEN Toronto-based centre. She would be co-President with me; I would handle organizing the new Centre in Canada until she returned. I was familiar with the work of PEN International, having been elected a member some years earlier. I was also familiar with the way the Montreal branch of PEN (which represented all of Canada) carried out its business which consisted largely of tea parties at which members read their work to each other. I told Atwood that while we should certainly participate fully in matters literary we should focus our efforts on the Writers in Prison programme whose aim was to free writers imprisoned throughout the world because their writings had offended their governments. Atwood was in total agreement; an outspoken critic, she was the very model of the writer *engagé*.

We were both very much aware that literary organizations like The Writers Union of Canada and PEN International had to be careful not to become too patently politicized—TWUC had among its members (and Chairs) Liberals, Conservatives, and New Democrats. But sometimes politics and literature could not be kept in separate compartments. When PEN was founded in 1926 by a group of writers that included Catherine Dawson Scott, John Galsworthy, Bernard Shaw, and H.G. Wells its mandate was principally to support freedom of expression for writers while taking into account the susceptibilities of the members' countries. This artificial distinction was blown apart at the 1933 PEN International Congress held in Dubrovnik, Yugoslavia, when Nazi book burnings and Nazi treatment of Ernst Toller, Thomas Mann and his brother Heinrich, and others so enraged the members that they expelled the Berlin PEN Centre. The Joycean concept of the artist as above and beyond his handiwork, indifferent, paring his fingernails, was seen as an abdication of responsibility in the years following the mass slaughter by European nations of millions of young men in World War One. Atwood and I decided that the English Centre of PEN Canada would take an activist role and that its primary aim would be directed to persuading governments worldwide to free those of its writers whom it feared enough to make them imprison them. PEN International had no guns but in the years following its foundation it had the moral authority of members such as Arthur Miller, Nadine Gordimer, Leopold Sedar Senghor, Mario Vargas Llosa, Norman Mailer, Rosamond Lehmann, and Kurt Vonnegut Jr. to challenge governments in the forum of international public opinion.

When I agreed to assist Atwood in establishing PEN Canada, I had another motive in mind although I did not divulge it to her at the time. It seemed to me that the period 1960 to 1980 represented the de-colonization of Canadian culture and was succeeded by a flowering of the arts, authentically Canadian in its genius. I also felt that in nurturing this flowering Canadian poets, dramatists, and fiction writers had been insulated from the international scene. Insulated because of the need to develop an identity distinct from the colonial past and the ever-present American juggernaut comprising a massive print, radio, television, and film culture. Isolated from the vibrancy of Europe because of the paucity of exchange programs and Europe's ignorance of what was happening in Canadian letters. Isolated in a sense by a Canadian grant system fostered by the Canada Council which culminated in the highest award offered the Canadian writer—the Governor General's Award whose very title reeked of a past colonialism. By linking up with PEN International I was of the opinion that Canadian writers would benefit enormously from foreign contacts. Shortly after we formed PEN Canada Atwood sent me a form letter from The Nobel Committee of The Swedish Academy inviting PEN Canada to nominate a candidate for the Nobel Prize in Literature. I replied to Atwood in a letter of 7 December 1984 that although I felt we had four or five writers in the country who were credible candidates that we not nominate candidates to avoid creating division within our membership at this early stage of our growth. But individual members of our organization should feel free to do so. I myself wrote in support of Robertson Davies when he was nominated some years later for the Nobel Prize feeling he was pre-eminently suited. I was disappointed when he did not get it.

Very soon we had a Constitution drawn up and we had our formal founding meeting in November 1984 when Atwood and I were elected as Co-Presidents. Other members of the Executive included Jack Batten, Susan Crean, Greg Gatenby, Graeme Gibson, Rick Salutin, and Eric Wright and among the membership were Pierre Berton, Northrop Frye, Robertson Davies, Margaret Laurence, Farley Mowat, and Alice Munro. Our executive meetings were held in the home of Atwood and Gibson and as we were joined by more and more people—Timothy Findley, Erna Paris, John Ralston Saul, and June Callwood, for example—Findley brought along his bridge chairs when the Atwood-Gibson house ran out of chairs. At the beginning we had very little money to do the things we wanted to do, so Atwood had one of her wonderful ideas. Our PEN Centre would produce a book based on the work of Canadian writers, past and living, who had written about food and which she would compile and illustrate. The title showed the Atwood sense of whimsy: *The Canlit Foodbook: From Pen to Palate—A Collection of Tasty Literary Fare.* The book was picked up by HarperCollins for about thirty thousand dollars and enabled us to hire an Executive Director and pay for sending money and essentials to the families of imprisoned writers. We raised support for the South Vietnamese writer and journalist Do Trung Hue who had been imprisoned in 1975 and were delighted to learn in March 1985 that he had been released. This was the perfect recipe to energize our PEN branch and to seek links with PEN International through its Congresses where writers exchanged views and became familiar with the work that PEN was doing throughout the world. Very soon it was decided that June Callwood and I should attend the PEN Congress in San Marino in June 1985 and that six members would attend the January 1986 Congress to be held in New York. We Canadians were shouldering our way into international affairs.

San Marino is a tiny country surrounded by Italy with a population at that time of about 20,000. It is not far from the Adriatic Sea and the popular resort of Rimini. It was on that trip that I got to know Callwood more intimately. One evening during the PEN meeting she and I had dinner in Rimini when she began to tell me of the death of her son Casey, twenty years old, killed by a drunk driver only three years earlier. As we sat there in that beautiful city by the sea, she spoke in a flat voice, empty of emotion, telling me in detail of Casey's death and of her pain. I wanted to stop her, I wanted to comfort her, but I didn't know how, I wanted not to be so involved in her pain. But I knew that she was condemned for a time to retell the event that wounded her more deeply than anything that had ever happened to her in her life. And as she talked, seeking closure, seeking consolation of some kind, I found the tears streaming down my eyes. People observing us must have thought we were a couple engaged in a quarrel, perhaps reliving a past that had turned out badly. The next day she was her professional self, writing an article for the *Globe and Mail* about the business of the San Marino meeting—writers and journalists imprisoned in so many countries including Cuba, Guatemala, Turkey, the Soviet Union, and Argentina where ninety four writers have "disappeared." Walter Kaufmann of East Germany wanted the USA condemned for its Star War defence program (while ignoring the total lack of freedom in his own country), the women delegates from Bulgaria rose on every occasion to speak of the freedom enjoyed in their country (one of the delegates was a government agent "protecting" the other two). I protested against the USA State Department's barring of writers Farley Mowat and George Woodcock from entering that country—a protest warmly approved by the American delegation. In her *Globe and Mail* column June noted that at a ball held by the San Marino Government "the Bulgarians wanted to dance with Prof. Benson" to show their solidarity with Canada! Although we saw each other in the years ahead June never alluded again to the death of her beautiful Casey.

There could not have been a greater contrast to the bucolic and sociable San Marino Congress than the Forty Eighth International PEN Congress held in New York City in January 1986 under the presidency of Norman Mailer, a presidency that was bound to be stormy. It was, especially since Mailer invited the US Secretary of State, George Schultz, to speak at the opening ceremonies. American Secretaries of State were not welcome because the writers were well aware that a previous Secretary, Henry Kissinger, had used the CIA shamelessly to oust the democratically elected president of Chile who was either forced to commit suicide, or assassinated, with US knowledge and complicity (the same thing had happened to President Diem of Vietnam, assassinated in 1963). What gave an added dimension to the tension surrounding Schultz's presence was the fact that the writer Isabel Allende, a relative of the murdered Allende, was present at the Congress. On a more prosaic note, writers from all over the world objected to being hustled about by armed Secret Service agents assigned to protect Mr Schultz who always seemed to me to be on the verge of an apoplectic fit.

Noted writers from Europe and the Americas were invited and Salman Rushdie, author of *Midnight's Children* and then at work on *The Satanic Verses*, wrote how intimidated he felt in the presence of so many famous writers. And well he might have been. A sampling included Joseph Brodsky, J.M. Coetzee, Umberto Eco, Carlos Fuentes, Günter Grass, Eugene Ionesco, Czeslaw Milosz, Octavio Paz, Wole Soyinka, Tom Stoppard, Mario Vargas Llosa, and Derek Walcott. A sign of Canada's growing presence on the international scene was the inclusion of four Canadians, Margaret Atwood, Robertson Davies, Mavis Gallant, and Alice Munro, as Guests of Honour. Greg Gatenby and I attended as delegates who were there largely to gather information on the organization of such an expensive and elaborate event and to learn how a Congress was run. In San Marino Callwood and I had met Alexandre Blokh, PEN International's Executive Director, about the possibility of Canada offering to host a Congress. He welcomed the idea suggesting we plan for 1989. I had a talk with Mailer on this. A small barrel-chested bantam of a man, widely known for macho views and controversial opinions, he proved to be a charming person, disarming in his candour. He said that in addition to raising money from such dependable sources as The National Endowment for the Arts and The Rockefeller Foundation he had raised money for his Congress from any source open to him, appealing often to the vanity of the newly rich. He would arrange readings, he told me, and invite men who had made their fortunes in running a chain of plumbing stores or flogging a new lotion that promised to reduce wrinkles. It was usually the wives who came, seeking "class" and eager to write cheques to validate their husbands' prosaic background through association with the likes of Susan Sontag and William Styron. When I looked up the donors to this PEN Congress I saw that Jacqueline Kennedy Onassis had given one thousand dollars and that Ivan F. Boesky had given somewhere between ten and twenty thousand dollars. Mailer certainly did take money from any source—about eighteen months later Boesky was charged by the SEC with insider trading and consequently went to jail after being fined one hundred million dollars.

The Congress became involved in controversy when women writers, mainly American, protested at the fact that there were one hundred and sixty male panelists and sixteen female panelists which by any count did seem unfair. When Mailer declared that there were too few women writers of sufficient stature, the women delegates booed and screamed and Mailer, ignoring his duty as President to run the Congress with impartiality, cursed the women in the most scatological terms he could find and was cursed as vigorously in turn. I was surprised to read that of the twenty-two American member Planning Committee at least ten were women. Why were they complicit in such disregard of female writers? At a Plenary meeting Atwood, representing foreign female delegates, pledged that the PEN Congress slated for Canada in 1989 would give a fair hearing to writers from all parts of the world (Rushdie had pointed out that he was the sole representative of south Asia) and that there would be equal representation of women. Her speech to the delegates had the delegates roaring with laughter as she gently made fun of Mailer and his macho posturing; she pointed out that Canada had four guests of honour, three women and one man—Robertson Davies—whom she felt was equal in beauty and accomplishments to three women.

The feisty Cynthia Ozick precipitated another storm when she attacked Bruno Kreisky, the former Jewish Chancellor of Austria, for having met with Arafat and Quaddafi of Libya. Kreisky participated as member of a panel whose theme was "The Statesman's View of the Imagination of the State." Pierre Trudeau, now safely retired from the political arena, leapt to the defence of Kreisky and was as loudly applauded for that as his implied rebuke to the many American writers from New York and environs who threatened to reduce the international work of PEN to their parochial interests. Callwood, writing in the *Globe and Mail*, also noted the political, national, and ideological extremism of many of the American writers. Nevertheless, the really useful and non dramatic work of PEN was being carried out at the committee level, work designed to emphasize the inalienable rights and responsibilities of writers throughout the world, and to devise strategies to free writers from prisons and from torture.

There was also a busy social schedule—a party at Gracie Mansion where the Mayor of New York acted as host, publishers' parties designed to "puff" selected authors, and, memorably, a final soiree at the Temple of Dendrun, the Metropolitan Museum of Art. The Temple, donated by the Egyptian government to America for its generosity in preserving ancient treasures threatened by the construction of the Aswan Dam, had been shipped to New York where it was unloaded, stone by stone, before reassembly in a huge room in the Metropolitan Museum. In this stunning setting the delegates assembled at the close of the Congress, all dressed suitably for the occasion, gowns aglitter with jewelry, entrances timed perfectly to create an effect, Nobel Prize-winning laureates Milosz of Lithuania and Claude Simone of France chatting with future Nobel laureates Joseph Brodsky, J.M. Coetzee, Nadine Gordimer, Günter Grass, Octavio Paz, Wole Soyinka, Derek Walcott. Even in this distinguished gathering Pierre Trudeau created a stir. He arrived fashionably late, a flower in his lapel and a strikingly beautiful woman on his arm, a woman at least forty years younger and four inches taller than he. The older men watched Trudeau with ill-concealed envy and the young woman with regret and lust, all thought of literature banished by audacity and beauty.

And so the 48th Congress at New York came to a close and the Canadian guests of honour and delegates prepared to leave the St Moritz Hotel. I was staying over an extra day to conclude some business but Atwood, keen to save our PEN funds, invited me to meet the novelist E.L. Doctorow who had offered his apartment located conveniently downtown. He showed us around but soon took off leaving Peggy and me to our devices. As she unpacked I noticed that she had a large file of clippings on the Grand Ayatollah Khomeini and his establishment of an oppressive theocratic state in Iran and another file on fundamental right wing preachers in the USA. These files, I later surmised, were part of her research for her dystopian novel *The Handmaid's Tale*. That evening we decided to have dinner out and see a movie. We spent twenty minutes scrabbling on the carpet for one of Peggy's contact lens (which we did not find) and searching the *New York Times* for a good movie. I suggested *Ran*, directed by Kurosawa, but Peggy, squinting through one eye, finally settled on *The Jewel of the Nile*, starring Michael Douglas and Kathleen Turner. As Peggy ooh-ed and laughed her way through the preposterous plot, I realized that this was how she relaxed—after a hard day of committee work, interviews ("How would you define Canadian spatiality, Miss Atwood?"), speeches, she did not want always to see Truffaut or Bergman or Kurosawa. When we returned to our apartment I saw another side of Margaret Atwood—the street smart, savvy New Yorker. She handed me the key and watched as I opened the door upon which she chastised me. This New York was a hard boiled city, mugging was rampant, one must be always on the *qui vive*, she lectured me. She shut the door, looked left and right (issuing instructions all the while), put the key in the door, looked left and right, and entered quickly. Survival! When I tell this story of Peggy Atwood and me spending a night, unchaperoned, in Doctorow's New York apartment, my listeners invariably ask, but what *happened?* And I always reply that I behaved as any man in an Atwood novel would behave in similar circumstances.

An important part of any large gathering—whether of geologists or medical doctors or writers—is the informal meeting in a café or bar or tea room. The hotel's Le Trianon Lounge was my favourite watering hole where I met old friends and got to know new ones. Among old friends was Greg Gatenby who had been running Toronto's Harbourfront Reading Series since 1974, making it, arguably, the finest forum of its type in the world. While he brought established writers to Toronto, he had an eye for promising young writers. He was also an ardent supporter of Canadian writers astutely showcasing them with established international authors. On the evening of one such reading Gatenby held a dinner party for the speakers of that evening—Robertson Davies, the American novelist Hortense Calisher, Mordechai Richler, and Allan Fotheringham. When my wife and I entered the dining room I found that we were to be seated to the right of Robertson Davies and his wife Brenda with Richler and his wife Florence to our left. The journalist Rick Salutin entered and was going to join us when he discovered that he was sitting next to Richler. He departed to another table in haste.

The dinner was a most peculiar affair. Richler was flanked on his right by Fotheringham and Calisher but he never deigned to talk to them nor they to him. I had expected Fotheringham to be a good table guest since he wrote an amusing column in *Maclean's* and was a panelist on various talk shows. But he sat silently that evening, looking like a rather self-satisfied, overfed Santa Claus, hoarding, perhaps, the *bons mots* he would dispense to a more appropriate audience. Calisher was a very fragile straggling wisp of a woman who had written many novels in what critics invariably characterized as an elliptical style. Occasionally Robertson Davies would address a remark to her but he eventually gave up. My wife chatted with Florence Richler, a pleasant woman, and I enjoyed talk with the Davies. Richler ignored us. When the time came for the waiter to take our orders Richler spoke for the first time to order another double whiskey and fish and chips for himself and Florence (without consulting her). Half way through the evening he finally asked me who I was. I told him my name which seemed to upset him. As the dinner wore on he became more truculent in his manner avoiding conversation with Florence or my wife. When he eventually he asked me if I was a writer I sensed that he wanted to vent his anger on someone, anyone, and if he didn't know anything I had written I was a suitable target. I said yes and continued my conversation with Davies. Richler interrupted to ask me what I wrote. Libretti, I replied, hoping to keep him at a distance. It worked. He looked puzzled, disconcerted, ordered another drink, and returned to the silence that enveloped him and his two dinner companions Calisher and Fotheringham. I was surprised at the failure of three people whose stock in trade was communication to communicate, but I remembered that when Marcel Proust and James Joyce once shared a taxi they only spoke of opening and shutting the taxi's windows. I was also surprised at Richler's rudeness, something that may be excused in a man of genius—there are many examples of record of Bethoven's boorishness. But Richler was not a genius, merely a very talented writer. And that is accolade enough.

At another of Gatenby's Harbourfront readings I first met Salman Rushdie. He had not yet published *The Satanic Verses* which made him the most talked about writer in the world, but his novel *Midnight's Children* was already recognized as one of the landmark novels of the twentieth century. Its theme was the partitioning of the Indian subcontinent into India and Pakistan in 1947 and the subsequent violence among Sikhs, Muslims, and Hindus that resulted in the massacre of two million people. Rushdie was then a rather retiring person with a slightly owlish look that sat well with his measured and deliberate manner. But when a subject engaged him he spoke with fluency and a wealth of allusions to world literature and politics. I had recently read Khushwant Singh's novel *Train to Pakistan* which we discussed briefly and Rushdie was interested to learn more from me how narrowly Ireland had escaped a blood bath when Partition was instituted there. We also spoke of the just published life of Lord Louis Mountbatten where biographer Philip Ziegler reported that while

Mountbatten, then Governor-General of India, was seemingly playing impartial arbiter in the matter of Partition, his wife, Edwina, was conducting a sexual affair with India's Prime Minister, Jawaharlal Nehru—and with Mountbatten's complicity. I thought that Rushdie with his corrosive wit might seize on this theme for a novel but perhaps it has proven too sensitive even for him. When I next saw Rushie after the New York PEN Congress it was in Toronto as he made his way into Convocation Hall, the University of Toronto, to give a speech—his first in Canada—under the auspices of PEN Canada. He was surrounded by policemen because the Ayatollah Khomeini had pronounced a *fatwa* calling on all devout Muslims to assassinate him for uttering blasphemies against the prophet Mohammed. I was within a few feet of him as he entered and saw plainly that he wore the air of a haunted man who dreaded death. But he spoke bravely that night before an audience that cheered him for his courage. As I watched I was filled with pride because here in Canada, Bob Rae, Premier, had extended to a writer the protection and the power of Ontario in defiance of Khomeini and his ignorance-driven, intolerant theocracy.

Another guest at Gatenby's Harbourfront readings in the 1980s was the playwright Harold Pinter. He was easily the finest reader I have heard in my life, trained actor that he was. But following that reading I was backstage when he cursed and shouted at Gatenby in the most vicious manner. It seemed that Pinter had asked for a bottle of whiskey to be ready for him when he finished his reading but Gatenby, who prided himself on pampering his writers, had forgotten. Some years later, when I chaired a panel of writers that included his wife Lady Antonia Fraser, I saw another side of Pinter—the solicitous (slavish?) husband. He sought me out to tell me how nervous she was before readings and when I went to escort her to the reading venue he was there again comforting her and impressing on me that I must not upset her in any way.

At this Congress in New York I first made the acquaintance of John Ralston Saul, a slim, tall man with light red hair and a high domed forehead, who, I soon discovered, had traveled extensively, mainly in South East Asia. I had no idea then that he had earned his doctorate in Economics at the University of London, or that he was a novelist, one of whose books had sold millions of copies in France. What I did know was that I had met a man whose views on politics and culture were deeply informed, that they were often provocative, and that he shared as deep a distrust of the military-industrial complex as President Eisenhower, that he was a good drinker with a rapid wit and an eagerness to be friends. In our conversations I did learn that he was at work on a very large non-fiction work that had occupied him for a number of years. When it was finally published under the title *Voltaire's Bastards: The Dictatorship of Reason in the West* I read it with the same admiring avidity that I had, years before, read Marshall McLuhan's *Understanding Media*. Combining philosophical speculation with economic analysis, *Voltaire's Bastards* is a seminal work in its attack on twentieth-century technological elitism that effectively gutted twentieth-century democracy.

On our return from New York we began planning for the 54th PEN International Congress to be held in Canada in September 1989, hosted by both the English and Quebec PEN Centres. Graeme Gibson, who had succeeded Timothy Findley as President, worked with Quebec's PEN President Jean Éthier-Blais so that each independent centre would complement the work of each other. The Executive Committee in Toronto was a brilliant group in the years 1986–89 that included Atwood, Callwood, Susan Crean, Louise Dennys, Gibson, Gatenby, and John Ralson Saul. I remained Vice President from 1985 until 1990. The Congress Organizing Committee consisted of Gatenby, Gibson, Saul, and myself. The first order of business was to settle on a theme acceptable to both English and Quebec PEN Centres. After much discussion it was titled "The Writer: Freedom and Power/L'Écrivain: liberté et pouvoir." Our Congress would explore questions arising from the prevalence of contemporary political and religious ideologies that allow dominant nations, in the name of freedom, to pursue their fight for global power. Our Congress would ask such questions as: how should writers engage with censorship; with the concentration of publishing houses; with the imposition by the superpowers of their vision of the world on the media? What was the responsibility of the writer to society in the final years of the twentieth century?

PEN Congresses usually have four elements—general literary sessions which address the theme of the Congress; assembly meetings where delegates conduct the business of PEN International (the Writers in Prison program, for example); readings where distinguished writers give readings which are open to the public; and special literary sessions which address issues not directly related to the theme of the Congress but which are of particular interest to participants. Under the latter category we in

Toronto featured readings and panels with the titles "The Next Generation" and "Children's Writing and the Rights of Children."

In choosing distinguished foreign writers and our own Canadian writers we sought to get wide representation. Rather than having only a Eurocentric and North American-dominated invitation list we also wanted to present writers from Africa and Asia. We also insisted on having representative writers from across Canada to balance those from the Toronto and Montreal areas. And of course we wanted fair gender representation. A few examples show the richness of the artistic fare that we finally offered. The opening panel, chaired by the popular CBC broadcaster Barbara Frum, featured Chinua Achebe of Nigeria, Atwood, Claribel Allegría of El Salvador, and Anita Desai of India. Another panel chaired by Adrienne Clarkson on the subject "Private Conscience and State Security" featured Duo Duo of China, Harold Pinter, Miriam Tlali of South Africa, and Achebe. The last literary session in Toronto called "Language as Power," chaired by Rosalie Abella, had Tadeusz Konwicki of Poland, Emily Nasrallah of Lebanon, Nayantara Sahgal of India, and Atwood. Canadian writers on various literary panels included Findley, Rudy Wiebe, Anne Hébert, Nicole Brossard, Austin Clarke, Michael Ondaatje, Irving Layton, and Josef Škvorecký. A notable omission was Mordecai Richler—he should have been on the Quebec list but so violently did the Quebec organizers dislike him that they flatly refused to invite him. I thought this a pity since Richler was always very fair when it came to apportioning censure and contempt on those people and institutions that he disliked. Nevertheless, the twelve Congress literary sessions offered the most international representation of authors ever seen in Canada.

The week-long Congress offered me interesting insights into some of the personalities involved. I attended a talk given by Northrop Frye and was surprised how untouched I was by it. The ideas he had developed years before in his *Anatomy of Criticism* now seemed dated and in his delivery it was as if he had been wound up like a toy. Perhaps the venue was unfair to him—the other participants were creative artists and although Frye had once attempted a novel he was a terminological buccaneer, not an artist. Betty Friedan was a very different kind of personality. Egotistic, domineering, she insisted on joining panels where she was not a guest and on monopolizing conversation. She very soon earned a reputation as someone to be avoided. At the closing banquet held in the Grand Salon of

Montreal's Hotel Meridian, the Montreal hosts, very well aware of Irving Layton's misogyny, mischievously placed him at a dinner table for four with Freidan. I watched him squirm as Freidan talked and talked at him ever more relentlessly.

Following the Congress I attended a final event to celebrate its success—a private dinner at the home of Adrienne Clarkson and John Ralston Saul with Atwood, Gibson, and Gatenby as guests. It was an evening of good talk and friendship covering politics, personalities, poetry, music, film, travel, food. I discovered that Clarkson had a great love of the poetry of Yeats and we traded quotations from our favourite poems throughout the evening.

> *Think where man's glory most begins and ends,*
> *And say my glory was I had such friends.*

Shortly after that evening I resigned from the Executive. I felt that I had done my share. Then too the burden of driving to meetings in Toronto in the late evening began to seem too heavy. I was approaching retirement from my university position and I felt some loss of energy as I came to terms with the death of some whom I loved dearly—my brothers Hugh, Jack, and Gerard and my sister Françoise, the last three buried far from their place of birth in Canada, Zimbabwe, and the USA. But despite the passage of the years I never gave up my interest in the PEN Canada or in The Writers Union of Canada. In the early 1990s I wrote various reports for TWUC but I was content to leave Union matters to younger hands. I was delighted to see that by the year 2010 Union membership had grown to almost two thousand and to see also how English PEN Canada had gained such recognition throughout the world, recognition signaled by the election of John Ralston Saul as International President—a worthy successor to such predecessors as Galsworthy, Alberto Moravia, Heinrich Böll, Arthur Miller, and Mario Vargas Llosa.

The Importance of Being a Writer

In 1989 when Len Conolly and I concluded our work on *The Oxford Companion to Canadian Theatre* we wrote in the introduction that we were "eyeing the rich literatures of the British Commonwealth, and expect to sally forth on an even longer voyage of editorial exploration than the one we have just concluded." Five years later we ended that voyage with the publication by Routledge (London and New York) of the two-volume work *Encyclopedia of Post-Colonial Literatures in English*. It was a massive book representing the work of five hundred and seventy-six contributors drawn from around the world, authorities in their fields, who wrote some one thousand six hundred entries on the literatures of Australia, Bangladesh, Canada, the Caribbean, East Africa, Gibraltar, Hong Kong, India, Malaysia, Malta, New Zealand, Pakistan, the Philippines, Singapore, Sri Lanka, St Helena, South Africa, South Central Africa, the South Pacific, and West Africa. Our editorial board—twenty in all—was drawn from the best-qualified people in these various countries—who identified what entries should be included and who should write these entries. Our job in Guelph headquarters was to keep in touch with our world-wide contributors, edit entries when they arrived, confirm material facts such as the titles of works and dates of first publication. With the development of search machines like Google and the ability to immediately access online the catalogues of such great libraries as the Library of Congress (more than thirty two million books and printed materials) and the British Library (more than twenty-five million books) the task of cross checking became much easier. Conolly and I and our staff had available to us the current bibliographies and encyclopedias of the nations whose literatures we were addressing; unfortunately, some of these were notoriously inaccurate. For example, the standard reference work purporting to be an accurate guide to Caribbean literature was totally unreliable, especially in regard to the dating of publications. In the case of many African countries it was difficult to find native academics to write our entries (as we would have preferred); too often, they had fled the violence and corruption of their homelands and were employed in the universities of Europe, North America, and Australia.

We had determined very early that there would be a text-generated index to enable readers to locate easily and quickly references to thousands of authors, books, publishing houses, theatre companies, individual short stories and poems, and other relevant literary materials to an extent that would be impossible otherwise. Mindful of the difficulties we had experienced in preparing an index to *The Oxford Companion to Canadian Theatre* I met with staff associated with the University of Guelph's Computing Services, most notably Les Dunn, to determine if it was possible for him to invent such a text-generating index. To take an example. If Robertson Davies' play *A Jig for the Gypsy* appears in the text I must flip the title so that it appears in the index as *Jig for the Gypsy, A*. For two years Dunn and I met regularly as he sought to do what I asked of him and eventually he found a method of getting what I wanted. I had identified eight functions that had to be executed in order to compile a comprehensive index and eventually Dunn, through trial and error, came up with a set of WordPerfect macros that could perform these eight functions. In order to simplify the task for our secretaries, each item to be indexed had to be colour-coded and the secretaries trained to know immediately which macro matched which colour. It was part of my work to do the colour coding—as painstaking and meticulous a job as I have ever undertaken. When the manuscript was in page proof stage Dunn ran the index, which took some eighteen hours to complete. The result was an index of more than a quarter million entries. So valuable was our index and so innovative our technique that the Association for Literary and Linguistic Computing (ALLC) invited Dunn and myself to give a paper on our work at their Nineteenth International Conference held at England's Oxford University in April of 1992, which they also published. As I sat in the great dining room of Christ Church with a portrait of Henry the Eighth looking down at me I think he would have been struck by the fact that I was the only member of that distinguished body, the ALLC, who had never booted up a computer.

The Routledge *Encyclopedia of Post-Colonial Literatures in English* was published to very favourable critical notices in 1994—the periodical *Choice*, which is the bible of librarians, listed it among the "Outstanding Academic Books of 1995." While the critical response, in general, focused on the literary character of the work, I saw the work as also a political statement—Eurocentric values had dominated most of the great publishing companies of the world to the neglect of writers from the colonies. The *Encyclopedia*, as I saw it, was intended to correct that cultural squint and to draw attention to such writers as Atwood, Soyinka, Raja Rao, and Ngugi wa Thiong'o who were likely to be handicapped by virtue of being regarded as mere colonials. Our *Encyclopedia* was a tool in the de-Anglicising of Empire.

It was at this time I was forced to enter the contemporary world and learn how to use a computer. With the publication of the *Encyclopedia*, our grant ran out and we had to let our small staff go. Additionally, in 1993 I reached the mandatory retirement age of sixty-five which meant that I could no longer draw to any great extent on the secretaries in the Department of English—if I were to continue to publish I would have to learn how to use a computer and its various programs. I did so, taught by Renate and my two sons. My retirement earned me a farewell dinner hosted by the Department of English, election to the rank of University Professor Emeritus by the Senate of the University (with unspecified benefits that I never did discover), and a vision of the future (feared by many retirees) of the years ahead now freed of committee meetings, students, and early morning classes. Most importantly, I was now freed from the grading of hundreds of essays at the undergraduate level which had with the passing years grown to be the most taxing duty of all.

But it had been a good inning as a teacher, an inning stretching back to my first school in the slums of Belfast to my one-room school in northern Saskatchewan to my three years with the young airmen of NATO. What made it so good and so interesting and, yes, exciting often, was the contact with young minds. To hear a child of five read a story with some fluency under my guidance was as rewarding as inspiring a university student to take up graduate studies, and to be able to counsel a brilliant student at any level was a privilege and usually a pleasure. There were also other rewards—invitations to read academic papers at academic conferences throughout the world, or to chair a panel discussion with international writers of distinction, or to help a young colleague find a publisher. And through those years there had been the sustaining rewards of family life—Renate always busy with her teaching and publishing and housekeeping, both of us looking after our children Ormonde and Shaun as they fulfilled those rites of passage that included school, high school, summer camp, university, marriage—Ormonde to Dione Holmes, grandchildren Elle and Lily, and holidays in Florida, Cape Cod, South Carolina, Cuba, and the Caribbean when the long winters gave way to welcome Spring.

What made it less difficult for me to retire from university teaching and research was the fact that the study of literature had been overtaken and subverted to some extent by a methodology owing more to cultural studies than to the study of literature as literature. Cultural studies, holistic by nature, deal with the political nature of contemporary culture as well as its historical precedents and embrace fields as diverse as sociology, anthropology, literary studies, and linguistics. No one would deny that a feminist reading of *Jane Eyre* or a Marxist interpretation of Dickens' *Hard Times* can shed new light on these novels, but too often such readings under the rubric of cultural studies are developed in a vocabulary entirely alien to that traditionally used in, say, English or French literary studies. For example, the German critic Roman Ingarden popularized the term "concretize"; she wrote that the term has two characteristics: on the one hand, "the purely intentional concretization, ontically heteronomous in form and relative to the subjective operation"; on the other hand, "the objectively existing concretization, characteristic, in form, of the respective ontic sphere." Even more startling (amusing?) is Jacques Lacan's musing on castration anxiety where he writes that the phallus can be equated with the square root of minus one, "the symbol of the signification produced above, of the *jouissance* it restores—by the coefficient of its statement—to the function of a missing signifier." This seems rather a complex way of explaining an erection. It would seem that the term "writing" itself would hardly require explanation. But if one adopts the definition offered by the French critic Roland Barthes, it certainly does: "Writing is the neutral, composite, oblique space where our subject vanishes, where all identity is lost, beginning with the very identity of the body writing." The problem with this definition is that it is formulated to substantiate Barthes' claim that the author is dead, that the living person who wrote a work is totally different from the author of that work. But such reformulation of literary terms meant that in far too many cases professors did not really understand the new language that had been foisted on them by a number of often conflicting schools with consequent damage to their roles as teachers. Additionally, these postmodernist texts were published in languages (French, German, Russian, Polish) in which too few American and British professors were competent, thus forcing them to rely on translations, some poorly done. Lest my comments seem extreme, even reactionary, it is worth pointing out that the only thing the critics I have quoted seemed to have in common was a mutual loathing of others in the field. Michel Faucault characterized Jacques Derrida's prose style as *obscurantisme terroriste* and critic Jürgen Habermas described Foucault's work as "an iceberg covered with the crystals of arbitrary formulations." Widespread objection to such postmodernist criticism was comically driven home by the physicist Alan Sokal who submitted an article, "Trangressing the Boundaries: Towards a Transformative Hermeneutics of Quantum Gravity," to *Social Text*, an academic journal of postmodern cultural studies. Intended by Sokal as a "pastiche of Left-wing cant . . . and outright nonsense," it was published by *Social Text* whose editors knew so little about science that they failed to recognize Sokal's parody of postmodernist terminology. When I read criticism by Coleridge on the poetry of Wordsworth or Northrop Frye developing his systematic study of the formal causes of art, I rejoice in their clarity of thought and expression. But I believe firmly that the worst excesses of contemporary criticism will fall victim to the astringent test of time and that whatever is valuable will so be winnowed. Schools of literary criticism are time-driven, unlike the works of art they profess to illuminate.

What was especially rewarding about those years was that each generation of students offered me a vantage point from which to examine the human condition—its politics, its arts, its sciences, human sexuality, power. In my childhood I had seen lamplighters light the streets of Belfast and I had seen a man walk on the moon. I had heard peace being promised in our time and I had seen the cities of Japan incinerated by giant American bombers. I had once yearned to be a priest but lived to read of a sexually abusive priesthood in Ireland that had flourished around me. In my lifetime millions of men and women and children had been butchered in human wars and everywhere, it seemed, humanity lives in poverty and suffering. Human existence was a pageantry of pain and aspiration, of great deeds and human cruelty, of hope and hope denied; but one could not despair, one could only go on living seeking some kind of truth amid the desolations of the contemporary. The poet Yeats offered me a kind of comfort:

> *Civilisation is hooped together, brought*
> *Under a rule, under the semblance of peace*
> *By manifold illusion; but man's life is thought,*
> *And he, despite his terror, cannot cease*
> *Ravening through century after century*
> *Ravening, raging, and uprooting that he may come*
> *Into the desolation of reality.*

I was fortunate also that in my retirement I was again able to complement academic work with a return to creative writing. In 1989, rereading Dickens' *A Tale of Two Cities*, I was struck by the dramatic character of this extraordinary novel. From its publication it had been a great success not only as a novel but also in an extraordinary number of stage adaptations—most than one hundred and thirty. I began to think about creating a book with lyrics for a musical based on the novel. But I soon discovered that two previous English-language musical adaptations had failed miserably—interestingly, a 1984 Japanese version presented by the Takarazuka Revue, featuring an all-female company, was very successful. The difficulty in adapting *A Tale of Two Cities* as a musical work lies in the vastness of the novel which must be condensed to a libretto of some fifty pages. There was also the added factor that a new 1980s French musical *Les Misérables* –or *Les Miz*, as it was popularly known—seemed to pre-empt the very territory that *A Tale of two Cities* covers. It didn't, of course, but so I was told. Undeterred I began work on the book and lyrics.

Although I had already written the libretti for three operas I found that I now had to learn a new craft—writing words for a musical. Musicals, it seemed to me, laid much more emphasis on the book and lyrics than opera did on the libretto. An opera could succeed despite a poor libretto, even a libretto that didn't really make sense, provided it had an outstanding musical score. Wagner, who wrote the libretto for his *Das Rheingold*, later commented, "I now simply cannot bear to look at the text by itself anymore." But his music is so extraordinary that audiences overlook the pseudo-philosophical farrago that constitutes his libretti. I do not believe such an imbalance of music and words is tolerated in musical theatre—the books and lyrics of commonly played musicals as different in character as *My Fair Lady*, *Oklahoma*, and *Sunday in the Park with George* show no such imbalance and, in fact, deepen our appreciation of the music. But despite the difficulties facing me in transforming *A Tale of two Cities* into a musical, I had a workable script by 1996 which I sent to the Stratford Festival in the hope the people there might consider mounting it. The years went by and I heard nothing from them.

As yet I had no composer. Charles Wilson with whom I had written three operas did not write for musical theatre and I knew no one who did. Through Mavor Moore I was aware of the work of Norman Campbell and John Fenwick who had written the music for *Anne of Green Gables* and *Johnny Belinda* but theirs was not the kind of music I had in mind for my *Tale of Two Cities*. In 1996 I heard an oratorio, *Revelation*, by the Canadian composer Victor Davies and was immediately excited by the way in which he had taken the vast theme outlined in *The Book of Revelation* and condensed it without losing its scope or apocalyptic voice. I was also greatly impressed by the richness and brilliance of his orchestration and by the fact that he had written so much classic music whose signature characteristic was its accessibility, a first and primary aspect of musical theatre. I wrote to him asking whether he would be interested in collaborating with me on a musical *A Tale of two Cities* and I was delighted, and surprised, when he wrote to say he was. I learned afterward that he had read the partial script I had sent him when returning from a visit to Los Angeles (he often wrote for film) where he had been disgusted by the greed and devious dealings of the producers he had met on his visit. The lines that caught his eye and persuaded him to join me seemed pertinent to his state of mind at that time:

> *Out of the darkness came your hand*
> *Out of the darkness you called my name.*
> *Out of the darkness a beacon light*
> *To guide me through the fearsome night.*

And so began a twelve-year collaboration that was at once rewarding in terms of personal friendship with Victor and his wife Lori and learning a new craft as we moved from hope to doubt, and from writing to rewriting. In the early stages of our collaboration we had no promise that our work would be performed because we had not been commissioned. This was a particular burden for Davies because he made his living by his compositions unlike most Canadian composers who hold university positions. But then one day, in 1999, quite unexpectedly, Antoni Cimolino, General Manager at the Stratford Festival, called asking me about the state of my book for *A Tale of Two Cities*. Events followed fast after that. It was agreed that Victor Davies would write the music and that we would met regularly with Jason Miller, a young man in charge of Special Projects at Stratford who knew a great deal about musical theatre and should be of help. Some months later the Stratford Festival contracted formally to support the creation of the music and the further development of the book and lyrics. The festival gave us five months to integrate book, lyrics, and music.

In January 2000 a workshop was arranged to take place in the Festival's Theatre, Rehearsal Hall No. 3. Victor and I met with selected members of the regular actors and Victor coached them in the music which they were singing for the first time. Since many of the songs involved chorus work and duets and trios it proved very difficult to get the kind of quality we wanted. We began at 11 am and had only five hours to prepare the entire musical for presentation. As I watched Davies rehearse the singers I was struck by the fact that twenty-six years earlier Jean Gascon (then Artistic Director) and Michael Bawtree had decided to stage my opera *The Summoning of Everyman* solely on the basis of an enthusiastic review in the *Globe and Mail*. At five pm Richard Monette, Artistic Director, Bert Carrière, Music Director, David Prossner, Literary Manager, and Antoni Cimolino filed into the room and we began our scaled down workshop. There was supposed to be a post-mortem but it consisted of a single question from Monette, "What are we going to do with this?"

As it turned out Stratford decided to do nothing with it. Davies and I were disappointed but we were not prepared to drop a project we had come to love. We turned to entertainment lawyer Dan Brambilla who had worked for Garth Drabinsky's Livent productions and who hoped to become an impresario in his own right. But that too eventually fizzled out, we went our way, and Brambilla went on to become CEO of Toronto's Sony Centre for the Performing Arts (originally the O'Keefe Centre). Davies and I continued work on our musical but other projects intervened until one day in 2003 Davies told me a small company in Vancouver was looking for a new small-cast chamber opera. Did I have a suitable libretto? I didn't, but within a day I remembered that I had taught Oscar Wilde's wonderful comedy *The Importance of Being Earnest* for many years and that I had marked in my copy a number of places where I thought there should be music. I phoned Davies, we began work which proved enormously enjoyable because we knew we were working with a masterpiece, one of the finest comedies ever written. But because the cast of the play was too large for the chamber opera we were writing, I was forced to take this masterpiece and cut the original nine-actor cast to five. Who should I eliminate? Murder? Eventually I cut the roles of the servants Lane and Merriman, the Rev. Dr Chasuble, and Miss Prism, leaving only the young couples and Lady Bracknell. To remove such memorable characters, a step not lightly taken, might seem too drastic but I was able to preserve their presence by reporting their actions.

Within a matter of months we had completed much of the opera—book, lyrics and piano score—only to learn that the Vancouver company had run out of money. Undeterred we pressed on with our work despite not having a commission or a promise of production. Then, quite by accident, Davies was in Stratford attending a play when he met John Miller, Artistic Producer of Stratford Summer Music, who asked him if he had anything musical that might fit the one remaining spot he had for the 2005 season. Davies told him of our chamber opera and a meeting was arranged for a week later in Stratford where Davies played some of the new music. Bruce Dow, a comic actor in the regular Stratford Festival Company who was present as prospective Director, gave his approval, and within an hour Miller announced that he would finalize his 2005 season by presenting a performance of our opera following a week-long workshop. Then began a search for four singers for the roles of Algernon Moncrieff, John Worthing, Gwendolen Fairfax, and Cecily Cardew. Because Miller's budget allowed him to use only non-Equity singers for these roles, we visited a number of universities where we held open auditions. The quality of performance was extremely gratifying and within a short time we found our singers. The role of Lady Bracknell went to Laura Pudwell, an experienced professional opera singer and university voice teacher. During these auditions which took place on four different days I had a severe headache each evening despite the fact that all my life I had been relatively headache free. Once the auditions had been completed, my headaches disappeared. The answer was simple. Listening each day, in the close quarters of a university studio, to opera singers whose powers of projection were so developed and whose professionally trained vocal tracts were able to project such extraordinary volume were the reason.

The workshop at Stratford during the first week of August was a delight since we, the creators, were now able to hear our words and music performed by a talented cast. The actual concert performance in the Auditorium of Stratford's City Hall was packed, the audience enthusiastic. It included many regular members of the Stratford Festival company some of whom had played in various productions of *The Importance of Being Earnest* and knew the text by heart. None of them voiced concern at my editing of the play although one person asked me if it would be possible to restore the characters I had cut. I said I did not think so given the way music and words were integrated.

A direct benefit of the concert version was that we had a tape of the performance and at this point our new opera crossed paths with our musical *A Tale of Two Cities*. Ever on the lookout for a producer we had met with Guillermo Silva-Marin, General Director of Toronto Operetta Theatre, in the hope that we might persuade him to mount our *Tale*. Silva-Marin was also the General Director of the prestigious Opera in Concert which had mounted my opera *The Summoning of Everyman* in 1994 which the critics felt was now a classic of the Canadian opera repertoire. He listened to the tape of our opera *The Importance of Being Earnest* and while he was enormously impressed by the work he stated firmly that if he were to stage it, it would have to be converted into an operetta that would fit the mandate of Toronto Operetta Theatre. We agreed to do so. With the greater resources that Silva-Marin would offer, it was now obvious that I could restore those characters I had exterminated in my opera version. And so the servants Lane and Merryman returned to usher in those delightful characters the Rev. Dr Chasuble and Miss Prism. In April 2007 the Board of Toronto Operetta Theatre approved the inclusion of our operetta for a February 2008 world premiere. This might seem like ample time, but Davies was then at work on writing the music for a full length opera *Transit of Venus* to a libretto by Maureen Hunter, to be premiered at the Manitoba Theatre Centre, Winnipeg, in November of 2007. To complete *Earnest, The Im-*

portance of Being, as our operetta was now called, would be a close thing. And so it proved—the last pages of the orchestral score were delivered to Silva-Marin and the orchestra two days before the opening.

Guillermo Silva-Marin is a complete man of the theatre. Born in Puerto Rico he came to Canada in 1971 as a young man and within the year secured a place in the Chorus of the Canadian Opera Company (he sang in *Heloise and Abelard*) before going on to sing leading roles in opera houses in Canada and the USA. Possessed of seemingly endless energy, he founded Toronto Operetta Theatre in 1985, often acting as director, singer, and set and lighting designer. While much of his repertoire was predictable—*Die Fledermaus*, *Countess Maritza*, *Wiener Blut*, for example—he staged more adventurous fare such as Bernstein's *Candide* and Calixa Lavallée's *The Widow*. He also introduced Canadian audiences to the *zarzuela* in such works as Torroba's *Luisa Fernanda* and Barbieri's *El Barberillo de Lavapiés*. But because he knew the history of opera so intimately, he knew the importance of presenting original work. After all, how many times does one want to stage such beautiful chestnuts as *Die Fledermaus* and *The Merry Widow*? That was why he seized so eagerly on *Earnest, The Importance of Being*—he loved the work, it would be the first true Canadian operetta to be written in over a hundred years, and he, Guillermo Silva-Marin, would bring it into being!

Guillermo's method of direction was a revelation to me. He had ten days in which to rehearse this new work, including orchestral rehearsals. He began by stripping my libretto of all stage directions, even such innocuous ones as "Ernest leaves." He sat on a chair in front of his singers and without a script or notes to hand began day by day to block the operetta. He never needed a reminder about the smallest of details and gradually I began to see the work unfold beautifully and admire how the singers could absorb directions so quickly and incorporate new ideas into already established routines. When he had finished his daily blocking and rehearsal of movement, the Music Director, Jeffrey Huard, took over to rehearse the singers. He had worked with Garth Drabinsky's Livent company conducting the world premieres of *Ragtime*, *Kiss of the Spider Woman*, and the Broadway production of *Phantom of the Opera*. When he asked me to supply a new phrase or reshape a line I did so without demure because I trusted him implicitly in such matters. Within the short space of ten days he and Silva-Marin had readied the cast for opening night and the world premiere of *Earnest, The Importance of Being* which took place on 22 February 2008 in the Jane Mallet Theatre, St. Lawrence Centre for the Arts. The operetta was a great success and Davies and I reveled in the laughter that rolled through the theatre as the wit of the great Oscar Wilde enlivened our lyrics and our music. An infuriating fact about the premiere is that because of union regulations Davies and I were forbidden to make any record of the performance which we could have used to promote the work with other producers and other companies. There does exist a tape and a filmed version but they must remain in the offices of Toronto Operetta Theatre where they can be viewed.

A final note on my treatment of Wilde's text. In the transformation of novels and drama to the medium of opera or operetta the librettist is free to make changes, even sweeping changes, to the original material. Consequently, it is sometimes difficult to recognize the source material—for example, Pepoli's libretto for Bellini's *I Puritani*, based on Sir Walter Scott's *Old Mortality*, is so confusing in its story line that most commentators, quite rightly, advise audiences to ignore what is happening on stage and just listen to the wonderful music, There is also the more nuanced business of adaptation as when Myfanwy Piper adapted Thomas Mann's *Death in Venice* for Benjamin Britten knowing that a key role would be sung by Britten's lover Peter Pears. When Oscar Wilde was writing *The Importance of Being Earnest* he was living a hidden life among a *canaille* of blackmailers and male prostitutes, and frequenting homosexual brothels in London and Algiers. Yet a surface reading (or performance) of his play shows little of this. It rather shows a world of innocence (the four young lovers are really children) and eternal sunshine. Although I was aware of Wilde's homosexual subtext, I decided not to draw attention to it; in one lyric, close to the end of the play where Jack seeks desperately and comically to discover who his parents are, I did give a hint of this subtext:

> *Who am I? What is my name?*
> *It seems that I have lost my way.*
> *I need to know, something to show,*
> *That I alone am not to blame.*

Although I had retired in 1993 I was not yet finished with academic work. In 1992 William Toye and I decided to update his *Oxford Companion to*

Canadian Literature, first published in 1983. It is the fate of reference works that they become outdated in many respects the day they are published. New authors appear, established authors publish new works, new genres emerge ("gay literature," "multicultural writing"), and new critical directions may necessitate re-evaluation of a literature. For the next five years Toye and I corresponded with almost two hundred people—mostly academics—as we updated first edition entries and added new ones. The final volume came to more than a million words documenting the state of Canadian literature, in both French and English. The first copy of the new second edition of *The Oxford Companion to Canadian Literature*, signed by William Toye and myself, was given to Timothy Findley at a 1997 Trent University conference celebrating his work.

From my vantage point as co-editor I noted many differences between the tone and substance of the entries of the first edition of *The Oxford Companion to Canadian Literature* and the second. By 1997 many of those writers who had helped to establish an authentic Canadian voice had died—we prefaced the second edition with a note in memory of Robertson Davies, Margaret Laurence, Hugh MacLennan, and Gabrielle Roy. Central to the work of these seminal figures had been their search for a Canadian identity as they witnessed, in their lifetimes, the dissolution of the country's colonial ties to the British Empire and the emergence of a threat to national unity because of Quebec's isolation from Canada (MacLennan's novel *Two Solitudes* touches on both issues). The second edition revealed a much different focus, one more concerned with personal issues often related to sexuality; new entries covered gay and lesbian writing that had been totally absent from the first edition. Equally prominent was the presence of multicultural writing as seen in such writers as Dany Laferrière, Nadia Ghalem, Marco Micone, Anne-Marie Alonzo, Michael Ondaatje, Rohinton Mistry, Dionne Brand, M.G. Vassanji, and Rohinton Mistry.

Just as *The Oxford Companion to Canadian Literature* demanded updating so too did the Routledge *Encyclopedia of Post-Colonial Literatures in English*. Again Conolly and I called upon our editorial team and on more than six hundred and seventy contributors from across the world, we updated first edition entries and bibliographies, and we added some two hundred new authors. Routledge the publisher agreed that we would again have an index but insisted that they would have it done "in house." In the second year of our work I learned that having the index done "in house" meant outsourcing the work to a firm in India. I repeatedly questioned London about the wisdom of doing this but was told not to worry, that the Indian firm was entirely qualified to do the job. Eventually, in mid 2004 Conolly and I received page proofs including those for the index and were appalled to discover that it was a total mess. The principal error was the omission of thousands of names and titles of books. Instead of the comprehensive index of the first edition we had an index that lacked any pretence to academic rigour. We pointed all this out to Routledge and asked them not to print the *Encyclopedia* with such a flawed index but they refused. Conolly and I spent two months trying to correct the index to some degree but when the *Encyclopedia* was eventually published in 2005 it still remained a dishonest and misleading document. Surprisingly, we did not see a single reviewer draw attention to this debacle which disturbed us so much.

This was my last engagement with academic work for I had now decided to give my attention to other tasks. I found that I had a renewed interest in creative writing and so I wrote a number of plays and three new libretti—*The Birthday of the Infanta, A love Letter from Oscar Wilde* and one that I especially cherish *Pride and Prejudice* based on Jane Austen's wonderful novel. I wrote to a number of composers in North America and Europe hoping that they would read these libretti with a view to collaboration only to receive the politest of replies telling me that they were too busy with commissioned new work to take on additional work. I was pleased to learn that opera composers were in such demand but sorry that I was unable to find a composer who lacked a theme. Eventually, in 2010, I came across the music of Canadian composer John Burge, who had just won a Juno Award for best Canadian classical composition; the fact that the work *Flanders Fields Reflections* was based on the poem "In Flanders Fields" by Guelph's John McCrae seemed auspicious and caused me to send him two of my new libretti. Burge replied immediately saying that he had reached the point where he wanted tackle an opera. When we finally met—to discuss my libretti, I thought—he asked me to read a children's story, *The Auction* by Jan Andrews, there and then. The slight story told of a small boy's conversation with his grandfather about past family events and why he had to sell the farm. What persuaded me to take on this project was the fact that it would be presented by the Westben Arts Festival Theatre whose concerts and operas take place in an actual barn.

It was the ideal setting. Burge had one condition—he wanted me to find a way to have a musical saw played. He was surprised when I told him that often in my childhood in Ireland I had seen and heard farmers who could play simple songs on the saw and that indeed the Hollywood siren Marlene Dietrich had played the musical saw for the troops during the Second World War. I did manage to integrate the saw in the text of my libretto in a functional way—I was influenced by Mozart's use of a magic flute in *Die Zauberflöte*. Premiered in the summer of 2012, *The Auction* was very well received—the critic John Terauds wrote: "*The Auction* fits into its Westben festival setting like a rooster on a fencepost."

Terauds used his review to question the state of Canadian opera. "It's mystifying that one has to leave Toronto in order to see the premiere of a new, full-length Canadian opera." There is, in fact, nothing mystifying about the matter. There still remains in this field that colonial cringe that had so dominated Canadian culture prior to the 1970s. When, for example, I corresponded with the Canadian Broadcasting Corporation about broadcasting *The Auction* I was stonewalled with a *pro forma* bureaucratic response to the effect that the CBC would not broadcast this new rarity—a Canadian opera—because it lacked funds to do so. I was finally reduced to writing to the President of the CBC, Hubert T. Lacroix, pointing out that broadcasting *The Auction* fitted exactly the CBC's mandate, that it was financially more attractive than paying for the Saturday broadcast of New York's Metropolitan Opera (how many times does one want to hear *La Traviata*, *Tosca*, *Carmen* to the exclusion of possibly exciting new work?). I offered many other reasons, but Mr Lacroix did not intervene. The grounds for refusing to broadcast *The Auction* were based, literally, on pure ignorance—no one at the CBC ever asked to read my libretto or to hear any of the music.

This same sorry state of affairs extends to Toronto and to its largest opera company—the Canadian Opera Company, the recipient over the years of millions of tax dollars. In the last ten years when I approached a number of prominent Canadian composers about collaborating on creating new work for this company I was invariably told that they had, in fact, written to Alexander Neef, its General Director, only to face indifference. Underlying his seeming disdain of Canadian opera is his belief that it lacks artistic merit which is ironic given, for example, the fiasco that was the 2012 presentation of Handel's noble *Semele* which Neef perpetrated on a bewildered public followed in 2018 by *Hadrian*, a *mélange* of pop music, quasi opera, and gratuitous male nudity. There is urgent need for the decolonization of the Canadian opera scene and a cleansing of those cultural bureaucrats who presently run our opera companies and the CBC—they have eyes to see, and see not, ears to hear, and hear not.

But Guillermo Silva-Marin continued to see Victor Davies and myself and to hear us and it came about that he listened to a number of the songs from our "musical" *A Tale of Two Cities* and decided that if Victor Davies and I would we would recreate it as an opera he would produce it. Accordingly, it was finally presented in July/August 2016 by Summer Opera Lyric Theatre of Toronto under his direction along with Offenbach's *The Tales of Hoffmann* and Handel's *Giulio Cesare*. It had been a long wait—some twelve years—but I never regretted the time spent on bring to life the tragic and heroic characters of Dickens' novel. I am presently at work with a twenty-seven-year-old composer on a musical with a Canadian subject that incorporates rap and hip hop elements; I do hope that it will be produced in my life time; after all, Verdi was still at work on his great masterpiece *Falstaff* when he was eighty-two years old and Picasso in his nineties was turning out paintings dominated by energy, sexuality, and genius.

L'Envoi

The writing of a memoir can be a pleasant task as one conjures up memories of time past and of family and friends. But memories can hurt. One counts the many loved ones that have passed away and so many treasured things that have been lost or destroyed by the passing of time. The death of my sister Mai was especially difficult because she had played such a central role in my life. As the oldest child, she had taken me for walks, told me stories, welcomed me always into her home as I grew older. She had been the repository of the family history to whom we all turned when we needed information on past events and family connections. When she died, I was acutely aware that I was the last of ten children and there was no one I could turn to as I had once turned to Mai.

In 44 BC the Roman author Cicero wrote a book on old age, *De Senectute*, in which he welcomed the end of his earthly pilgrimage: ". . . as I approach death, I seem to be sighting land, and to be arriving to port after a long journey." When at the age of forty I wrote the libretto for the opera *The Summoning of Everyman* I included a refrain from a fifteenth-century Scottish poem *Lament for the Makers*: "*Timor mortis conturbat me*" ("The fear of death haunts me"). The artist who drew the poster promoting the opera portrayed Death with his cloak protectively around the men and women he is conveying to the next world as if to assure them safe passage to a better place. Among the men and women Death has gathered in his cloak are many who enriched my life—Aloys Fleischmann, David Riley, Niki Goldschmidt, June Callwood. When I first saw June on an evening more than thirty years ago, she was a creature of such beauty and aspiration and vitality that I could not have imagined that she could be taken away. And I could not know that one day The Writers Union of Canada would ask me to write her obituary. Niki Goldschmidt had seemed beyond Death's reach, but in 2004, at the age of ninety-five, he too was taken. I attended his service in Roy Thomson Hall which was filled to capacity with friends and artists who had been touched by Niki's extraordinary personality and art—that afternoon was summarized for me by a weeping Maureen Forester, also ravaged by the years, as she stumbled her way from the hall. Two years later the Guelph Spring Festival which had played so important a part in Niki's life, and mine, ceased to exist and in 2012 Murdo MacKinnon, the Festival's co-founder, died. The family called on me to deliver his elegy. *Atque in perpetuum frater, ave atque vale.*

And now death has taken my Renate. Dementia ravaged her as she lay in a Toronto nursing home, tended and fed by strangers, that fine intellect ruined without hope of cure. And everywhere about me reminders—the books we translated over so many hours, her German cookbooks, a wardrobe full of her clothes that will never be worn again, my first love letter to her. And I am undone, raging against the cruelty of age and time.

But we must take consolation in what remains and what remains are memories, memories enriched and burnished by the years. Memories of the first time I entered St Peter's Basilica, the first time I saw the murals of Rivera, Orozco and Sequeiros in Mexico City, and the Taj Mahal (with Renate in the foreground holding a red umbrella against the glare of the sun), the first time I held my sons in my arms. And I note how time has taken so much from me in order to leave the things that have sustained me so well throughout the years—Sophocles' *Oedipus the King*, the plays of Shakespeare, Tolstoy's *The Death of Ivan Ilyich* and Mann's *Death in Venice*, the odes of Keats, Shelley's *Prometheus Unbound* and Yeats' later poems, the operas of Mozart and Schubert's *Lieder*. And one memory over all. A sunlit morning in 1933, church bells ringing, my mother and I on our way to Mass. Indestructible.

Old age is rich in one special area—that of dreams. And so often now two dreams come to me as I drift asleep. In the less frequent dream I am in the middle of a vast arena that is flooded with sunlight. There is a red door. Music plays and the crowd roars. I watch the red door. It opens. And there is the bull, pawing the ground, readying itself.

In the other dream I am standing at a river that is like a flood of light flowing past me. On the far bank I see people calling and waving as if beckoning me to cross. It is my family—my father and mother, and Mai, Charles, Hugh, Jackie, Françoise, my twin Bernadette, Gerard. Philomena, young, unchanged, happy. Renate! Nightly they come in dreams and call me to come to them. Yes. Yes.

As I write these final lines, this farewell, I am in my study overlooking the garden that Renate and I planted more than fifty years ago where we played with our children and where I now watch our grandchildren, twins Elle and Lily, at play. The snow of a hard winter is almost gone, and flowers are pushing their way through the soil, and the birds of spring have returned. At Easter the bells of the churches in Guelph rang out to celebrate the resurrection of Christ. I too rejoice in this personal resurrection, but with the passing years I have come to associate Easter with Spring, to think of Resurrection as the return of those birds to my garden each year, the flowers beneath the earth that struggle upwards to the light, my children and grandchildren who are my only guarantee that I endure. "And nothing 'gainst Time's scythe can make defence / Save breed, to brave him when he takes thee hence."

In the last scene of my libretto for *The Auction,* the central character, an old man, is interrogated by his younger self who questions whether life is worth living. Yes, the old man answers, yes:

> *I see my life and it was tough as nails,*
> *But if I had the chance I would not change a thing.*
> *I met the finest woman in the world*
> *And we loved each other as true lovers should.*
> *I have seen these arms, once strong as steel,*
> *Wither as the years closed in on me,*
> *But I am glad, yea, glad with all my heart*
> *Because they once embraced the one I loved.*
> *So do not ask me if the price was right,*
> *And do not speak to me again of death,*
> *Or the drawing of the shades at night.*
> *For I have loved and been loved and that*
> *Is all that any man can ask.*
> *And so I will avow till my last breath.*

Guelph, 2018

www.ingramcontent.com/pod-product-compliance
Lightning Source LLC
Chambersburg PA
CBHW030903080526
44589CB00010B/131